MW00659037

AN AUTHENTIC ENGLISH LANGUAGE ARTS CURRICULUM

This book provides ways of thinking for preservice and new teachers to transition from the theory behind curricular design to engaged teaching and learning in the classroom. It offers a comprehensive framework for the creation and implementation of one's own authentic and effective ELA curriculum. In addition to strategies for preservice teachers to develop their own pedagogies, lessons, and teaching techniques, Costigan also demonstrates how to design tools for teaching in the current testing- and standards-driven context of the educational reform movement. Containing real-life examples of reading and writing instruction, this book empowers preservice teachers to translate the concepts of curriculum design to actual ELA classroom practices that will engage students.

Arthur T. Costigan is Associate Professor of English Education and Co-Director of the English Education program at Queens College (CUNY), USA.

AN AUTHENTIC ENGLISH LANGUAGE ARTS CURRICULUM

Finding Your Way in a Standards-Driven Context

Arthur T. Costigan

Routledge
Taylor & Francis Group
NEW YORK AND LONDON

First published 2019
by Routledge
711 Third Avenue, New York, NY 10017

and by Routledge
2 Park Square, Milton Park, Abingdon, Oxon, OX14 4RN

Routledge is an imprint of the Taylor & Francis Group, an informa business

Library of Congress Cataloging-in-Publication Data
Names: Costigan, Arthur T., author.
Title: An authentic English Language Arts curriculum : finding your way in a standards-driven context / Arthur T. Costigan.
Description: New York : Routledge, 2019. | Includes bibliographical references and index.
Identifiers: LCCN 2018019894 | ISBN 9780815348412 (hardback) | ISBN 9780815348429 (pbk.) | ISBN 9781351167161 (ebook)
Subjects: LCSH: Language arts—Curricula. | English language—Study and teaching. | Student teachers—Training of.
Classification: LCC LB1576 .C7366 2019 | DDC 428.0071—dc23
LC record available at https://lccn.loc.gov/2018019894

ISBN: 978-0-8153-4841-2 (hbk)
ISBN: 978-0-8153-4842-9 (pbk)
ISBN: 978-1-351-16716-1 (ebk)

Typeset in Bembo
by Swales & Willis Ltd, Exeter, Devon, UK

To all my talented and generous English Language Arts education students at Queens College, without whom this book would not be possible.

CONTENTS

PREFACE

Welcome to This Book

This book is an introduction or a "way in" to teaching English Language Arts (ELA). It presents you with an approach, or an orientation, to the teaching and learning of the important and essential elements of the ELA curriculum. Through this way of approaching English, you will be able to develop your own pedagogies, activities, lessons, and teaching strategies. While this book does present you with actual techniques, it could never present you with all the pedagogies you would need to teach, even in your first semester of teaching. In fact, this book maintains that just giving you a set of pedagogies, student activities, or lessons, is not enough. Despite the reality that teachers are always looking for activities and lessons that engage students, giving you individual packages of pedagogies might actually be the worst thing the book could do, because in this case, you would never know the thinking *behind* those strategies. Instead, this book will demonstrate that it is by coming into a particular conversation about teaching English, a particular way of looking at English teaching and learning, that you will be empowered as an educator. This book gives you the scaffolding behind those activities, the structure or blueprint for what is possible for you to do in your own classroom with writing, reading, and speaking.

Another way of looking at this is that the book advocates a particular *ecology* of teaching English. The word *ecology* comes from the Greek word *oikos*, meaning "habitat," "environment," or "the place a being resides." This book maintains that once you enter a particular landscape, environment, or "place," you will be empowered to come up with English teaching strategies, activities, lessons, pedagogies, and techniques that will engage and empower your students.

There are very many books that already deal with the teaching of English in comprehensive ways, all of them on one end of the scale from the purely practical and "hands on," with many activities that teachers can borrow (and steal) for themselves, to the more theoretical, giving teachers the theories behind the way young people are engaged linguistically (Burant, et al., 2010; Burke, 2013; Christenbury & Lindblom, 2016; Smagorinsky, 2007; Wiggins & McTighe, 2005). This book adds to this rich conversation by providing a scaffolded and a foundational approach, one that looks at the blueprint *behind* the edifice of ELA, an edifice that contains the many strategies for writing, reading, and speaking.

Overall, I hope this book allows for an investigation into what type of classroom you want to create, one that values democracy, social justice, and equality, and dare I say, one that will be a place of exploration, investigation, engagement, and even joy for you and your students (O'Reilly, 1993). Given this stance of creating an ELA classroom, this book is intended to give readers who are preservice teachers, student teachers, beginning teachers, and even experienced teachers, a "way in" to conceiving of the ELA classroom. This book maintains that good teaching comes from a particular attitude, stance, or ecology rather than the "gimmicks and tricks" of delivering lessons (Macrorie, 1985). Once a teacher understands what is *behind*, or what undergirds and scaffolds ELA teaching and learning, then possibilities open up for designing a meaningful curriculum that focuses on student learning rather than the teacher's performance. This book addresses, in specific, the literature, the writing, the reading curriculum.

In the literature curriculum, this book covers how to conceptualize, design, and implement units that are arranged around what I call a *Line of Inquiry* (LOI), a *Way In* (WI), or the *Big Human Issue* (BHI) present in a work of art. These are similar to essential questions (EQs), which are questions that are not answerable with a one-answer finality, but rather are used to stimulate thought, and to provoke inquiry and further questioning (Wiggins & McTighe, 2013). As we shall see, my idea of the LOI in curricular design is to link the essential question to the work of art or literature under consideration: *To what degree is humankind basically inclined to good or inclined to evil? Does privilege or being disadvantaged have anything to do with one's sense of responsibility? Or ability to form healthy relationships?* and, *What responsibility do average people (like us) have for the continual state of war sustained by the United States*? In this book, these become Lines of Inquiry, or Ways Into works of art, or the Big Human Issues for designing curriculum around works such as *Lord of The Flies, The Great Gatsby*, or Ira Kaminsky's poem, "We Lived Happily During the War" (Kaminsky, 2013; see Chapter 1).

In writing, the book builds upon the tradition of writing as a *process*, rather than just as the production of a correct-as-possible *product*, and it builds upon the traditions of a collaborative worship model of the writing workshop (Blau, 2003, 2010; Elbow, 1998; Macrorie, 1985). In regards to the reading curriculum, this book addresses how basing reading on a psycholinguistic approach, what I call the *organic* approach, can be applied to the 7–12 ELA classrooms

(Pinker, 2007; Smith, 2006, 2009). This organic approach, in turn, influences how we go about teaching both nonfiction and literature through approaches that focus on the reader's transaction with the text (Rosenblatt, 1978, 1983). This meaning-making then, in turn, is democratically negotiated with one's peers in a workshop-type environment that is investigatory and collaborative (Beach, Thein, & Webb, 2016; Blau, 2011; Wilhelm, 2016). And, of course, all these practices are negotiated in an era of accountability, high-stakes testing, and externally imposed standards (Crocco & Costigan, 2006, 2007). While the Common Core State Standards (CCSS) are being replaced in many states, it seems as if the standards movement is here to stay in one form or another (Costigan, 2014). The ELA jury is out on these, and opinions vary widely from those who embrace standards, to those who find them reasonable enough to negotiate their way through them, and to those who find them at best a hindrance to authentic education and something to be subverted (Beach, Thein, & Webb, 2016; Gallagher, 2015; Smith, Appleman, & Wilhelm, 2014).

And, of course, there are many specialized books from reputable publishers that deal with the varied subareas of English, such as Young Adult Literature (YAL), teaching the writing of poetry, creative writing, expository writing, organic writing processes, exploratory talk, public speaking, teaching controversial topics, various assessment modalities, close reading, reader response practices, and so on—to name a few of many subareas that comprise English. And of course, now there is as much that is available on the internet and electronically as there is available in hard copy books. Lastly, there are all the types of curricula presented in national conferences such as the National Council of Teachers of English (NCTE) and the American Educational Research Association (AERA), and the Modern Language Association (MLA), among many others. But I cannot know everyone who is writing about ELA, and I can't read everything, and I do have some original things to say based on 32 years in the teaching profession, almost 14 as an urban high school teacher, and 18 mostly as a teacher educator and director of a large, urban, teacher education program.

Teachers use a lot of techniques and pedagogies, more than any one book can present. For example, for a research project I solicited the kind and number of teaching techniques and pedagogies used in three one-semester long graduate courses containing a total of 39 beginning teachers who were in their first to third years of teaching. These teachers typically had the normal teaching duties of five classes per day for a 90-day semester. All told, they came up with 93 different techniques they were using in the records they kept for just one semester of classes. Just the techniques beginning with the letter "A" were: *Accountability talk, active engagement, aggressive monitoring, aims (eliciting of), alternative ending options, argumentative writing, anticipatory set, art gallery walk, attach the prompt.* (You can look at Appendix A to this preface to see all the types of teaching lessons arranged by: (1) ELA techniques and pedagogies used; (2) ELA unit themes, topics, and issues; and (3) ELA literature or works of art taught.) Note that because of the pressures of testing and accountability systems, the list is extremely varied. Teachers and administrators just don't know how to respond to all the demands. I call this the *idiosyncratic curriculum* (Costigan, 2017).

This book will be an attempt to sort this out and to separate those techniques and strategies that are aesthetic (that is, engaging and alive), authentic (real-world based), meaningful (likely to engage students), and that enhance student learning (effective), from those that are artificial (don't look like reading and writing in the real world), *an*esthetic (without feeling), and disengaging (make students dislike learning).

How Does This Book Work?

Chapter 1, *The English Orientation* sets the tone, structure, and content of this book. So, this chapter presents you with the importance of a "way of thinking," or a "way in," or an *ecology* (landscape, habitat, or place a being resides) that a teacher can have to the approach of teaching English. Rather than just giving you lessons, techniques, and approaches to teaching writing, reading, and speaking, this chapter gives you an orientation to the teaching of English Language Arts (ELA).

Chapter 2, *The Foundations of Practice: Where We Come From and Where We Are Now* presents you with the background of where our curriculum currently comes from. I'll take you from Dewey through the changes in the ways of thinking about how students learn in the last century, up to current approaches or "ways in" to teaching reading and writing today. The chapter differentiates between the *commonsense* and *uncommonsense* traditions (Mayher, 1991), the first stressing the passing on of information, and the second conceiving of the learner as an active construer of knowledge. The chapter demonstrates how this has impact in particular upon how teachers go about teaching literature, reading, and writing.

Chapter 3, *English Language Arts: What Is It, How Is It Learned, and How Do You Teach It?* Explains the how the modalities of the ELA curriculum—writing, reading, and speaking (and listening and movement)—are essential elements of the ELA curriculum and how this can be a basis for creating a curriculum of units and lessons. Once teachers understand that they can create a text out of a text (intermodality), many possibilities open up for creating lessons that get the work of art, or text, under consideration, "in the head," that is, in the long-term memory.

Chapter 4, *Expanding Our Understanding of Intermodality* does just that, providing further examples of the ways in which teachers create lessons that focus on the work of art under consideration through the many modes of writing, reading (literature), speaking, as well as listening, and through movement (kinesthetics). The chapter presents how to design a literature unit using the Line of Inquiry, Way In, or Big Human Issue to enhance students' transactions with works of art. The chapter also call into questions some learning techniques that may not be as effective as students transacting authentically with writing, reading, or speaking: graphic organizers, unrehearsed public reading, plot and theme, and contextual information as enhancing meaning making of a text.

Chapter 5, *The ELA Classroom in the Context of Contemporary Schooling: Educational Reform, Standards, and Assessment* puts the previous chapters' ideas about creating curriculum in the context of the educational reform movement, which includes high-stakes tests, increased student and teacher accountability, and the imposition (often by non-teachers) of so-called objective standards and rubrics, such as the CCSS. The chapter gives the history and politics behind these reforms and explains how this has influenced in particular the ELA classroom. The chapter contrasts this thinking with how best to assess students with authentic assessment practices.

Chapter 6, *Multiple Literacies as Culturally Sustaining Pedagogy in English Language Arts*, by Limarys Caraballo. In the current context of standardization and accountability, English language arts curricula are often focused on literacy skills that do not honor the interrelated nature of students' multiple identities, languages, and literacies—particularly those of students from historically marginalized communities. In this chapter, Limarys Caraballo explains how a multiple literacies approach can help teachers create and implement curriculum that includes and sustains the cultures, languages, and literacies of all students.

Appendix A

Teaching Done by 59 Teachers in Three Separate One-Semester Long ELA Methods Courses

TABLE 1.1 ELA Reading and Writing Techniques

[Advance!] lesson plan format for lesson planning	Character analysis
Accountable/accountability talk	Character chart
Active engagement	Check for understanding
Aggressive monitoring	Citing evidence
Aims	Class read
Alternative ending options, argumentative writing	Cold call
Alternative plan for when things go wrong	Compare and contrast assignments
Anticipatory set	Critical lens perspective
Art gallery walks with sticky note board	Danielson Method lesson plan format
Attach the prompt	Debate a certain theme
Back pocket questions	Differentiated instruction
Baseline assessment	Do now
Batch feedback	Do now inquiry starter
CCSS standards on board	Elicit the aim
	Entrance tickets
	Entry point
	Exemplar responses

Exit tickets	Prompts for writing
Four corners sharing	Prompts: sentence starters
Freytag triangle (2)	QRI 5 Inventory
Goal: content	Quick homework quizzes
Goal: language	Related quote to begin class by interpreting with class
Graphic organizers: for every essay	Rules and routines of a respectful classroom
Graphic organizers: T-charts	Scaffolded questions
Group discussions: cooperative	Scaffolding
Group work	Share out (2)
Guided instruction	Show-call
Guided practice (2)	Socratic seminars
I will be able to (instead of students will be able to)	Standards-based grading policies
Independent practice	Starter task
Informational texts	Stretch-the-question
Jigsaw activities	Student led discussion
Learning intentions	Students will be able to . . . (Swabat)
Learning objectives	Teaching point
Learning targets	Think-pair-share
Literature circles	Tiered instruction
Medial summary	Time stamps per section (of lesson)
Mini lessons	Turn and talk
Modeling	Vocabulary instruction, direct
Motivation	WITSI (Writing is Thinking with Strategic Inquiry)
Multiple activities	Workshop model
Multiple ways of learning	Writing argumentative essay
Notice and note	Writing TIED paragraphs based on text
Peer editing	
Pivotal questions to lead discussions	
Planned misconception	
Popcorn reading	

TABLE 1.2 Themes, Topics, and Issues Taught

AIDS and stigma in Young Adult novels	Explorer unit
Argumentative essay (5)	How to analyze
Block Essays	How to research
Celebrating privacy	Identifying Perspectives
Character traits	Independent reading
Citing evidence	Individual poem units for each class
Collaborative annotations	Inferences
Comparing and contrasting characters	Introduction to literary devices
Dealing with content	Introductions, ice breaker game
Drama unit	JFA: Journalistic Feature Article vs regular essay
Emotional appeal	Literary devices (2)
Explication writing	

(continued)

TABLE 1.2 *(continued)*

Literary essay	Short answer response, how to
Marginalization	Short Stories (7)
Memoir	Sonnets (2)
MOSL test taking strategies	Spelling Bee
Novels	Text to self connection (2)
Patriarchal Society unit	The American Dream
Persuasive strategies	Thematic essay unit
Plot sequence	Transitional phases
Poems	Understanding the theme of "visual"
Point of view	Unusual language (in novel)

TABLE 1.3 Works of Literature Taught

A Long Walk to Water (2)	Of Mice and Men
A Street Car Named Desire (3)	Romeo and Juliet
Call Me Maria	Rules of the Game
Dracula	Sold
Dreaming of Heidi	The Addict
Fences	The Autobiography of Malcolm X
Frankenstein	The Color Purple
Go Ask Alice	The Great Gatsby
Go Tell It On the Mountain	The Hangman
Greek Myths	The Jacket
Johnny Tremain	The Naked Truth
Julius Caesar	The Pearl
Lyddie (3)	To Kill a Mockingbird (novel and film)
Maus	Tuesdays with Morrie
Might	Two Kinds
Monster	

References

Beach, R., Thein, A. H., & Webb, A. (2016). *Teaching to exceed the English Language Arts Common State Standards: A critical inquiry approach for 6–12 classrooms* (2nd ed.). New York: Taylor & Francis.

Blau, S. (2003). *The Literature workshop: Teaching texts and their readers.* Portsmouth, NH: Heinemann.

Blau, S. (2011). Fostering authentic learning in the literature classroom. In J. Milner & C. Pope (Eds.), *Engaging American novels.* Urbana, IL: NCTE.

Burant, T., Christensen, L., Salas, K. D., & Walters, S. (2010). *The new teacher book: Finding purpose, balance, and hope during your first years in the classroom.* Milwaukee, WI: Rethinking Schools.

Burke, J. (2013). *The English teacher's companion* (4th ed.). Portsmouth, NH: Heinemann.

Christenbury, L. & Lindblom, K. (2016). *Making the journey: Being and becoming a teacher of English Language Arts* (4th ed.). Portsmouth, NH: Heinemann.

Costigan, A. T. (2014, August). Demythologizing educational reforms: Thirty years since A Nation at Risk. In A. T. Costigan and L. Grey (Eds.), *Demythologizing educational reforms: Responses to the political and corporate takeover of education* (pp. 1–19). New York: Routledge.

Costigan, A. T. (2017). "I'm Not Teaching English, I'm Teaching Something Else!": How New Teachers Create Curriculum Under Mandates of Educational Reform. *Educational Studies.* Available at: www.tandfonline.com/eprint/YW6Y5F2UhED4vHVF5B3p/full.

Crocco, M. S. & Costigan, A. T. (2006). High-stakes teaching: What's at stake for teachers (and students) in the age of accountability. *The New Educator, 2*, 1–13.

Crocco, M. S. & Costigan, A. T. (2007). The Narrowing of Curriculum and Pedagogy: Urban Educators Speak Out. *Urban Education, 42*(6), 512–535.

Elbow, P. (1998). *Writing without teachers* (2nd ed.). New York: Oxford University Press.

Gallagher, K. (2015). *In the best interest of students: Staying true to what works in the ELA classroom.* Portland, ME: Stenhouse.

Macrorie, K. (1985). *Telling writing* (4th ed.) Portsmouth, NH: Boynton/Cook.

Mayher, J. S. (1991). *Uncommon sense: Theoretical practice in language education.* Portsmouth, NH: Heinemann.

O'Reilly, M. R. (1993). *The peaceable classroom.* Portsmouth, NH: Heinemann.

Pinker, S. (2007). *The language instinct: How the mind creates language.* New York: HarperPerennial Modern Classics.

Rosenblatt L. M. (1978). *The reader, the text, the poem: The transactional theory of the literary work.* Carbondale, IL: Southern Illinois University Press.

Rosenblatt L. M. (1983). *Reading as exploration* (3rd ed.). New York: Modern Language Association.

Smagorinsky, P. (2007). *Teaching by design: How to create and carry out instructional units.* Portsmouth, NH: Heinemann.

Smith, F. (2006). *Reading without nonsense* (4th ed.). New York: Teachers College Press.

Smith, F. (2009). *Understanding reading: A psycholinguistic analysis of reading and learning to read.* New York: Taylor & Francis/Routledge.

Smith, M. W., Appleman, D., & Wilhelm, J. D. (2014). *Uncommon core: Where the authors of the standards go wrong about instruction—and how you can get it right.* Thousand Oak, CA: Corwin.

Wiggins, G. & McTighe, J. (2005). *Understanding by design* (2nd ed.). Alexandria, VA: Association for Supervisors and Curriculum Development [ASCD].

Wiggins, G. & McTighe, J. (2013). *Essential questions: Opening doors to understanding.* Alexandria, VA: Association for Supervisors and Curriculum Development [ASCD].

Wilhelm, J. (2016). *You gotta be the book: Teaching engaged and reflective reading with adolescents* (3rd ed.). New York: Teachers College Press.

1

THE ENGLISH ORIENTATION

Your English Orientation

This book is different from many others in that it does not just present techniques, pedagogies, and activities, but rather talks about an *orientation*, an approach, a "way in," to teaching English. Just as you have an orientation to a certain type of music, or a specific culture's food (think classic French, Thai, Sichuan, or Tex Mex), you also have a certain vocabulary or discourse (a way of speaking and thinking), and you have an *orientation* to English. Of course, you also have a sexual orientation and a gender orientation which color the core of your life and your relationships. Some of us have scientific or mathematical orientations, others have artistic orientations, and others have an orientation to athletics. In fact, you probably have several orientations and don't have several others, just as I don't really have a mathematical orientation or a basketball playing orientation. I argue that your English orientation is also an important part of your life. You would not be reading this book unless you had an orientation to reading and writing and to sharing it with other human beings, your current or future students.

Orientation can be defined as "the direction you are facing," or "alignment with what is important to you," or "facing the right way." Orientation literally means "facing East." The Orient is where the sun rises, and many cultures pray facing eastward. An orientation is the way you approach the important issues and phenomena that you are focused on, or concerned with, or slanted towards, or in favor of. So too, you have become an English teacher, or are in the process of becoming an English teacher, because in all likelihood you already have an orientation, inclination, and instinct towards the use of, and study of, English. You read novels, or write poems, or keep a diary, and you enjoy deep conversations with your friends and colleagues about books, movies, music, and important human issues. You are a writer, a reader, a speaker, and a conversationalist, and you want to share this orientation or focus or way of living with your students. I know this because over 17 years I've asked each potential student applying to one of the four ELA education programs I direct: (1) Why do you want to be a teacher? and, (2) why do you want to be an *English* teacher? Almost every candidate without exception states that they want: (1) To pass on their love of literature and/or writing; and (2) to make a difference in the lives of young people.

Another perhaps simpler way of looking at this is that, while this book looks at the outside skin of the building of ELA (what teachers and students do), it's more authentic focus is the complicated structures on the inside (the groundwork, support, and scaffolding) of how teachers think about what they do in the ELA classroom. Let's move on two examples which I have brought together from the several types of lessons I've often observed. One lesson leans towards what my mentor John Mayher classifies as *commonsense* (traditional) practices, and the second heavily favors *uncommonsense* (we'll get to the names) practices (Mayher, 1991).

Two Teachers, Two Classrooms, Two Curricula

Let's imagine two teaching scenarios for two different teachers whom we'll call Maria and Derrick. Both are novice second year English ELA teachers teaching in a school we'll call Hamilton High. I think both of these teachers can tell us much about two basic approaches to the teaching of English.

Before I get to each teacher's story however, I need to point out that these lessons are in the context of these teachers' typically busy, if not hectic, day. Maria and Derrick teach five "pupil periods" (that is, class sections) per day, and these are divided between two different class preparations, or "preps"—say, in a fall semester, two freshman class sections, and three senior class sections. However, it really isn't just two "preps" per day, along with the two accompanying lesson plans, because many individual classes will contain students who have special needs, thus each lesson plan will have to have several adaptations, or have "differentiation," for these students. For example, one or several students might have Individual Educational Programs (IEPs) and need Special Education services. Alternatively, the class may contain English Language Learners (ELLs) or other students with special needs. Additionally, it may not be just teaching "two sophomore ELA classes," as one class section might be Advanced Placement (AP) and one might be remedial. And this diversity can get rather absurd: The most difficult class I ever taught, the last period of the day, was a remedial English class whose students were placed in my class because they had consistently failed the state *math* test—go figure. So, each ELA lesson doesn't just "get taught," it needs to be differentiated for different students with different learning styles, abilities, and needs. And, as any teacher can tell you, even two "on level" classes (however that is defined) that *should* be the same, may actually have quite different classroom personalities, sometimes markedly so. In fact, I've never taught, in high school or college, two of the same type of classes on the same level that have had the same class personality.

It is also worth noting that the two lessons described below occur during an eight-period day: Five are teaching periods with two "preps," but there is also one period to prepare lesson plans and materials, called a "prep" period. Another is a "professional period," which is really a "building assignment" such as monitoring a hallway or working in the attendance office. The third non-teaching period is 40 minutes for lunch. A day chopped up into roughly 42-minute sections is rushed. Additionally, in each of these five short 42-minute lessons, a teacher in an urban district may have up to 34 students (or more) per class, which at five periods per day, comes to 170 students per day (or more). (Think of reading 170 student assignments or homeworks per day!) All this is the result of the factory model of education, which was intentionally created in the 1920s to process masses of students as a result of the then novelty of compulsory or mandatory education. Today's middle and high schools are still designed to move as many students as possible on an assembly line from Math, to Science, to Phys Ed, to the lunch room, and so forth, much like a Model T Ford moved on an assembly line in 1922.

I bring this up because this is the reality of teaching today. It's a rushed, complicated, exhausting, and almost impossible task, one that society does not seem to appreciate, and one that educational reformers certainly don't understand. I am giving this description of the realities of teaching because we should not forget that it is in this context that our discussion of the ELA curriculum takes place. I never forget, in the writing of this book, that this is the context in which we teach and our students learn. Turning now to Maria and Derrick, let us focus on how these new second year novice teachers go about producing a lesson.

Maria's Story

Maria Sanchez has just arrived in the teachers' lounge and is just sitting down at 8:10 a.m. on a Monday morning and getting comfortable with a cup of coffee before her busy day. Just as she takes the lid off her coffee take out cup, there's a knock on the door of the room. In comes a young man holding a note and a manila folder, He asks for Ms. Sanchez. Maria says, "That's me," and the student hands her the note and the folder. The note is from the Assistant Principal (AP) and tells her she is to do a class coverage for a teacher's absence, something that is required of teachers to do several times a semester. Maria sighs and the young man leaves. In the folder are copies of Percy Bysshe Shelley's "Ozymandias." Maria is a bit concerned that the teacher has not left a lesson plan, as she was supposed to do. Maria only has enough copies of poem for the class. She says to herself, "OK, I can do this. I was a major in English in college, I had a course in Romantic Poetry where we covered this, I'm getting my master's in Education and I've been provisionally and initially certified, so I know something about how to teach poetry. She re-familiarizes herself with this well-known poem and reads,

1. I met a traveller from an antique land,
2. Who said—"Two vast and trunkless legs of stone
3. Stand in the desert. . . . Near them, on the sand,
4. Half sunk a shattered visage lies, whose frown,
5. And wrinkled lip, and sneer of cold command,
6. Tell that its sculptor well those passions read
7. Which yet survive, stamped on these lifeless things,
8. The hand that mocked them, and the heart that fed;
9. And on the pedestal, these words appear:
10. My name is Ozymandias, King of Kings;
11. Look on my Works, ye Mighty, and despair!
12. Nothing beside remains. Round the decay
13. Of that colossal Wreck, boundless and bare
14. The lone and level sands stretch far away."

The bell rings and Maria is off to Room 222 to an unknown class of Juniors to somehow engage them with this poem.

Maria arrives a bit out of breath as the students are entering the class. Using her best "teacher voice" she tells the students to settle down and that she will be reporting back to Ms. Simpson (the regular teacher) about how they behaved. And she will be collecting their writing that day and it will be graded. Fortunately, the students settle down and Maria hands out the poem.

"We're going to read today a Romantic poem, does anyone know what that is?" The class is silent. "OK, then, these are poems which were written in an era when feelings were considered very important, so the poet want us to *feel* things in the poem. Let's begin by reviewing any vocabulary words that we don't know. Can each of you circle words that are strange to you in the poem, because this was written hundreds of years ago." Fortunately for her, Maria thinks, the students do the task, and she thinks that this must be a "good" class of students, willing to do what they are asked.

The students come up with various words, such as, "trunkless," "visage," "colossal," and so forth. Maria puts them on the board and has the students copy them in their notebook, telling the class, "Remember these vocabulary words might be on your next exam." After spending about ten minutes reviewing the words, Maria begins the class proper. She starts reading the poem to the class line by line. Beginning with the first line, Maria states, "Remember a *trunk* is the main part of your body, and *vast* means enormous." She begins to read, "I met a traveller from an antique land, / Who said—"Two vast and trunkless legs of stone / Stand in the desert." She asks, "Can anyone translate this for us?" One student says, "I think it means that the poet met a guy when on vacation, and there was a statue of legs without a body just standing there in the desert." Maria congratulates the young man on "getting it." She continues this way through the entire poem, that is translating or interpreting each line, being sure to take time to summarize and explain after several lines have been "translated." This takes most of the period. Maria is relieved that the students have the academic ability to "get" the poem and she will compliment Ms. Simpson when she next sees her.

The end of the class is approaching and Maria tries to wrap it up, "So, what do you think is the message or theme of this poem?" She continues, "A traveler, tourist if you will, hears a story about someone who says there is a broken statue in the desert with an inscription about how great this king is, but all there is remaining is his broken statue, or *visage*, which means appearance." One student, obviously the academic leader in the class, raises his hand and says, "I think he is saying that fame doesn't last." Maria says, "Good, I think you've understood the poem . . ." It is now the end of the period and the bell rings. Maria says, as the students are rushing out of the room, "Thanks for your wonderful contributions today, I'll be sure to tell Ms. Simpson what a wonderful class you have been." Maria is happy that this might be a poem which is useful for the students on the state exam, which always requires an essay comparing two works of literature. However, Maria wonders what she would have done if the students were non-native speakers of English, or did not have a background in analyzing poetry, or were just disengaged from formal schooling, to "get" the theme of the poem. She feels fortunate today.

Derrick's Story

Derrick has a similar schedule to Maria and gets his "coverage" just as he's opening up his coffee—this *always* happens. Derrick, unfortunately, is unfamiliar with the poem. However, he reads it and he thinks he "gets" it enough to teach it. He runs to the English Department office and finds a pair of scissors. He is going to "scramble" the poem.

With very little time before the first bell of the day, he cuts up the poem and places the slips of paper containing the lines on the glass of the photocopier in random order. He pushes the button and prints out ten copies so that groups of from two to four students will each have one copy of the scrambled poem. Derrick's thankful that the copying machine is working today. If Derrick had time, he could have cut up the poem's lines into strips himself and put them in individual envelopes for groups of students. The scrambled poem now looks like this:

SAMPLE 1.1 Sample Assembled Poem

And on the pedestal, these words appear:
And wrinkled lip, and sneer of cold command,
Half sunk a shattered visage lies, whose frown,
I met a traveller from an antique land,
Look on my Works, ye Mighty, and despair!
My name is Ozymandias, King of Kings;
Nothing beside remains. Round the decay

(continued)

SAMPLE 1.1 *(continued)*

Of that colossal Wreck, boundless and bare
Stand in the desert. . . . Near them, on the sand,
Tell that its sculptor well those passions read
The hand that mocked them, and the heart that fed;
The lone and level sands stretch far away."
Which yet survive, stamped on these lifeless things,
Who said–"Two vast and trunkless legs of stone

(Note that the lines are simply arranged in alphabetical order, something you can do easily on an Excel spreadsheet.) Derrick now hurries to Room 222, running a bit late, and opens the door to find a rowdy group of students, some walking about the room talking to each other, others socializing, others on their cell phones—totally against school rules. Derrick sighs at the difficult task in front of him and uses his "teacher voice" saying settle down and get to your seats. I have the seating chart here and I *will* get back to Ms. Simpson on how you behave today."

The students settle down reluctantly. Derrick begins, "OK, I'm new here and don't know any of you. Who can tell me who is the most important person in this room, you know, who is the best person here?" The students look a bit confused. "I mean who thinks he or she is the best person or most important person in the room? The leader? I need to know before I begin the lesson." Several hands go up and there's a few "Me, Me! Me's!" from the class and Derrick calls on the most energetic young man. "OK, you," he looks at the seating chart, "Juan, why are you the most important or best person in the room?" "Yeah, I'm The Man. I'm the greatest person in the room." The other students start dissing Juan with "You ain't the best," along with some inappropriate insults and comments, which Derrick ignores. "Well, *why* are you the best? How can you prove it?" Juan states that he is the best at basketball, the best lover (the kids start groaning and laughing), and the "richest most chill guy in the room." "Well that's very interesting, Juan, but some people in the room disagree with you. Let's hear from some other people." Derrick sees that there are more male hands going up than the females, so he is sure to call on some female students. This goes on for about seven minutes, during which each student explains why they are the most talented, all, of course, with questionable evidence.

"OK, then," Derrick continues, "I want to tell you a story about who was the greatest person in the world. He was a king who lived a long time ago, in a place like ancient Egypt. He ruled the known world at the time, like a Pharaoh, but that was a long time ago, thousands of years, actually. So, just last week someone, a traveler, like a tourist, comes across his statue in the desert, and it's huge, but it's broken in half, only the enormous legs remain sticking out of the sand, but the body, the trunk, is missing. The traveler then reads what is inscribed—that means written—on the huge pedestal or foundation of the statue, and that's what in the poem."

"Here's a copy of the poem, but I've mixed up the lines of the story. I want you to get into pairs and put the lines together in the order you think is the best. Each pair will probably come up with a different order for the lines, so don't worry. What we really want to find out is if this poem is telling us anything we don't know about being great. And see how you yourself compare to Ozymandias, this Greatest of the Great Kings who ever lived." The students work at the activity for about ten minutes, and Derrick sees that the period is about to end. He asks one group to read their "assembled poem" and asks the other groups to compare their order-choices with the one that was read. Two other groups then read their poems, and the students compare their results. All the groups are different, but all seem to have "gotten" the poem. What Derrick notices is that of the six groups of five people, four groups began the assembled poem with, "My name is Ozymandias, King of Kings," and the other one began, "I met a traveller from an antique land." Four groups ended the poem with the original ending, "The lone and level

SAMPLE 1.2 Two Sample Assembled Poems

I met a traveller from an antique land,	My name is Ozymandias, King of Kings;
Who said—"Two vast and trunkless legs of stone	I met a traveller from an antique land,
Stand in the desert. . . . Near them, on the sand,	Who said–"Two vast and trunkless legs of stone
Half sunk a shattered visage lies, whose frown,	Stand in the desert. . . . Near them, on the sand,
And wrinkled lip, and sneer of cold command,	Half sunk a shattered visage lies, whose frown,
Tell that its sculptor well those passions read	And wrinkled lip, and sneer of cold command,
Which yet survive, stamped on these lifeless things,	Tell that its sculptor well those passions read
The hand that mocked them, and the heart that fed;	The hand that mocked them, and the heart that fed;
And on the pedestal, these words appear:	Nothing besides remains. Round the decay
My name is Ozymandias, King of Kings;	The lone and level sands stretch far away.
Look on my Works, ye Mighty, and despair!	Which yet survive, stamped on these lifeless things,
Noting besides remains. Round the decay	Of that colossal Wreck, boundless and bare
Of that colossal Wreck, boundless and bare	And on the pedestal, these words appear:
The lone and level sands stretch far away.	Look on my Works, ye Mighty, and despair

sands stretch far away," and one group ended with the line, "Look on my Works, ye Mighty, and despair!".

Now, the point of this activity is not to see who can get closest to the original form of the poem; rather, this is a meaning-making activity where readers make poetic choices based on structure, word order, and occasionally (and curiously seldom) rhyme. Let's look at two versions side by side and see how two groups of readers were making sense of the poem. Note that these are the two that are most different in the class (see Sample 1.2 on p. 7).

Derrick notices that the groups made similar choices; namely, that a line followed a line in the reassembled poem often in the same way as the poem, because that was the way it made sense.

By the end of the class, Derrick wishes he has more time. He says, "Ms. Simpson will continue with this poem when she returns, but I'm giving you a homework assignment and she will collect it and give it to me to read. I want you to write a paragraph about, 'Something you can do that would make people remember you a thousand years from now'." The bell rings.

Derrick feels that the lesson went well because the students were engaged in his discussion of who was "the greatest," and they were engaged in the activity of assembling the poem, but he wonders if the students have the poem "in the head." There was no time for classroom discussion of the assembled poems. Yet the poems that the students constructed all seem to make sense, and Derrick feels that the students did understand the poem better than if he had simply read it to them and stopped every line for a class discussion or explanation of "the facts" of the poem. He feels they have begun to, but he wishes he could follow up the next day as this is a poem that would take more than one day, perhaps two or three.

Two Teachers, Two Lessons, Two Approaches

I think it is readily apparent that these are two very different types of lessons. One is more traditional, using vocabulary instruction, having the teacher read and stop to ask factual or informational questions (or plot questions if this was a story) with the objective or purpose to, at the end of the class, arrive at a summative message or "theme" of the poem. Derrick's, on the other hand, seems to violate some of these traditional techniques. There is no direct vocabulary instruction, there is no teacher asking students to "stop and question" the facts, information (or plot) of the text, and there is no arriving at the "theme" or message of the poem. In fact, even if Derrick had time, he was not going to do these things. Furthermore, Derrick even tells a story directly related to the poem, which some teachers may see as "giving it away." In fact, most teachers who teach poetry, or Shakespeare, or a short story, spend much of their time having the students read the text and try to "figure out what it says," whereas Derrick just simply tells the students so that the students can transact or engage with the text without struggling with "figuring out the meaning."

The "stop and question facts" approach is quite common in most of the ELA classrooms I have observed, and I suspect it may be the most typical approach to teaching literature, not only nationwide, but in other countries (as I observed in a school for five days in the United Kingdom). It is almost as if we are penalizing students because they can't "figure out" what a poem, a Shakespeare scene, or a short story is saying; that is, without any point of reference or prior understanding that would help them access the text. Note that here Derrick does the exact opposite: He "gives it all away"; the students only have to engage or transact with the text. Derrick uses an *aesthetic* approach. Actually, "giving it all away" is what you do when you go to the movies or watch a TV show. You know pretty much all about it before you pay for your ticket or turn on the TV. It is the variations in the text that are interesting. That is why I watched the recent TV special *The Alienist* with interest. I wanted to see how the director and actors "played with" the presentation of serial murders in nineteenth-century New York, which I had read about in Caleb Carr's book. This "playing with" the text, not "getting the plot/facts/information," is what is important, and this is why books get turned into movies, movies are remade, and one story is changed from one media to another all the time. It's the "playing with" of the particular modality that gives us all the fun.

The question now arises not necessarily of which is the better lesson, but of which class is more likely to have engaged with the text. I think it is Derrick's students who have the poem more "in the head" or in their long-term memory. Derrick's students have been aesthetically engaged with the poem, that is, engaged through the senses. I should also add that in a few months hence, when students are asked to write "the literature essay" on a state exam, that it would be Derrick's students who are more likely to remember the substance of the poem. Here we note a curious, contradictory, and counterintuitive fact: Maria's students did all the analysis and explaining, but they have not been really engaged with the poem, they have not engaged or *transacted* with the poem, they have approached it informationally or *efferently* (from the Latin *effere*, "to take away") (Rosenblatt, 1978, 1983); Derrick's students, however, have done no analyzing or explaining, and they have the poem "in the head." Derrick's students have engaged in an activity that is called *unarticulated response* (Anderson & Rubano, 1991). This too is aesthetic education. It is a common myth of educational reformers and many others that one has to read efferently (for facts and information) before they are engaged aesthetically (have a transaction) with the work. Actually, the opposite is true: If a reader is not aesthetically engaged with a text, they will have grave difficulty getting any information from the text (Anderson & Rubano, 1991).

I think if you try this "assembling the text" technique, you will find not only that the students are engaged with the activity, but that they get it far more "in the head"—that is in the long-term memory—than if you use the "stop and question" or "translate and interpret lines/sentences" technique. I suggest you try it with "Ozymandias," or with another relatively *short* poem (there is only so much cutting and assembling that can be done in a short middle school or high school period). You can use a poem found on one of the old state exams, or a sonnet (only 14 lines), or you can try a more contemporary poem, such as "We Lived Happily During the War" by Ilya Kaminsky (2013):

> And when they bombed other people's houses, we
>
> protested
> but not enough, we opposed them but not
>
> enough. I was
> in my bed, around my bed America
>
> was falling: invisible house by invisible house by invisible house.
>
> I took a chair outside and watched the sun.
>
> In the sixth month
> of a disastrous reign in the house of money
>
> in the street of money in the city of money in the country of money,
> our great country of money, we (forgive us)
>
> lived happily during the war.

Here's a sample of an assembled poem done by preservice teachers in a graduate methods course. See if this version makes sense in their way of viewing the poem. Note that the spacing of the original poem could not be a factor in assembling the lines, but compare it to the original version. The arranged version also had lines starting with capital letters so the arrangers would not have a clue to sentence beginnings in the poem. To make the poem fit on the page, I have had to "wrap some lines," so the boxes will give you an idea of the original lines (see Sample 1.3 on p. 11).

While we always respect the canonical version the author wrote, there are two questions we can ask about the assembled reader response version: (1) Is this a valid meaning making of the poem; and, (2) by assembling the lines of the poem, did the readers respond to the structure of the poem so that it will remain more "in the head," that is, in their long-term memories? I think the answer is, "yes." Moreover, (3) did they enjoy transacting with the poem?

Your Students' Orientation: "Good Students" and "Not Good" Students

One of the principals of Aesthetic Education (AE) is that you teach the same way, if not on the same level, to successful students as to students who are disengaged from schooling. In other words, you do the same transactional activities *qualitatively*, if not *quantitatively*, whether the students are advanced placement high school seniors, or non-native English-speaking seventh graders, or with AP students, or with students who are disengaged from formal schooling. This

SAMPLE 1.3 Original and Assembled Poems Compared

Original Version	*Sample Assembled Version*
And when they bombed other people's houses, we	In the sixth month
protested	Of a disastrous reign in the house of money
but not enough, we opposed them but not	In the street of money in the city of money in the city of money in the
enough. I was	Our great country of money, we (forgive us)
in my bed, around my bed America	Lived happily during the war.
was falling: invisible house by invisible house by invisible house.	And when they bombed another people's house, we
I took a chair outside and watched the sun.	Protested
In the sixth month	But not enough, we opposed them but not
of a disastrous reign in the house of money	Enough. I was
in the street of money in the city of money in the country of money,	In my bed, around my bed America
our great country of money, we (forgive us)	Was falling: Invisible house by invisible house by
lived happily during the war.	I took a chair outside and watched the sun

is because all humans, of whatever maturity or intellectual attainment, engage in the process of learning in the same way. This is a concept that my education students don't agree with at first, and I can understand why readers of this book may think this statement is not only wrong, but outrageous. All I ask is that you give me time to demonstrate something about aesthetic education and practices and you will see that "learning is learning." My graduate students love the "assembling the poem" activity, and it's the first activity I do in my methods class. Note that it would work with fifth graders, and even in grades lower than that. Aesthetic approaches are a "way in" to teaching and learning, and they are the ways in which all learners organically learn. A doctoral candidate does not "learn" in any essentially different or qualitative way than a kindergartener, though quantitatively they are on vastly different levels. Gravity, the laws of motion, or how we process vitamin D from sunlight works by the same qualitative processes in all people, even if the sizes and capacities of differing people cause these same processes to quantitatively happen more slowly, or faster, or more, or less on or in the individual.

Creating Students Who Are Not Only Good at English, But Are Good at Loving It

As we discussed at the start of this chapter, you have an orientation to English—that's why you became a teacher. However, your students may not, even the academically successful ones. Let's do a thought experiment to illustrate this. I warn you, it's a bit unfair, but anyone who has taught for only a few days knows that there is some truth and usefulness to what we're examining here. Let's suppose we could divide, split, or bifurcate our students between "good" and "not good" English students. That's it, right down the middle, sheep and goats. I know we can't do this and that each student is unique and complicated. But let's suppose that we did categorize students between the "good," who are essentially engaged by formal schooling, and the "not good," who are essentially disengaged from formal schooling. Put simply, the engaged would be those who "buy into" schooling as a means for social and economic advancement, or as something necessary to a successful life. You will note that I did not mention anything about the good students liking, or being aesthetically engaged, with ELA studies of writing, reading, or speaking. The original "Coleman Report" (1966) made the point that the best students were not particularly the brightest, but those who had a support system of family and friends, and a local culture that valued the social and economic benefits of schooling; they valued the extrinsic rewards of academics, if not the intrinsic reward of learning in itself. Additionally, Coleman found that the students who got good grades were those who were willing to work at relatively boring tasks, not quite knowing the purpose of what they did, except they had to do it to be successful. They were able to delay gratification. Thus, students who are good at English might be different from their teacher (that's you) who is good at English and likes English. You see, there are students who get good grades in English and like writing, reading, and speaking. And there are students who get good grades in English and only tolerate writing, reading, and speaking for what it will get them down the line when they are adults. In short, school worked for us teachers in some important way, and the English curriculum has worked for us and we were successful at it. This is not to say, however, that most successful students *like* reading novels, writing poems, or any of the other elements of the ELA curriculum.

The second category is students who are disengaged from schooling for some reason—a reason which they often don't, won't, or can't articulate. But this does not mean they are stupid, just disengaged. However, I always tell my education students that these misbehaving students are often the most interesting and those who have great potential. These are the ones who arrive late, skip school regularly, often for days at a time, who don't do their homework, and who generally don't seem to care enough to do the minimum work to maintain passing grades. The mechanics of formal schooling are not working for them. We've all had students like this and they baffle us. I found very many of these in the urban schools where I taught in in poor and working poor neighborhoods in New York City. I think, if you've been teaching for more than a day, you have encountered these students. Even in my first teaching gig at a private boys' college prep school, there were the readily identifiable troublemakers.

One very dedicated Math teacher I know used to often moan about his underperforming students, "They are snatching defeat from the jaws of victory!" He just couldn't understand why many students rejected his offer of excellent mathematics instruction which would help them pass the state exams. As he noted, it's not hard to just simply pass most middle and high school classes by doing basic mathematics.

If I may digress a moment, my solution to this was to tell chronically absent students, or students who didn't do any work, to take some time when they *did* come to class. I used say, "Go to the back of the room, find a seat, and write me a letter telling me, 'Why I have been absent for two days a week', or, 'Why I won't do any work'. Tell me about yourselves." And then they'd *tell me*, and then I would learn exactly why they were "not good" students. They often were homeless, or living in three different overcrowded apartments, or some other awful social or economic conditions—in the city poor students are typically domicile challenged due to what Jeremiah Moss calls *hypergentrification* (Moss, 2017). Or, often they had had very little preparation, or no preparation, for the techniques and strategies that would have prepared them for the rules and rigors of formal schooling. Or perhaps they were in abusive relationships. Or, they simply did not have a reason to care, given their autobiographical experiences. You have to have access to success to be successful, no matter what the challenge is, and education is no exception. It's called the *Law of Proximal Opportunity*. George Bush was already close to the presidency when he became president. That's why it was easy for him. "Not good" students are often those who do not have *proximal opportunity* for academic, social, or economic success.

I'm writing of New York City because that's where I've lived for over 30 years. But the same goes for any urban, suburban, or rural district. Public schools anywhere have students with very problematic home lives, and any of our teaching is contextual. For instance, I often remind my education students here in New York City that, at best, 75 percent of New York City public students *never graduate from high school at all*. And that's the official estimate which is "messaged" with a lot of data missing, such as not including all the students who simply disappear from the rosters every year. I think the dropout rate in the city is closer to 45–50 percent (Costigan, 2000). Can I repeat that and I want to scream it: *About half of New York City students never graduate from high school at all.* That's outrageous in the twenty-first century. All this is to say that these students who are "not good" students are very different from you who, as a teacher, probably had a history of being a "good" student.

I am relating this, as I stated at the beginning of this section, because I have found that a good ELA lesson does the right things: engages all students, the academically disengaged, and the "good students" who also may be disengaged from reading and writing, but not from social advancement. And, no I'm not being naïve about this. Your goal, and my goal, as teachers is to engage all the students in our class every day. It never happens perfectly in the real world, but you can come very, very, very close. Your "bad students," who I should more charitably call "disengaged students," are what I call "bellwethers"; they tell you if your lesson is working or not. The "good" students tend to remain silent and play the "silence game"; that is, be as passive, acquiescing, and pleasant as possible to get a good grade. The bellwethers tell you if you're coming across (Costigan, 2004, 2005).

As the above sentences indicate, there are as many issues with "good" students as with "bad" students. It is not necessarily the case that these high achieving students love, or even like, the study of English literature, or writing, or talking about literature, or any academic subject area or discipline. In ELA, academically high achieving students don't *necessarily* like to read novels, read or write poems, or put their thoughts on paper in an essay, nor indeed do they like any other of the many parts of the English curriculum. Again, it bears repeating, we've known for over 50 years that students often value schooling for the extrinsic rewards of some future payoff of a good college, which leads to a good job, and not for any intrinsic value of what is studied in school (Bronfenbrenner, 1970). As a colleague of mine states:

> American life is now a competition to get into the best kindergarten, to go to the best school, to get into the most highly selective college, to get the best job, to have more money than other people. All to get into the best nursing home and die.

While this may seem cynical, I have been on the board of directors of a highly selective kindergarten in a very wealthy area of New York City, one where tuition was close to $40,000 per year for a *half* day, not including all the extra fees. Like most privileged parents, the parents of students in this school were desperate to get their children into a "good" school, not necessarily because it offered a fine education (which it did), but for the opportunities for advancement on to Harvard and Yale and then a successful career and a wealthy, and thus happy, life. However, as David Hursh points out, well-being is not well having (Hursh, 2016).

What Does This Have to Do with English?

Both engaged and disengaged students alike do not necessarily share your orientation towards the use of, and study of, English. Nevertheless, regardless of whether you are teaching young people who are disengaged from formal schooling, or teaching academically high achieving students, this book is designed for you to claim—or if you are now teaching, to *re*claim—your English orientation and to share it with your students. Whether they are academically achieving or not, your students don't necessarily "buy into" English as a value in their lives. That is, at least not yet. At least until you have had a go with them in your classroom. And as I will maintain throughout this book, the things that engage one set of students will engage every other set of students, if you maintain a certain attitude, or live in a certain ecology of doing things.

One of the ideas behind this book is that teaching is not just a "skill set." That is, teaching is not just a set of learned "teaching behaviors." Who you are—as a person and as a teacher—matters. Who your students are doesn't just matter, it is essential. You are not just a teacher holding a bucket of ideas, information, facts, skills pouring the contents of that knowledge-jug into your ever-ready students' heads. You are full of thoughts, feelings, wishes, dreams, and ideas. Your students are also living creatures who have personal autobiographies and who come from families and communities with certain values, and discourses (ways of thinking, speaking, acting, and communicating). The first step is acknowledging that learning is autobiographically based, particularly as your autobiography meets the biographies of your students. It is in this light that we look at Maria and Derrick, above. One, you will see, is information-based and one is autobiography-based. One teacher creates a classroom in which knowledge is seen as something that is passed on independently from the lived lives of real people, while the other creates a classroom in which knowledge is constructed from the lives of real people. In Maria's class, students receive information about a very fine poem, but they are not really transacting with it. In Derrick's class the student is actively doing *something* and is engaged: this is what we call the aesthetic approach. How we got here will be covered in the next chapter.

Thinking About Learning and Doing Teaching

Each chapter of this book will end with either a lesson you can do, or thoughts about a type of curriculum you might want to consider. This is an example of curriculum design and/or implementation (teaching) that both summarizes the chapter and brings up issues presented in the chapter. Let's begin by looking at one.

When the students arrive in class and take their seats, they notice on the teacher's desk (or on a table in the room) many pictures scattered about. Some visual representations have been cut out of magazines. Some are postcards. Some are other kinds of reproductions of artworks. There are a few more visual representations on the desk than there are students in the room. It is important however, that each picture has at least one human presented in it.

After taking attendance and getting the students settled down, the teacher, named Jennifer, announces, "Today we're going to do a writing project, but the writing will be based on a picture, photograph, or visual representation that you choose. This will lead to a reading or writing unit. So, we're going to go up row by row and select one picture with which you'd like to work."

In about five minutes, each student is seated at his or her desk with a picture. The teacher asks them to turn over the pictures so they are not yet looking at them. Jennifer then states, "We're going to do some *guided freewriting* [Elbow, 1998], can anyone review what that is?" Jennifer picks on a volunteer and the student explains, "That's when we just try to keep the pen moving and keep writing. Spelling, grammar, punctuation, neatness, don't count." Jennifer adds, "Yes you're right, but guided means that I'm going to give you starters (or prompts) which you can try to write about. This is also, for now, *anonymous writing* in that you're just writing for yourself, and it's *low stakes writing* because I won't be grading it. However, you will be turning it into an original piece of writing that I will eventually collect." The teacher then asks, "By the way, what do you do if you can't keep your pen moving, if you get 'stuck'?" Jennifer calls on another student, and he says, "Well you can just write about what is really on your mind instead of the prompt, even if it isn't what Jennifer suggests, or you can just keep writing, 'stuck', 'stuck', 'stuck'." Another student adds, "Or, if you're stuck on the word, you can just keep writing the word over and over again until something comes through."

"OK, let's begin," Jennifer announces, "I want you to take a moment and *not* write, just look at the picture. What do you notice? What do you see in the picture? What do you think is happening in the picture? What is the 'story' of what is going on in the picture?" She pauses for a few minutes to let the students actively observe the picture they each have. (Alternatively, note that two students could be sharing a picture if resources are limited, though they will be each writing as individuals.)

"OK, now It's time to write. Start freewriting about what you see in the picture." Then, depending on the class's writing experiences, they write from about three to five or more minutes. Then Jennifer states, "OK, I'm going to ask you to continue to write while I ask you to consider different things in the picture. You can move on in your writing based on what I'm suggesting, or you can stay with the thought you're on if you're going with the flow. Let's begin." Jennifer consults her lesson plan and decides from among a number of *starters* (prompts) to get the students to continue writing about their visual representations. Each of these writing segments after each prompt lasts a few minutes, and Jennifer paces herself on giving successive starters by observing how the students are writing. The starters may include:

- *Focus on one of the people in the picture. Write down the thoughts going on in their head.*
- *If there is another person in the picture, what is one saying to another? If there is not another person in the picture, what is the person in the picture saying to someone just outside the picture? Write the dialogue.*
- *What do you think happened before this picture was taken or painted or created?*
- *What do you think is going to happen after this picture was taken or painted or created?*
- *Given what is presented in the picture, what do you think is the end result of what is happening in the picture?*
- *What is happening outside of the picture, outside of the frame or four corners of the picture. What is happening on the left, right, top, or bottom of the picture?*
- *What are you absolutely sure of in the picture?*

- *What questions do you have about the picture? What do you wonder about? What are you unsure about in the picture? What is unclear in the picture? What do you find confusing in the picture?*
- *Take a moment and tell lies about the picture.*
- *What feeling does the picture give you? What emotions does the picture present to you? What in the picture causes you to feel this way?*
- *Take a moment and notice something in the picture you haven't noticed before. What do you notice? Write about the thing you now notice in the picture.*
- *Is there anything else you haven't yet, so far, paid attention to?*
- *Is there anything else you would like to say about the picture? What final thoughts do you have about the picture?*

As you can imagine there are other starters a teacher can use. The idea is to keep the students writing. Following Elbow (1998), at the end of the writing session, Jennifer asked the students to *postwrite* (metacognitive writing = *meta*, beyond; *cognitive*, thinking) on, "How did your writing go today? Did it go well, because . . .? Did it not go well because . . .? Was it successful because . . .? Write one sentence about how you wrote today." Jennifer explains that though this is low stakes writing (not graded) it is *public writing* (published, made public); namely, that this will be shared with the class.

After the writing session, the teacher asks the students at the minimum to share their postwriting. Or, she may ask the students to underline (or put a star or asterisk next to) one or several lines they wrote, and to share their writing, either as volunteers or in a "read around." If a read around, students can read all, some, or just one or two words of their writing, or they can say "pass" without penalty. After they have shared, there might be a short class discussion about what they discovered in their writing, or the teacher may ask the students to share in pairs or small groups something about their writing.

Depending on whether the focus or point of this ultimate unit is *writing*, or whether the point is *reading*, the teacher will probably introduce a model of the type of reading or writing she wants the students to do. (Another type of lesson or unit could have the focus or point of speaking, but I don't recommend this for novice teachers, as explained in the next chapters of the book.) It is obvious that the freewrite could be turned into a writing narrative, a descriptive essay, a poem, a story, or dialogue (drama). In each case teacher would supply a text that modeled and contextualized the student generated writing genre under consideration. If this were a *writing lesson*—as is the most typical use of this type of lesson—the student would write a narrative, poem, story, or dramatic dialogue once provided with a model (contextual support). This model, in turn, could be used to engage with a specific published genre of a work of literature. Thus, the freewrite response to the visual representation would last probably for one lesson, and the subsequent lesson could last from a few days to several weeks depending on whether this was a *writing unit* (where students produce their original narratives, poems, or dramatic dialogues) in engagement with a published work of art (contextual support); or, whether this is a *reading unit* where student transact with a particular genre of a work of art (descriptive essay, story, poetry, drama) in light of their own writing.

I hope you can see—as I do when I myself teach or observe this type of lesson—that it is highly engaging. Students have "fun," because they are engaged in an authentic, autobiographical, social (sharing with others eventually) writing and reading activity which looks like reading and writing in the real world. This lesson looks different from many reading and writing lessons I often observe in 7–12 classrooms where students read to "get" a predetermined message or "theme," or when they write according a formulaic four-paragraph essay: (1) Introduction, (2) Body A, (3) Body B, and (4) Conclusion. Nevertheless, I need to make several important points about this lesson for you, the reader, to consider:

1. I no longer use the term *creative writing*. I do believe that students should create their own narratives, autobiographies, biographies, stories, poems, and plays, but creating fiction, poetry, and drama is not more creative than what I do when I write scholarly articles and books such as this one. The writing process is the same. Writing is writing.
2. This lesson is in no sense original. I have seen this type of lesson several times. It's as TS Eliot was supposed to have said about poets, "Bad poets borrow, good poets steal." Same with teachers. I tell my education students to *steal* all the time. Good teaching pedagogies are not copyrighted.

What is important for this chapter and this book is the strategies behind this lesson, its structure or scaffolding, if you will. The lesson is not important because I have "given you a lesson," but because I have given you the way the lesson works behind the scenes, the ecology of the lesson, literally "where it lives." Let's consider some major elements of the lesson.

Theoretical Framework, or Conceptual Framework, of Lesson

This is an aesthetic, transactional writing project using reader response techniques as applied to the text of a work of art, which is visual representation (photograph, picture, other visual representation or reproduction). The theoretical framework of the lesson could be represented Figure 1.1; this is explained further in the next chapters of the book.

Thus, the instructional ELA "point" (text, modality) of this lesson is *writing*: For students to create a descriptive narrative based on a visual artifact or text or modality (photograph, picture, postcard, reproduction, visual image). The secondary wing is speaking (teacher gives instructions, students work collaboratively, the lesson ends with a *read around* where students share all or some of their writings). This wing is secondary because, while it is a part of the lesson, it is really using the normative type of speaking used in the ELA classroom, not directly addressed in this lesson.

Point (or Focus of Lesson)

Writing: Descriptive Narrative or Descriptive Essay

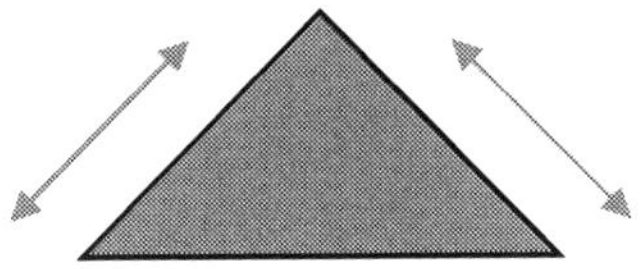

Secondary wing (support) ↔ **Primary Wing (support)**

Speaking — Reading visual representation

FIGURE 1.1 The Intermodal Triangle: Point and Wings.

Thus, note that: (1) A lesson with the focus or point of reading is supported by the wings of reading and writing; (2) a lesson with the focus or point of writing, is supported by wings of reading and speaking; (3) a lesson with the focus or point of speaking (e.g. speeches, debate) is supported by the wings of writing and reading. Additionally, as this lesson has the point of writing, the teacher must also provide a model, scaffolding, or sample of professional writing in this genre to *contextualize* the writing for the students. The freewrite is done on the students' own, but if this is turned into a formal public piece of writing (published, to the teacher or to other students), then a context or model must be provided.

The Theoretical Framework or Conceptual Framework of this curriculum (lesson or unit) contains the following elements:

1. **Aesthetic education and aesthetic reading:** Involves learning through the senses and personal student experiences.
2. **Constructivist learning:** Students create or construct their own meanings based on what they already know. They actively create meaning by the engagement of new information with what is already known.
3. **Reader response/aesthetic reading/aesthetic transaction:** Students transact (engage, interact) with the "text" (modality) of a picture, photograph, or other visual representation in the same way they would with a text of literature, or even an efferent (informational-based) reading (Asher, 2003).
4. **Intermodality:** The lesson and students' meaning making is created by the interaction of various modes of differing texts or modalities of knowing: The mode of writing interacts with the visual mode, which interacts with the modality of speaking (students share final writings).

5. **Student-centered (and autobiographical) practices:** The lesson is based on who the students are, what they are thinking, and how they individually respond to the representations. While the lesson has formal and technical aspects of the ELA curriculum, these are grafted on to the who the students are, their autobiographies.
6. **Materials:** A few years ago I would get these representations from postcards of paintings in a museum (every museum had postcards, but now less so, if at all). Or, I'd ask for old magazines from the school librarian and just cut out pictures. Or I'd ask students to cut out interesting pictures from magazines at home. The library or my friends always had old magazines lying around, but magazines are mostly online now and printing them out can be time consuming and/or costly. Nowadays, you could put several pictures on a screen as these are readily available online, or if you had several computers in your room, you could put a representation on each computer and have the students walk around and place themselves at one image that interests them. The following pictures, which can be viewed online, would really work:

   - Johannes Vermeer, any picture with two people in it, such as *The Love Letter*, or *The Girl with the Wineglass*
   - Théodore Géricault, *The Raft of the Medusa*
   - Edward Hopper, any picture with two people in it. *Nighthawks* (if they don't know the painting), or *Room in New York*, or *Summer Evening*
   - Picasso, *Guernica*
   - Van Gogh, *Into the Undergrowth*
   - Georges Seurat, *A Sunday on La Grande Jatte*
   - Renoir, *The Boating Party*
   - Walker Evans, just about every photograph will do.
   - James Van Der Zee, *Couple in Racoon Coats, Wedding Party*. I'd avoid the pictures of dead people, which was the fashion in the early twentieth century.
   - A Jacob Lawrence painting; check out the Black Lives Matter exhibit on the webpage of MoMa (Museum of Modern Art, New York City) at www.thedailybeast.com/black-lives-matter-at-moma; or research Jacob Lawrence by searching for him online, or looking for his Migration Series.

The list is endless, of course. I've played (fairly) safe and conservative with the above list as some of these images are fairly well-known to any educated person in the United States, but they might not be known to your students. You can take it further, of course and do more unfamiliar works, but I'd probably avoid (without careful preparation) naked people and prostitutes: both (and often both are the same figures) are not unknown in the photography and painting world.

Summary

I have used this lesson to illustrate concepts that follow in the book. If I were to have to give it one word it would be *intermodality*. This means that students take one text (modality), namely a visual representation, and they create another modality (free-writing) to make meaning of it. This, in turn, gives the students access to two other possibilities, such as a descriptive writing unit, or in support of a reading unit with the theme of description (think of the number of "To a . . ." poems that use description. By creating a text out of a text, a modality of meaning making out of a modality of meaning making, learning is strengthened and enters the long-term memory.

This type of learning is active as students are actually engaged in *doing* something (rather than listening), and it is constructivist because students are actively construing and building up knowledge based on what they already know. The constructivist nature is, in turn, both *autobiographical* (or student-centered) because it is based on the students' personal understandings and ways of thinking, feeling, and understanding, as well as being *socially construed*, because the writing, and reading, is actively shared with other students. This works, I think, much better than in reading having a teacher "read, stop, translate" a work of art, or in writing, having a teacher "give instructions in the genre, have students plan (outline), have students write." In the interaction of modalities of texts, not only is the students' long-term memory accessed (getting it "in the head"), but students are involved in authentic life-based and real-world writing, reading, and speaking activities.

And, if you, as a teacher, absolutely had to teach "the literature essay," or the "four-paragraph essays," or "the five-paragraph theme," this authentic reading or writing activity could, after it has been engaged in, be turned into artificial, schoolish writing. Here's a general rule I've developed:

- Students who can do real writing, reading, and speaking activities can do schoolish writing, reading, and speaking tasks.
- Students who can only do schoolish writing (artificial essays), and schoolish reading (reading for plot, information, and "theme") cannot necessarily do authentic reading like it exists in the real world.
- And a student who is adept at schoolish speaking (answering the teacher's question with a correct—or not—one or few word answer) cannot do real-world exploratory talk for discovery and communication with others, but of course, a student who is really learning to speak with articulation and cohesion can also answer a teacher's question with a word or two.

The subsequent chapters of this book will take you through how to create a more authentic curriculum, one that is purposeful and engaging for your students, so that, if they have to do schoolish, standards- and test-based learning, they can do it much better than if you only taught "to the needs of the school-room," or "to the standards," or "to the test."

References

Asher, R. (2003). Murals as interdisciplinary teaching. In D. Kaufmann, D. M. Moss, & T. A. Osborne (Eds.), *Beyond the boundaries: A transdisciplinary approach to teaching and learning* (pp. 131–144). Westport, CT: Praeger Publishers/Greenwood Publishing Group, Inc.

Bronfenbrenner, U. (1970). *Two worlds of childhood: U.S. and U.S.S.R.* New York: Russell Sage Foundation/Basic Books.

Coleman, J. (1966). *Equality of educational opportunity* ("Coleman Report"). Washington, DC: National Center for Educational Statistics.

Costigan, A. T. (2000). How teachers construct their learning histories. Dissertation in English Education, New York University.

Costigan, A. (2004). Finding a name for what they want: A study of New York City's Teaching Fellows. *Teaching and Teacher Education: An International Journal, 20*(2), 129–143.

Costigan, A. (2005). Choosing to stay, choosing to leave: The New York City Teaching Fellows after two years. *Teacher Education Quarterly, 32*(2), 125–142.

Hursh, D. (2016). *The end of public schools: The corporate reform agenda to privatize education.* New York: Routledge.

Kaminsky, I. (2013). "We lived happily during the war." Poetry Foundation. Originally published in *Poetry Magazine*, May 2009. Accessed January 4, 2018 at: www.poetryfoundation.org/poems/91413/we-lived-happily-during-the-war.

Mayher, J. S. (1991). *Uncommon sense: Theoretical practice in language education.* Portsmouth, NH: Heinemann.

Moss, J. (2017). *Vanishing New York: How a great city lost its soul.* New York: Dey St/William Morrow.

Rosenblatt L. M. (1978). *The reader, the text, the poem: The transactional theory of the literary work.* Carbondale, IL: Southern Illinois University Press.

Rosenblatt L. M. (1983). *Reading as exploration* (3rd ed.). New York: Modern Language Association.

2

THE FOUNDATIONS OF PRACTICE

Where We Come From and Where We Are Now

Where Does ELA Teaching Come From?

In this chapter, I am going to discuss the history and current state of English Language Arts (ELA) instruction and the theories behind them. I know that that sentence will probably make you want to skip this chapter and go to the next where you will find more practical suggestions about how to teach ELA. Please don't. There are three reasons why I think this chapter is essential for understanding how to teach writing, reading, and speaking. The first is that this chapter gives you the background on how we think about the teaching of English, the foundations of practice and pedagogy. Knowing where you come from is essential to figuring out where you are going. The second reason is that without a solid foundation in the thinking behind what we now know in ELA instruction, you are at risk of teaching day to day and at the whim of what administrators want and what students are used to (Lortie, 1975). I would even say that if you are in a school that uses scripted or prepackaged curricula, knowing how students actually write, read, and speak will assist you in making those lessons not only your own, but ones that engage your students. The third reason is that I will end the chapter with some concrete writing, reading, and speaking activities you can use in your 7–12 ELA classroom, but only after I give you some information about the foundations in the teaching and learning of literacy. Let me try to explain this from my perspective as a former high school English teacher of nearly 14 years, and as a teacher educator for over 18 years.

When I arrived in New York City to teach, I had worked my last shift on a Saturday and left Boston literally on the midnight train; by Monday morning, I was at Erasmus Hall in Flatbush, Brooklyn. I was given a Delaney Book—an attendance card filing system that I had never seen before and didn't know how to use—as well as a class schedule; that was my entire introduction to urban public school teaching. The bell rang and I was off to find my room to teach my first class as one of 42 English teachers in a school of about 7,500 students. Then I began my five-period-a-day teaching job. Out the window went my Dewey-based, constructivist, student-centered ideas, which I had learned in my master's program. My first day, and my first year of teaching, was about survival. I taught the curriculum I was given in the way I remembered from my very traditional educational background. There is even a term for this—*wash out theory*—where teachers fall into teaching as they were taught simply because of the day to day pressures, the expectations of students and administrators, and the weight of our own traditional background as students watching the commonsense things teachers do (Britzman, 1986, 2003; Zeichner & Tabachnik, 1981). Eventually I returned to a more constructivist outlook—hence this book—but that's another story. The point here is that I didn't have a strong enough foundation to not teach in the ways that I had been taught, or to discover ways to teach that were beneficial for my students. Rather, I taught just to survive, and I'm sorry to say I just did things that I was told to do, or things that I had to come up with day by day. My teaching may only have been somewhat effective, and only somewhat beneficial for my students. That's not the way to thrive in the teaching profession.

Let me tell you another related story to make the case for this "the foundations of where we come from, where we are now" chapter. Once, in an ELA teaching methods course, my class were sharing the lesson plans they had created as part of the course's requirements. During the class, as we were sharing lesson plans, I realized each of the 15 or so student teachers in the class came up with lessons simply based on what seemed commonsensical from their extensive in-school observations required by the program: Graphic organizers, vocabulary lists, writing parts of "the argumentative essay," and, "reading for textural evidence" predominated. The last two concerns in writing and reading are due to a local misinterpretation of what administrators and teachers believe the Common Core State Standards (CCSS) demand (Costigan, 2017).

In short, the core lesson activities presented in their lessons were weak, gathered from what they had observed in their schools, using pedagogies whose effectiveness they never questioned. They were teaching things just because they thought they should, but they couldn't explain: (1) Why they were using a particular pedagogy; (2) how that pedagogy would enhance student learning and engage learners; and, most importantly, (3) how these activities helped students enjoy reading and writing so that they become engaged and lifelong readers and writers. I asked the class a question they certainly didn't like: "Would you like to be a student sitting in your own class?" The answer for the class seemed to be, "Not really." I then asked the unpopular question, "Then why are you teaching the way you are?" The answer was that they did not have any basic foundation (yet) in what actually were the ways in which young people learn to write, read, and speak.

Thus, there are several questions I've come to ask myself and teacher education candidates when designing lessons, and I think they bear articulating:

1. How is this writing, reading, or speaking activity engaging the students I have before me, and how do I know is it enhancing their learning?
2. If I, as a teacher, hated to do this when I was a student, why am I doing it to my students?
3. If this activity is something that will make my student hate rather than like reading or writing, why am I doing it?
4. Lots of students learn to hate reading and writing in school. What can I do to reverse this trend and make them love reading, literature, and writing, as much as I do?

In the class I am describing, I thought a minute and told them to take out the methods text we were using, and I assigned every two students a chapter, saying something like, "OK, in each chapter are techniques that you can use in your lessons. Rather than coming up with something on your own, I'd like you to find two techniques or pedagogies you can use to enhance your lesson and engage your students." As you may have guessed, the vast majority of students in the class found at least two or three pedagogies or activities they could use that would enhance student learning, and actually engage students with writing, reading, and speaking.

Another issue for new (and experienced) teachers is that we reinvent the wheel. This is what I did in my first years of teaching. When I taught *Macbeth*, or the mandatory "persuasive essay" for the state exam, or poetry reading, or anything else, it was as if *no one ever did this before*. Like my students in my methods class, I "came up with things" on my own, never considering that there was a mass of literature written by educators and researchers who had thought about these things and had taught these things, from the National Council of Teachers of English (NCTE), and from reputable publishers, all of which could save me the time and trouble of having to come up with learning activities on my own.

This chapter argues that, rather than just unreflectively mimicking the pedagogies currently in use in our school, or coming up with lessons on our own, we need a further step, and that is to ground ourselves in the foundations of what is writing, what is reading, what is speaking. Should one use a graphic organizer in a lesson? The answer depends on your understanding of what the reading and writing process is, how you define it, the requirements of the content you are presenting, and the learning needs of your students. And all that cannot be determined unless you are aware of, and can articulate, your "English orientation," the ecology or environment of the way you think about ELA. And you can only have that orientation if you have a foundation in your head of what is language, how it is acquired, and how it is expressed in the processes of writing, reading, and speaking.

I am reminded of a first year Social Studies teacher I was interviewing for a research project. He said, "Tomorrow I need to teach nineteenth century immigration, and all we're covering in my methods class is how to use primary documents to create a unit on the Civil War era." A little reflection reveals that what this new teacher lacked, at this point in his career, was a foundation (or the groundwork or ecology) that could be applied to either immigration or the Civil War (how to use primary documents with his students). Giving him a lesson on immigration would help him tomorrow, but it wouldn't provide him with a foundation, an approach, an orientation, to teaching the vast and complex issues of the Social Studies American History curriculum, or any History or Social Studies curriculum. I was the same way when I started teaching. I'd think, "I need to begin a *Macbeth* scene tomorrow," and I'd never consider what I have learned about reader response criticism, kinesthetic learning, the writing process, or anything else. Dan Lortie (1975) identified this nearly a half century ago as *presentism*. It's still with us today.

The next chapter of this book will have a more direct discussion about how to design units, lessons, and activities, but I want to go over the foundations of the way we think about the ELA curriculum, of how and why we are where we are. I think this will help you begin to think about overall theories and practices you can use to orient yourselves toward teaching and learning. It will begin the conversation about how students *learn* best (which always comes first) and how best to *teach* (which always comes from the first consideration). Knowing the history of approaches to teaching and learning, and knowing where we are now can, I think, only help you in framing your "teaching ecology" or "teaching environment" rather than figuring it out on your own. So, let's speak a bit about the foundations of literacy so that we have something on which to build our teaching curriculum.

The Beginnings of the Story

At the start of the twentieth century, the philosopher John Dewey in lectures, in his teaching, in his books, and in his experimental school where his ideas were tried out, spoke of a "Copernican Revolution" in education (Dewey, 1900, 1902, both in Dewey, 1971). By this he meant an educational system of teaching and learning in which learning centered not on the "sun" of the content (information and skills) taught, but on the "sun" of the child and how the child was naturally disposed to learning. In Dewey's first writings on education, *The School and Society* (1899) and *The Child and the Curriculum* (1902), he advocated a child-centered, activity-centered approach to education (Dewey, 1971). This approach, of course, was a reaction to the memorization and information- and fact-based methodology of most education in the United States of that day (and this is one that is still prevalent today—as Maria's lesson in Chapter 1 shows). If you ever heard "toe the line" (not "tow the line"), you are referring to a "recitation" where a student would literally put her toes on a line in front of the teacher to recite what she memorized, perhaps something like the multiplication tables, or French irregular verbs, or the rules for a participle or gerund. You will note that these examples have little to do with solving mathematical problems, speaking French, or writing standard English. Nevertheless, today recitation is still with us, and if we no longer toe the line, we take examinations, we summarize a work of art's "theme," and we believe there actually exists in the real world something called The Four-Paragraph Essay. In examinations and in many classrooms, you will notice, we engage in writing, reading, and speaking practices that bear little resemblance to what writers and readers do in the real world. Dewey, however, was about *bringing the outside in*, that is bringing the real world into the classroom, or rather, making classroom learning look like how people actually learn in the real world.

What is important is that in the pre-Copernican universe of education, the curriculum is fact- or information-based, as the novelist Charles Dickens wrote in *Hard Times* (1854). He put these words in the mouth of his relentless school board superintendent, Gradgrind:

> Now, what I want is, Facts. Teach these boys and girls nothing but Facts. Facts alone are wanted in life. Plant nothing else, and root out everything else. You can only form the minds of reasoning animals upon Facts: nothing else will ever be of any service to them. This is the principle on which I bring up my own children, and this is the principle on which I bring up these children. Stick to Facts, sir!

When you read the CCSS, or when you read about what Bill Gates or any another reformer wants to do with online or electronic education, or when you give your students a high stakes standardized examination, or when you teach reading for "supporting details," and writing "the argumentative essay," you will see that the advocacy of facts (or information) is as strong as it was in the nineteenth century. This battle is still going on between those of us who are educators who are process-based, student-centered, inquiry-based, constructivist, aesthetically oriented, and who use authentic assessment practices, and those of us who are information-centered, transmissive (passing along), and whose ultimate goal is for students to recall information on examinations and to defend a predetermined point in an essay. I assume, if you are reading this book, you are inclined more toward Dewey's point of view. And if you're not, as I wasn't given my traditional background, I hope this book will make a case for a more uncommonsense education (Mayher, 1991)

An essential point to make is that Dewey was not advocating an intellectually weak curriculum. Indeed, he notes in his early texts that child- or student-centered teaching and learning requires *more* effort, and that the child needs to be directed by careful guidance and positive criticism (Dewey, 1971). For those of us in ELA, this would be centering on:

1. *Writing as a process* much like real writers use, writing the real texts that actual writers write in the real world, rather than the artificial four paragraphs "literature essay" or "argumentative essay." And it would mean writing using multiple drafts, with many revisions, rather than writing it at one sitting under the high pressure as in a test. Writing would emphasize the process of writing rather than getting an as-perfect-as-possible product.
2. *Reading like real writers read* at home in armchairs, in libraries, or even at the beach, on a bus, in a dentist's office, or in the bathtub. It would mean reading for engagement, for an aesthetic *transaction* with the text, not for something called "plot" or "theme" and never reading under the time constraints and pressures of a test (Rosenblatt, 1978, 1983).
3. *Speaking for exploration*, for sharing, for working things out, just like real speakers speak after a movie, over coffee, on the bus, or in the school cafeteria. It would not be speaking to give a short one, two, or three word answer to a teacher who has "called on" you to get the correct preexisting fact or piece of information before "calling on" the next person.
4. *A multimodality or multiple literacy approach* that combines (1) writing, (2) reading, and (3) speaking as autobiographical and social (democratic) process, just as they are combined in the real world. Working on projects that combine all three modalities (among other modes of texts, as we shall see in the rest of this book). Working on projects that are autobiographies, biographies, qualitative research projects, investigations, collaborative projects—anything that uses the whole person and develops the whole person. (Note that Chapter 6 of this book on multiple literacies by my colleague Limarys Caraballo will take this even further.)

Indeed, one of the reasons I am writing this book is that I want you to think about these things now, and to avoid where I was, many years into my teaching when I and my students were bored with the formulaic, boring, artificial, schoolish things.

I remember, in particular, teaching a remedial (class) of bright but academically disinterested young the "persuasive essay" then in vogue. The paragraphs one through four were:

1. Introduction (Who, what, where, when, why, how; rephrase the question/directions; last line of introduction: "My opinion is . . .")
2. Body A, first supporting fact or reason A ("My first reason is . . .")
3. Body B, separate supporting fact or reason B ("My second reason is . . .")
4. Conclusion ("Therefore, my opinion is . . .").

How easy could it be? But the students just didn't do well on this simple template. Eventually I had an Ah! Moment, saying to myself, "Of course, I'm asking them to do fake, artificial things that exist only within the walls of the school.

This is simple, but counterintuitive. It's not the way real writers write. Why don't I start doing real, authentic things that exist in real life, like real writing (and reading, and speaking) in my classroom?" This is what Dewey was writing about at the start of the twentieth century. Sadly, this is still what we're struggling with today. Here is a general rule I've come to live by in my teaching:

A. Teaching students to do a fake (artificial) but simple thing is almost impossible to do—and they will come to hate doing these things.
B. Teaching students to do a real (authentic) but complex thing is always achievable—and they will come to love the challenge of doing real things.

Slight reflection reveals there are many corollaries to the above: A is painful, B is pleasurable; and A is counterintuitive, B is intuitive; A is unnatural, B is natural; A is not human, B is human, and so on . . .

When you think about your own education, or the education that you observe in most schools, it will become clear to you that learning in school still does not resemble the way learning takes place in the real world. In the ELA curriculum, the types of writing that students do (the persuasive essay, the argumentative essay, the literature essay, the five-paragraph theme) often do not resemble the types of writing that real writers do in the real world (a *New York Times* editorial, a blog entry, a short story in *The New Yorker*, a poem in *Poetry*). Nor do students in most classrooms in the United States go about reading and writing as *processes* that resemble what writers and readers in the real world do, nor does reading in most schools resemble the psycholinguistic processes that actually go on in the mind. No reader in the real world reads for a text's "message" or "theme." No reader in the real word reads for "textual evidence" or "supporting details." You could even divide the two approaches into the traditional/transmissive/commonsense one, which focuses on learning as a *product,* and the progressive/constructivist/uncommonsense one, which focuses on learning as a *process*.

I understand that each new teacher thinks of themself as a performer, an orchestra leader, the impresario in front of the room. They come to think (again, as I did) that everything depends on them and their lesson. It's all about the teacher. Granted, what the teacher does and how he plans his lesson, and how he executes it, matters very much; but what Dewey and these other early educational thinkers were saying is that the young person in front of you is where you are to begin, assuming that is that you know your content area. If you don't believe this, walk around any school and you will see teachers "delivering lessons" that have nothing to do with the way the people in front of them are able to learn. In short, too much of what goes on in ELA classrooms, and indeed most classrooms, violates the way young people learn. Let me put it another way: If you do not attune your teaching to the organic ways in which your students are able to learn, can learn, and do learn, how can you teach them anything?

Another point about Dewey is that this stuff isn't new. He was in a long tradition of educational reformers who began by looking at how children actually developed, namely, Johann Heinrich Pestalozzi (1746–1827), Friedrich Fröbel [Froebel] (1782–1852), and Maria Montessori (1870–1952). Granted these were mostly dealing with the kindergarten grades (a word, by the way, coined by Froebel). By the time of Dewey, scientists were also discovering the stages of human development in the womb, and they thought, "Why wouldn't this development continue through childhood and adolescence?" This is why I call this approach to education the *organic approach*, which sees humans as having a built-in system of development simply because they are humans, as opposed to the *building block approach*, which conceives of humans as a blank slate to which everything must added. The former pedagogy attempts to guide and refine a student's natural abilities; the later pedagogy attempts to add things to a student who is seen as lacking and deficient.

Montessori was a physician, someone who by definition is an empiricist using deductive methods. She came to schooling by beginning to observe the ways in which students actually learned and interacted with the real world, and based her educational system on that; hers is a system that continues to be used today. For instance, at one developmental stage (the organic approach) children become very neat. So, why not build in neatness and "putting away things" into the curriculum to develop this organic process. Thus, the overarching idea in all of these early reformers and practitioners is that learning builds upon the way that children develop organically. However, this is not just letting students do what they want and learn what they wish, which is a common misunderstanding of progressive educators and education. Rather the idea is to build upon the growth processes that are already there, and that develop organically by careful guidance and assistance. In teaching we have a choice: To build upon how students are hardwired to learn, or to try to counter that organic development with lessons and activities that are not natural and are counterintuitive.

It seems very clear that the child-centered, inquiry-centered, project-centered curriculum of Dewey (and the others mentioned above, along with many others not mentioned) is not the one that has been ascendant in United States public schools. First of all, it requires an intensive hands-on participation by teachers; it is labor-intensive. Thus, historically it was hard to do when, starting in the early part of the twentieth century, schools had to process masses of students, particularly immigrants and non-native speaking English students, who needed to be efficiently "educated" in classrooms of 30 to 50 students. Progressive education is not cost effective to the managerial and political class. And, of course this is true today where educational reformers would like students sitting in front of computer terminals learning information guided by algorithms—none of which

TABLE 2.1 Two Paradigms of Teaching and Learning (After John Mayher)

Uncommonsense		*Commonsense*
active	—	passive
activities	—	lecture
activity-based	—	memorization-based
aesthetic (values feeling)	—	anesthetic (ignores feeling)
authentic assessment	—	examination-based assessment
authoritative	—	authoritarian
autobiographical	—	collective
classroom like real world	—	classroom different from real world
collaborative	—	winners and losers
cooperative	—	competitive
democratic	—	autocratic
experience (doing-based)	—	information (fact-based)
in the body (kinesthetic)	—	disembodied (inert)
intrinsic rewards	—	extrinsic rewards
John Dewey (1859–1952)	—	Edward Lee Thorndike (1874–1949)
knowledge is constructed	—	knowledge is transmitted (by teacher)
knowledge is constructed	—	knowledge is received (by learner)
learning by doing	—	learning by watching and listening
learning by doing	—	learning by listening or seeing
learning is natural	—	learning is artificial
learning is pleasant	—	learning is painful
like play	—	like work
likes complex activities	—	likes simple and clear information and facts
manipulative	—	receptive
messy, complex	—	orderly steps, breaking down
multilayered	—	linear, backward design
multiple literacies	—	reading, writing, and arithmetic only
natural	—	artificial
organic	—	manufactured
original works of art	—	textbooks, workbooks, and computer fill ins
pleasurable	—	feelings unimportant
portfolio-based assessment	—	symbolic assessment (numbers)
process is important	—	product is important
progressive	—	traditional
project-based	—	lesson-based
real-world-based	—	school-based
real writing	—	schoolish writing
social	—	individual
student-centered	—	teacher-centered
teacher as coach	—	teacher as expert
uses bodies	—	ignores bodies
uses the senses (aesthetic)	—	ignores the senses (anesthetic)
who student is: important	—	who student is: irrelevant

need costly educators with their health plans, vacations, and retirement benefits. But there is an ideological reason the uncommonsense, student-centered, inquiry-based, process-based, real life-like, education of Dewey and others hasn't caught on. The person perhaps more responsible for traditional schooling, and the division of learning into "subjects," with bells, examinations, and the like, is Edward Lee Thorndike (1874–1949), who was roughly contemporaneous with Dewey. He was also one of the of the people who refined the intelligence test. Thorndike was incredibly influential. I risk grossly oversimplifying a complicated man and an immensely complex output, but Thorndike told teachers to teach what should be taught—that is to teach English to learners of English, not Latin as they believed in the late nineteenth century and as many teachers believe now. He advocated breaking down the teaching of English into manageable units (sometimes now called "backward design"), to reward or praise students when they learned it (behavioristic extrinsic reward), and to test that they had learned what they were taught. Perhaps it is due to Thorndike, more than any other single person, that our schools look like they do today with Math separate from Science, and English separate from History, with 42-minute periods, bells, with students sitting in rows, and of course with testing.

You might say that Dewey and Thorndike represent two trends in education today (see Mayher, 1991). At the risk of oversimplification, here's what the two approaches might look like by way of comparison, much of which I have borrowed from John Mayher's work (1991). Remember that these are trends and polarities (see Table 2.1 on p. 31).

So that, in no particular order, is the general background of the two ways we approach ELA.

The Foundations of English Language Arts Conversations: Literary Theory

There are many schools of literary theory (criticism), but we are really only going to talk about two: New Criticism and Reader Response Criticism. This is because these are the ones that have most influenced the 7–12 ELA classroom, whereas the dozens of other "schools" have not had anything like this influence.

New Criticism Theory

The one that was ascended to most colleges by the mid-twentieth century was New Criticism. It's still around today. The key concept in New Criticism is *close reading*, where an educated, literate, and informed reader looks at a text as *the text in itself*. That sounds like a tautology, but remember that before this, people read the text to reveal the ideas of the "great man" who wrote it, or for the lessons and insights it brought to the reader (I say "man" because that was the way people thought in Victorian days about writers). To oversimplify, the New Critics said, "Who cares who Shakespeare was, we don't know that much about him anyway, what we care about is that *Hamlet* is a self-contained text (object) which only refers to itself." Indeed, the work of art is always *greater* than its creator—and let's face it lots of authors were very imperfect, and sometimes purely awful people. You would be interested in Tennessee William's thoughts on *The Glass Menagerie* if he were still alive, but he would not be the definitive last word on this great play because the play exists as a text in and of itself outside of the creator. The fact that Christopher Marlowe was killed in a barroom brawl, might have been a spy for Elizabeth I, was most likely an atheist, possibly said some nasty things about Christianity and religion, and was probably gay—all this is interesting—, but what matters is the aesthetic object (text) of *Edward II* and "Come Live with Me and Be My Love." In New Critical thinking, the fact that the poem may have been written to a male is interesting, but the close reading does not want to go outside the four corners of the text. This is because to the New Critics, all that matters is *the text* and you'd better be a very educated reader to make sense of it through a process called *close reading*. The New Critics were trying—against the Victorians—to make reading a work of art as objective and scientific a process as possible, and the result is a certain detached, impersonal, and even cold reading of a text. (By the way, when the CCSS or an examination asks about "the author's intent," they are violating the very principle of New Critical theory, which indicates that we can never know the author's thinking, and even if we did, it would not necessarily influence our close reading of the text.)

"What does this have to do with me?" you ask. Well, whenever you talk about *plot* and *theme* in your discussions of literature in your class, you are using a sort of debased and simplified New Critical approach. Whenever an English test asks questions about a "reading passage," they are relying on a sort of simplified and debased close reading New Critical theory. Remember, there is no complex phenomenon that cannot be reduced and simplified for the classroom and in schooling. With "plot and theme" discussion there is little room for personal student interpretation, for aesthetic response, or for genuine feelings.

Reader Response Theory

In contrast, coming originally from Europe, there was another literary theory emerging which was, and is, in direct contrast to New Criticism. This is called Reader Response theory. To oversimplify greatly, this viewpoint maintains—in almost direct contrast to what we've been talking about—that the text doesn't really exist *unless there is someone to read it.* Only then does it become alive. The reader *actively construes* the text. Let's do this through a dialogue between the New Criticism (NC) person and the Reader Response (RR) person:

NC: Well then, if the text only exists if there is someone to read it, how do you know that you are having a correct reading? Readers make all sorts of misreadings all the time. How do you know you're not reading it *wrong*? What if a student said, *Hamlet* is about people from Mars? Any individual reader can make all sorts of misinterpretations. They do all the time.

RR: Well, I don't think any sentient young reader would say that *Hamlet* is about people from Mars, unless he was totally deluded. That's not commonsensical. But I will admit that when one reads a text, my reading may be at variance with yours, and both our readings may be at variance with traditional readings of the text, but our readings are at variance only *to a degree.* Furthermore, we don't read alone, well not really. Readers discuss what they read all the time. That's only natural. And, in any English class, reading any work of art, you do have individual readers, but it doesn't stay there. You have an interpretive community—the class discussion—which and who negotiates meaning.

NC: But that's not scientific. It's just what several people think.

RR: It doesn't attempt to be scientific. Reading is an *aesthetic act.* We don't even bother with *analyzing*, we deal with engaging—that is *transacting*—with the text (Rosenblatt, 1978, 1983). The aesthetic transaction is what is negotiated in the class, and this is how we negotiate meaning. By the way New Criticism isn't particularly scientific, either, even if that's what I.A. Richards and Cleanth Brooks were aiming at back in the mid-twentieth century; it is more of an art. Nevertheless, I'll tell you how the more reader response inclined readers come to some tentative conclusion about the meaning of a text. What we do is to get all the information we can about how people respond to the text—differing "readings," if you will—and then we democratically negotiate those readings. This is what a good teacher does in a literature class. Reading is a *conversation*, not an analytical act. Reading is a democratic act, and reading is a social act, and meaning is negotiated (Pradl, 1996).

NC: Well, I guess, that's similar to what we New Critics do, as when someone responds to T. S. Eliot's essay, "Hamlet and his problems," they are adding to the conversation of what Eliot said about this problematic play (Eliot, 1921/1998). In a sense we're in dialogue with T. S. Eliot and we're in dialogue with the people who are in dialogue with him.

RR: Maybe we're more similar than we thought.

As you probably have guessed, the writer of this book (that's me) is firmly in the reader response category, though all my background was in New Criticism techniques, which I think primarily made me feel inadequate reading literature and scared me when I was asked to analyze texts. Nevertheless, I am not necessarily against some New Critical approaches. I remember in particular a graduate poetry seminar on the then-called seventeenth-century Metaphysical Poets, mainly John Donne and George Herbert. All the eight of us did for almost a full two hours was to read and discuss one or two poems under the guidance of an expert professor. I can only say that the two hours of close reading were fascinating. I was never bored.

I should point out also that I'm in the minority of English educators by thinking (1) that New Criticism has some good things going for it, and (2) that New Criticism and reader response share some significant similarities. However, I might not be wrong in this. As Andrew Rejan recently explained in a NCTE publication, *English Education*, "The great tragedy in the misunderstood legacies of Rosenblatt and the New Critics lies in the failure to see the substantial common ground between two camps unnecessarily defined in opposition to one another" (Rejan, 2017, p. 37). Nevertheless, many current reader response advocates, particularly those in education, don't value New Criticism at all, and they have a point if only because the New Critical approach, even as it is watered down in 7–12 classrooms, has had deleterious effects (Wilhelm, 2016).

Originally reader response theory was a fairly heavy duty highly academic theoretical approach, particularly with theorists such as David Bleich, Stanley Fish, and Wolfgang Iser. Then came along Louise Rosenblatt's *Literature as Exploration* in 1938, which brought reader response into the "regular" college level literature classroom (Rosenblatt, 1983). Rosenblatt lived for a long time (1904–2005) and was highly influential, particularly because she was a teacher educator. Her second book *The Reader, The Text, the Poem* (1978) delved further into how literature has no set meaning, but is negotiated among readers in conversations that are exploratory, open-ended, democratic, and social. Along with another long-time and well-published practitioner, Maxine Greene (1917–2014), Rosenblatt helped generations of teachers realize that the very reason a work of art is *a work of art* is because it does not have a set meaning. As Greene states, "In many respects, teaching and learning are matters of breaking through barriers—of expectation, of boredom, of predefinition" (Greene, 1995, p. 14).

What, after all, is the meaning of *Moby Dick*, or of *Hamlet*, or of *I Know Why the Caged Bird Sings*, or "Variations on a Blue Guitar"? Who knows? We know that *Hamlet* is not about people from Mars, but in a democratic fashion we can come to some agreement (if still dissenting on particulars) about what *Hamlet* is meaning to us. As Greene would point out, the more a work of art is *a work of art*, the more literature is *literature*, the more it has no one "set" meaning and the more questions it raises (Greene, 1995).

Literary Theory in the ELA Classroom

I observe many ELA classes that use a debased New Criticism approach where the teacher is all about trying to get the class—or at least most of it or some of it—through plot analysis to the "theme" or "message" of a text as if there were one "set for all time" meaning of the text. There are three problems with this in practice: (1) it's like pulling teeth because it's really not the way people read; (2) it really doesn't help any individual in the class engage with, or transact with, the text; and, worst of all, (3) it doesn't make young people (students) like reading at all. In fact, it makes them dislike reading intensely.

I was not convinced of the usefulness and trustworthiness of reader response, namely that we can come, through social/democratic negotiation of meaning, to a canonical (for us) reading of a work of art until I was teaching *Hamlet* in a tenth grade classroom. Each literature circle was discussing different texts, and one was reading *Hamlet*. I'd set each group to some task which I now forget, and one obviously bright, rather excited, but otherwise academically disengaged student called me over and said—and here I paraphrase from memory: "You know, Mr Costigan, this is so wrong." "Why," I asked. "Because Hamlet is acting crazy. There ain't no reason for him to act so crazy." I was flabbergasted. Through reader response processes with his group about midway through the unit and the text, the young man had arrived at the central problem of *Hamlet* that T. S. Eliot had outlined in his "Hamlet and His Problems" (Eliot 1927/1998). Namely, that Hamlet (the character) has problems, but *Hamlet* (the play) has problems because the play provides no sufficient reasons for him to act the way that he does. Anyway, in my class, we had a great discussion of why Hamlet/*Hamlet* is a problem character and a play that presents us with problems. We will talk more at the end of this chapter about reader response practices, but for now we need to go back to what is involved in the organic processes of *reading*, that is, those processes that readers actually use to engage with a text.

The Foundations of English Language Arts Conversations: Reading

You have probably heard of the big controversy between a *phonics* approach to language instruction (what I call the *building block approach*) and *whole language* approaches to language instruction (what I call the *organic approach*). And you may be aware that there are some who say you can combine these two approaches into something called *balanced literacy*, and others who say you cannot do so. So, let's straighten out what language is, how it is acquired, and then we can speak of how we teach it, particularly in the teaching of reading and in the teaching of literature.

When I used the terms *phonics* and *whole language*, you probably thought of the elementary grades. This is because usually *reading* is what is taught up to, and perhaps a little into, the middle school years (grades 7–8). During the middle school years, when presumably a student has "learned to read" in at least a minimally acceptable matter, the teaching of *reading* turns to the teaching of *literature*—and now in the era of CCSS, this includes *informational texts*, what we used to call non-fiction and journalism. For now, you can see that the teaching of reading/literature is very complicated. As I will explain in the next chapter, this is because in the teaching of writing a student produces something (some-*thing*), a *product*, an *artifact*, a *text*. This text is a physical thing; it can be manipulated, changed, rearranged, added to, subtracted from, the process we call *editing*. In reading/literature, a person really doesn't produce anything, it's all "in the head." This is (1) why teaching reading is ephemeral, vaporous, harder than teaching writing, and more confusing, and (2) why this book will advocate that reading is always accompanied by the creation of a text to firm it up and get it objectified. So, first to a discussion of language.

Language: Acquired or Innate?

By roughly the eighteenth century, when everyday people like businesspersons, workers and artisans, and servants, rather than just academics started to read—the time, incidentally, when the novel took off—language was thought to be something that was *acquired*, learned mainly from one's parents, less so from one's childhood peers because they weren't all that good at it, and that also was presumably improved by instruction from one's teachers (if you were rich enough to have them) or in a "grammar" school where you learned the building blocks of language. The important point is that language was seen as being learned, just like you learned to ride a bicycle, or to bake a cake, or to pitch a baseball. Language was like any skill. It was built up in stages (the building block approach) from goo-gooing as a baby, through any number of incremental steps of language learning, to verbally defending your doctoral dissertation or writing your novel. Sound out that letter, which may be a *vowel* (which is like a note on a flute), or a *consonant* (which closes the sound by a type of click of the tongue), move up to *syllables* (combinations of letters, the sound parts of words), then to *phonemes* (what allows sound units to be differentiated), to *words*, to *sentences*, to *paragraphs*, and—ta da!—to the four-paragraph essay! (You now also know why "w" and "y" are sometimes with the vowels "a, e, i, o, u," and sometimes are consonants "b," "c," "d," f," "g," and so on; because sometimes they are the open pipe sounds [vowels], and sometimes they click off the ongoing note of the pipe [consonants].) What I have just described, however, is a behaviorist approach because language is viewed as being learned from the original state of being a *blank slate*, through being rewarded for imitating the sounds of those around you. This view of language is *additive*, or quantitative, not qualitative and *organic*.

Around in the midpoint of the last century this type of thinking was challenged. Not only was it challenged, people attempted to reverse it. The chief figure associated with this movement was Noam Chomsky who, when he wasn't getting on President Nixon's "enemies list" because of his politics, was studying how we humans acquire language. While the behaviorist B. F. Skinner held that the mind was a blank slate and developed language (like everything else) by learning through stimulus and responses and rewards and punishments, Chomsky and others came to hold that this was absolutely wrong. Language was not something that was *acquired,* it was a *process.* But the process was innate, part of being human, something humans do by their very nature. We are *hardwired* for language. Just as a cat doesn't have to learn how to meow, or a dog to bark, humans don't have to learn to speak. They just do it as part of their nature. Of course, if someone is deprived of human interaction and human speaking from an early age, their speaking would not be as fully developed as those babies who have rich verbal and vocal interactions, or, more importantly the child would find a language somewhere. However, the point is that using language is something we are born to do, part of our nature. This is why sign language is as much a language as any vocal language—it's all a human thing.

Furthermore, as Chomsky pointed out, there is a *universal grammar*; that is, all humans acquire, process, and use language in the same way. If a Martian came to the earth and tried to communicate with an English speaker, a French speaker, and a Russian speaker, or a speaker of Cantonese, the Martian would most likely see only language and one grammar. "Blue" and "bleu" are intensifiers, and it matters not if it is "the blue cow," *la vache bleue*, голубая корова, or 蓝色的牛. Now, I'm oversimplifying greatly, but it makes a difference to us as teachers if we have a building block approach, as many teachers still do, or if we favor the organic approach. It makes a difference if you value phonics and workbooks, and knowing how adverbs differ from adjectives, and if you teach grammar as it will help in writing, or on the other hand whether you see your role as enhancing and assisting the processes of language acquisition that are already there.

One of the leading reading experts, Frank Smith, lucidly and cogently presents what I call the organic approach, and here I am following his ideas (Smith, 1987, 2004, 2006). We all have had the experience of reading a paragraph over and over and over and never "getting it." This is not because we can't "sound out words," or that we don't have a practiced "skill" in reading, as the building block people say. This is because, we're missing what's *outside of the page.* You have to have an *appreceptive mass* (not Smith's term), a previous experience or background knowledge of information and emotions before you approach the page and ask questions of it. In other words, you read something because you have a prior knowledge of it and you want to know more about it, and ask questions of the text about it. Without questions for the text, a way to investigate the text, and without the prior knowledge that allows you to ask these questions the text does not make sense:

> If a pupil holds one wrist too high in playing, the only remedy that I have found, is to get someone to hold a small flexible stick which is passed over the faulty wrist, and at the same time under the other wrist. If the defect is the opposite, the reverse must be done. But this stick must not absolutely hinder the freedom of the player. Little by little this fault will correct itself; and this invention has been of great service to me.

I am sure you are at least mildly befuddled with the above paragraph. It is not about a middle school teacher doing weird things to a student playing some strange sport. Rather, it's from an eighteenth-century French treatise (translated of course) about playing the harpsichord, which is sort of like a piano but which plucks strings instead of hitting them with a hammer and which died out by the time of Mozart (but has since been revived). Here Francois Couperin "Le Grand" is talking about how a music instructor is to remedy the placement of the hands on the two keyboards of a harpsichord (Couperin, 1717/1933). To understand the passage, you have to know where it comes from, who Couperin was, what a harpsichord is, how it differs from the piano, and, most importantly, you have to be interested enough in the subject to want to ask questions of the paragraph.

Here's another passage from a novel:

> One afternoon, just as the bell of Nuestra Senora was sounding Terce, the lament of the peacocks announced a return of the storm. Since mid-day their plangent, disquieting cries had foretold its approach. Moving rapidly to and fro in their agitation, their flowing fans sweeping rhythmically the ground, they traced fevered curves beneath the overarching trees, orchestrating, with barbarity, as they did so, their strident screech with the clangour of the chapel bell that seemed, as it rang, to attract toward it a bank of tawny gold, cognac-coloured cloud, ominously fusing to sable.

As an experienced reader—and as a future or present ELA teacher, you are an experienced reader—you can probably guess a lot about this text. I give this as a sort of "test" to my students in a graduate reading curriculum class. I ask them to read the text several times and to write about how they *feel* about it. Being heavily educated in New Critical theories and practices they almost never write about how they *feel*, but what they *think*. And often they feel inadequate when faced with this text, as if they are supposed to "get it." But the point is, they don't have any information or feelings outside of the four corners of this paragraph to make any great sense of it, except for a few basics. And why should they? As experienced readers who have taken many literature courses, they do get a number of things about it; namely, that it is probably English (the prevalence of the letter *u*). What they don't have—which is something we know is essential from a psycholinguistic approach to reading—is enough of an appreceptive mass to ask questions of the test. They never had an experience that I had many years ago, and that is a friend who said, "What do you mean, you never read the novels of Ronald Firbank!? You should start with *Valmouth*." To borrow a phrase from Frank Smith, I *joined the Ronald Firbank literacy club* (see Firbank, 1919, p. 49; Smith 1987). Readers of this book have probably not. Why should you?

I would like you to note that what I have just asked you to do is exactly what an English test asks you to do to a reading passage. The reading passage assumes some faulty things about reading, namely that reading is a "skill" that can be acquired, practiced, and developed; that it doesn't matter what you know about the *content* of the reading passage. Reading, in this paradigm, is not an organic process that can be developed, but a skill that is acquired on the blank slate of a young person's mind. This supposes that some people have better skills at reading than other people, and that this skill can be assessed, measured, quantified, and given a number (on a test). I think this is absolutely wrong and invalidates what reading organically is.

Another important effect of a skills-based approach to reading is that rich people always do better on tests than poor people. Not only do privileged people have more opportunities and leisure time to read, but the test is more in line with advantaged peoples' apperceptive mass than poor people. As a high school student of mine from Washington Heights once pointed out, the SAT is not likely to ask someone the difference between a green plantain, a yellow plantain, and a black plantain, but it expects you to know what is a *regatta*.

The Organic Approach in Reading

So, how does a young person learn to read? The short answer is that we don't "sound out words," we don't add up letters into syllables into phonemes into sentences into paragraphs, and so on. We really don't even read "words," so to speak. Rather, than eating words (not to mention syllables) one by one, we gulp them like we eat raisins, in meaning groups. I liken reading more to smelling than anything else; we *smell out* groups of words on the page. Think of how you read your last novel for pleasure and how you transacted with the text. I think you almost sniffed your way through that novel. Thus, the job of the English teacher is to open up that apperceptive mass, that outside perception, that makes the student able to transact and engage with the text.

The Foundations of English Language Arts Conversations: Writing

Writing, I believe, is infinitely simpler than reading. This is because the writer is producing something, a product, an artifact, a text. Frank Smith says, "reading is thinking" (Smith, 2006), but we can also say that "writing is thinking." If you come to believe that writing is a form of thinking, a process, you are on your way to being in conversation with the writing process. Peter Elbow's seminal work in this area, *Writing Without Teachers* (1973), countered the old (again) building block approach to writing where it is a two-step process: First (1) you think about what you are going to write, then (2) you write it down. You then (3) may go back briefly to correct the draft (proofing), but no real editing is done. This is the type of writing we do on essay exams. This is also vastly different from how real people write, which is usually not only alone, but in vibrant communities, something that the National Writing Project has advanced.

I remember in the eighth grade being made to write a formal outline before I wrote any essay (the teacher was also fond of teaching grammar, of course) and it drove me crazy. When I started to write however, everything changed. This is because *writing is thinking*. I ended up cheating for the sake of the teacher by creating the outline *after* I wrote the essay—but what a waste of time. There are still very many teachers who believe in this artificial, building block, two-step processes. The problem is it is not the way real writers write, it's unnatural. Elbow likens writing to cooking, a messy organic process (Elbow, 1973). When Hemingway wrote, for instance, he often rewrote his short stories from the beginning each day (Samuelson, 1984). *That* certainly is an organic process. But whatever Hemingway did when he wrote, he didn't think first, then write second. He thought as he wrote. And if that's good enough for him, it's good enough for me.

The writing process is certainly the model that is advocated in many schools these days. Exactly how that is done and what it is, of course, up for debate. However, it involves writing and *getting it all out in a draft*, which can be called prewriting, or freewriting, or just plain writing. Then the real hard part of writing is rewriting, or revision. And more revision, and more revision—and revision, revision, revision. Revision, put simply is adding to, subtracting from, changing, and rearranging. Writing is not a solitary activity because a writer needs feedback, and that is only through one's follow writers, one's peers. In the writing process, the writing is never finished—not really. As the saying goes, *a poem is never finished, it is abandoned.* Same with any writing—you let it go, knowing that it can always be returned to. The final step is proof reading or simply proofing. And this is the last and least important part of the process, because it is mechanical. Where "building block" or "two-step" writing teachers go wrong is when they confuse proofing with editing. A correct draft is not necessarily a good draft, and a good draft might not be the more correct draft, though I have found, if you give students meaningful things to write, they tend to have far fewer errors, if only because they are invested in what they write. I have a colleague who is always complaining about the quality of her college students' writings. I ask her, "But what writing assignments are you giving them?" I can only say that if I had to write on the topics that this professor gave her students, I wouldn't do a very good job. When students are writing about the things they are interested in, they tend to write well.

A writing project always goes along with reading, as we shall see in the next chapter, but whether the focus is the writing modality that is responding to a reading/text (for instance a reading journal leading to a narrative or essay about a particular work of art), or a writing modality that uses reading (for instance, the creation of an autobiographical essay by students allied with the reading of autobiographies), the question then becomes how to engage students with this process. Once you have a writing assignment that is meaningful to the writers (students) in a particular class, the issue then becomes how to enhance and assist the process of writing, rewriting, and revision. The best model that writing teachers and classroom writing researchers and practitioners recommend is the workshop model where students are writers, with the teacher as a writing coach, and where there is created a community of writers (I refuse to cite anyone here because everyone should know this in 2018). Doing this is easier said than done, of course, as everything is in the world of teaching and learning, and this will be the substance of the chapters that follow.

Moving Forward

I do need to add that I have left out the growing body of critical theory in gender, women's, LBTQ, and increasingly transgendered literature, but I will address these in the next chapters. I also have not really addressed the *speaking curriculum* because I need to discuss in the next chapter how this fits in with the writing and reading curriculum. Additionally, note that I haven't touched on the dozens and dozens of other literary theories out there (Deconstructionism, Semiotics, Hermeneutics, Post Structuralism, among many, many others) because they have not had nearly as much impact on the ELA classroom as New Criticism and reader response theories and practices (Appleman, 2009; Eagleton, 1983/2008; Guerin, et al., 2005; Scott, 1963).

And, of course, in these days of test- and accountability-based education and the era of so-called educational reforms, there is the 300-pound gorilla of the standards-, testing-, and accountability-based educational reform movement, such as the CCSS; some practitioners think it is beneficial, some think it is something to be negotiated, and some think it is detrimental (Beach, Thein, & Webb, 2016; Gallagher, 2015; Smith, Appleman, & Wilhelm, 2014). What this chapter has done, I hope, is to lay the foundation for an organic approach to literacy on which we teachers can build our lessons and lesson activities in the ELA classroom. Let's talk about how this can happen.

Thinking About Learning and Doing Teaching

This book maintains that the key to teaching ELA is the creation of a *text*. The text is a modality of knowing. In writing, this is to create a text by the processes of writing and revision that real writers use. In reading, it is to create a text "in the head" out of a text "on the page," which is what practiced readers do as they variously: Read by imagining; daydreaming; being reminded of their own lived lives; remembering an event they have experienced; getting into "flow" (the state where you lose sense of time and place); getting facts and information; as well as reading the passage over and over again and not getting it. And, as we shall see in the next chapter—and as suggested in the grid below—speaking too is a form of a text or modality.

In reading, for example, this book suggests that to assist emerging readers, the teacher should help the reader (student) to create a (secondary) text out of a (primary) text on the page so that the learner engages with the primary text. This is what practiced readers do naturally "in the head," but which novice readers need help to do. This secondary text is not "secondary" in a qualitative sense, because in reader response practice the so-called secondary text is simply the way the primary text becomes alive; it literally doesn't exist until the reader is creating a text "in the head." As we shall see, the primary text can be print on the page, or it can be any work of art (painting, sculpture, photograph, movement or dance, even speaking or sound). So too, if the primary text is traditional print on a page or a computer screen (poem, short story, novel, essay), then the reader can be assisted in transacting with the text by creating a secondary text, which can be writing, drawing, speaking, or anything else. For instance, a middle school teacher does this when she asks her students to draw a key element of the story (a conflict, a character, or a possible ending), and then explain the drawing in a few sentences. A graphic organizer (bubble chart or T-chart) is supposed to do this also, but I am not sure that the graphic organizer as authentic a text as real writing (or drawing).

I used to call the creating of a secondary text out of the primary text *intertextuality*, but perhaps a better term is *intermodality* (Costigan, 2008). (This is similar to multiple literacies which will be discussed in Chapter 6.) The reason for this change in terms is that intertextuality is a term used in many disciplines. For instance, in media studies it is used to describe when one movie might reference another. It might also be when one TV show references another, say, when a current show references *The Flintstones* or *The Honeymooners*. It is used also in literary criticism when one text references another, for instance when James Joyce's *Ulysses* references the Catholic mass, "He held the bowl aloft and intoned:—Introibo ad altare Dei." Or it is when J. K. Rowling's Harry Potter series references J. R. R. Tolkien's Lord of the Rings trilogy. The term intertextuality is also used in semiotics and post-structuralism philosophy, which I am not competent to get into

I use the term intermodality in the ELA curriculum of writing, reading, and speaking. This is when one modality (such as reading) is engaged, enhanced, and firmed up in the learner's mind by using activities in another mode (such as speaking or writing). Note that the "mode" is also a form of a "text." This is something that many, if not most, teachers intuitively do already, as when they have students respond to a reading text with a writing activity or a classroom discussion. What I am trying to do is to make intermodality—that is, creating a certain kind of text *out of another kind of text*—as a conscious and deliberate part of curriculum design and implementation.

Below are some suggestions (modalities) for reading, writing, and speaking in the ELA classroom. I did not create the majority of these, but they are in the public domain of the conversations ELA practitioners are having. Nevertheless, in the creation of a text *out of a text*, there are some rules. The primary rule, which I learned from teaching in urban schools with students who were often

TABLE 2.2 ELA Activities and Modality Mapping

Reference #	*Activity Name and Type*	*Reader Response*	*Writing*	*Reading*	*Speaking*	*Description*
1	Cafeteria talk, bus stop talk, subway talk	O	—	O	SP	Students discuss a life-based issue (Line of Inquiry, Essential Question, q.v.) or a text as if they just met in a common public place.
2	Essential Question(s) (EQ)	O	O	O	SP	Similar to Line of Inquiry (q.v.), but based more on the big issues of life than a text in a unit. EQs are not ultimately answerable, but rather stimulate thought, engage inquiry, and lead to more questions, which are provocative and generative (see McTighe & Wiggins, 2013). "What makes a meaningful life?" "What are the causes of, and remedies of oppression?"
3	Exploratory talk, strategy 1	RR	—	RD	SP	Discovery groups to investigate what they can learn about a text.
4	Exploratory talk, strategy 2, interviews	O	WR	—	SP	Interview another student about a text or an issue in life. May interview people outside of school also about a life issue or Essential Question (q.v.). Do not take notes during interview, but as soon as practicable write everything remembered about the interview.
5	Exploratory talk, strategy 3, the questioning circle	O	—	O	SP	Teacher asks a question about a text or an issue. Calls on one student. Student does not answer questions, but asks another question. Questions continue until all students are called on. (See Wells, 2012 for questions as writing.)

6	Exploratory writing, strategy 1, prewriting	RR	WR	RD	O	Students write before they read, for instance what they know about Shakespeare, or how they like Shakespeare, or what their experiences are with Shakespeare (or another author, or poetry, or novels, and so forth).
7	Exploratory writing, strategy 2, discovery writing	RR	WR	RD	O	Student(s) write to discover what they know about an issue, or to investigate a text or part of a text. Could be a double-entry journal of knowns/unknowns, or facts/questions.
8	Freewriting, guided	O	WR	O	O	Students freewrite, but do so based on a topic (word, prompt, starter) given by the teacher. Could also write about a life issue, issue in text read, speaker of poem, conflict, or character.
9	Freewriting, memory chain, stream of consciousness	O	WR	O	O	Students write a word (their own or the teacher's, write another word, and keep the pen moving in a stream of consciousness writing. Usually this is unguided freewriting (q.v.), though the teacher might give the first word for the class.
10	Freewriting, post writing, metacognition	O	WR	O	SP	Students metacognitively write a sentence or a few sentences about how their freewriting session went. Could be rated on a numerical scale with an explanatory sentence. Post writing is usually shared with others and usually is not anonymous writing.

(continued)

TABLE 2.2 *(continued)*

Reference #	*Activity Name and Type*	*Reader Response*	*Writing*	*Reading*	*Speaking*	*Description*
11	Freewriting, unguided, classic	O	WR	O	O	Writers keep the pen (or fingers on the keyboard) moving for a set number of minutes (3 to 5 minutes usually). Spelling, usage, grammar, punctuation, neatness do not count as this is low stakes writing (q.v.). May be shared or anonymous writing (q.v.). See also "Freewriting, post writing."
12	Journal: double-entry, right left	O	WR	O	O	Write about a life issue, or a text with a paper divided in half. One issue on right, another issue on left. Writing is back and forth. May be freewriting.
13	Line of Inquiry (LOI)	O	WR	RD	O	An open-ended life-based question in a work of art. A literature unit has a LOI as part of its design: "How does the novel *Jack* show us how labeling is a necessary but complex part of our lives?" See also "Essential Question."
14	Metacognition, strategy 1	RR	WR	O	O	A pair or small group of students create a study guide about a section of a work of art.
15	Metacognition, strategy 2	RR	WR	O	O	A student, pairs, or groups of students create their own essay question(s) about a text. Create short answer questions or multiple choice questions.
16	Movement, kinesthetic learning, Reader response	RR	O	RD	SP	Students in movement present (act out) an event from a text. This can be done with words or without words. See "Cafeteria talk, bus stop talk, subway talk." Can be a living sculpture or tableau or with words.

17	Pair and share	O	—	O	SP	Similar to "Turn and talk" (q.v.). Two students simply turn and share what they know, or think, or feel about a topic, EQ (q.v.), or text.
18	Poem, found	RR	O	RD	O	Take select words from a text (poem, part of a chapter, scene from a play) and create a poem out of a specific number of words (e.g. 7–10). Students can either add words of their own or just use the words taken from the text.
19	Poem, rearranged, assembled	RR	—	RD	O	Student(s) are given a poem cut up into strips (see Chapter 1) and arrange the poems in a way that makes sense to them. Students discuss choices. Poems are shared with whole class and compared to canonical version to see what choices the author made. Important that there is no "correct" assembled poem.
20	Reader response strategy 1	RR	WR	O	O	Create a dialogue (as in a play) between two characters, or between yourself (reader) and a character.
21	Reader response, strategy 2	RR	WR	O	O	Write a psychological profile of a character or the speaker of a poem.

(continued)

TABLE 2.2 *(continued)*

Reference #	*Activity Name and Type*	*Reader Response*	*Writing*	*Reading*	*Speaking*	*Description*
22	Reader response, strategy 3, unarticulated response	RR	WR	RD	—	Student(s) rate the lines of a poem or text on such things as agree, disagree, likes, dislikes, understand, don't understand. Students may (1) apply numbers on a scale to each line, or (2) rate lines in front of them from 1 to last number of line.
23	Reader response, strategy 4, standard, classic	RR	WR	O	O	Write about a life issue of a text with the starters (prompts): "I like, don't like; I see, don't see; I (don't) understand, I notice, a question I have is. . ." (other starters can be used). Students use all or some of the starters, or make their own. May be freewriting.
24	Reader response, strategy 5	RR	WR	RD	O	Describe a situation similar to something that happens in a text.
25	Reader response, strategy 6	RR	WR	O	O	Describe the background of a character. Evaluate a character.
26	Reader response, strategy 7	RR	WR	O	O	Describe the scene from another character's point of view.
27	Reader response, strategy 8	RR	WR	O	O	Describe a character's thoughts (may be stream of consciousness).
28	Reader response, strategy 9	RR	WR	O	O	Describe an alternative ending to the text, or what the ending might be before it's read.
29	Reader response, strategy 10	RR	WR	O	O	Put a character or the speaker of a poem on trial.
30	Reader response, strategy 11	RR	WR	O	O	Describe an event that happens outside of the text.

31	Reader response, strategy 12	RR	WR	O	O	Describe a similar situation to something that happens in your or people's life or lives.
32	Reading for textual evidence	—	—	RD	—	See "Reading for information."
33	Reading for theme	—	—	RD	O	A form of debased New Criticism, which usually does not work. The operative myth is that if a student can figure out the plot, then they can arrive at a preset (by the teacher, textbook, or test) summative message or theme. In reality, however, the greater the work of art, the less the theme it has and the more it has multiple, changing, open-ended meanings (see Greene, 1995).
34	Reading poems for literary devices	—	—	RD	O	If literary devices must be taught (because of mandates or standardized examinations), teach these after aesthetic engagement.
35	Reading, aesthetic	RR	—	RD	—	Reading is on a scale from purely efferent reading for information to reading for aesthetic engagement or the transaction with the text.
36	Reading, efferent	RR	—	RD	—	Reading to take away information from a text (Rosenblatt, 1978, 1983). See "Reading, transactional," "Reading, aesthetic."

(continued)

TABLE 2.2 *(continued)*

Reference #	*Activity Name and Type*	*Reader Response*	*Writing*	*Reading*	*Speaking*	*Description*
37	Reading, for information, efferent reading	RR	—	RD	—	Students do not read for information first, then for aesthetic engagement (transaction); rather, students must read for aesthetic transaction first in order to "get" the information. Without an aesthetic transaction with the text, the reader cannot apprehend information or facts (Anderson & Rubano, 1991; Rosenblatt, 1978, 1983).
38	Reading, for plot	—	—	RD	O	Student must be engaged aesthetically with the text before they can summarize the plot. The operative mythic is that once students can figure out plot, they can arrive at a work of art's summative message or theme.
39	Reading, transactional	RR	—	RD	—	See "Reading, aesthetic."
40	Reading, Young Adult Literature (YAL)	—	—	RD	—	YAL is a growing genre of literature which demonstrably engages students. All YA novels have the theme of the main character emerging from a simple clear-cut world to the complex, but richer, realities of complex adult life.
41	Sharing, carousel, speed sharing	O	—	O	SP	Sharing, carousel (sharing, speed). Students form two groups, one facing in, one out. The pairs share. After a few minutes the outer group moves to the right to form a new sharing group. Repeat.

42	Sharing, four corners	O	—	O	SP	Take four parts of an issue (character, event) or four issues (characters, events) and have students go to four corners to discuss. May have a leader for each corner to report to whole group.
43	Sharing, speed	O	—	O	SP	See "Sharing, carousel."
44	Sharing, talk and turn, pair and share	—	—	—	SP	Students talk to their neighbor for a few moments to process a text or an issue.
45	Speaking interviews, insta-interviews	O	WR	O	SP	Students go around during lunch or free time and quickly ask a simple question of as many people as they can in a time period: "What do you think about Shakespeare's plays?" "How do you feel about poetry, English/writing/reading/novels/writing essays/school. . .?"
46	Speaking or writing, believing, doubting game	—	—	—	—	Based on a life-based issue or on a text issue, student(s) take two sides of an issue, finding reasons to believe it and doubt it.
47	Speaking, interviews	O	WR	O	SP	Students interview each other (or family and friends) about a life issue or a text issue. Do not take notes, but write up interview after it is completed.
48	Speaking, problem solving	O	—	O	SP	Students in pairs or groups discuss an issue and come up with several possible interpretations or solutions.

(continued)

TABLE 2.2 *(continued)*

Reference #	*Activity Name and Type*	*Reader Response*	*Writing*	*Reading*	*Speaking*	*Description*
49	Speaking, surveys	O	WR	O	SP	Student(s) fill out a questionnaire about a life issue or a text issue by interviewing colleagues (see "Speaking, interviews").
50	Speaking: writing conferences	O	—	—	SP	Teacher discusses student's/students' writing singly or in pairs.
51	Writing conferences with peers	O	—	—	SP	Students in pairs or small groups share and discuss each others' drafts.
52	Writing response, character	RR	WR	RD	O	Evaluate a character or the speaker of a poem.
53	Writing response, narrator, speaker	RR	WR	RD	O	Exploratory talk, evaluating a character or the speaker of a poem.
54	Writing response, rules, how to respond to others' writing	—	WR	—	SP	Do not judge (or grade), or if you must, make it the last thing you do. Write about (1) what you see or notice in the draft; (2) what questions you have about the draft; (3) what you might change in your draft. Decide if written comments should go into text (marginalia) and at the end, or on a separate sheet of paper. Or, write about what surprises you (!); questions you have (?); or changes you could make (.).
55	Writing, alternative ending	RRW	WR	RD	O	Student(s) complete the story (or chapter, or scene) with an alternative ending. This can be done in writing, drawing, or a combination of both.

56	Writing, anonymous 1	O	WR	O	—	Writing or freewriting (q.v.) which is only for the writer's eyes. Or, writing which is collected by the teacher, but without name or identifier on it. Sometimes with reading cards (q.v.) and exit cards (q.v.) the teacher can read the anonymous cards out loud.
57	Writing, anonymous 2	O	WR	O	O	Students freewrite, or simply write what they wish and they are not asked to share, though the teacher may ask volunteers to share. This is similar to low stakes writing (q.v.).
58	Writing, comments on	O	WR	O	—	Teacher or students (if carefully prepared to do this) comment on students' writing (a) in text (marginalia), and (b) at end of text, telling writer (1) what is "there" or read/seen in the writing, (2) questions the reader has, and (3) (optional) suggestions for improvement. If a grade must be given, it is after stages 1 through 3.
59	Writing, dialogue	O	WR	RD	O	Write a dialogue about an issue with two characters of your own creation. Write a dialogue between two characters in a story (or the speaker in a poem).
60	Writing, entrance card(s), exit card(s)	—	WR	—	O	Metacognitive writing at the beginning or at end of class about what was learned or what transpired in class. Could be a question. Public writing collected by teacher. If about a text used in class, could be a reading card (q.v.).

(continued)

TABLE 2.2 *(continued)*

Reference #	*Activity Name and Type*	*Reader Response*	*Writing*	*Reading*	*Speaking*	*Description*
61	Writing, high stakes	O	WR	O	O	Writing which is assessed and/or graded by teacher. This is public writing. Should be used only for final draft after multiple opportunities for revision. See: "Writing, comments on."
62	Writing, intermodality	RR	WR	RD	O	Take a text (poem) or part of a text (essay or story) and create another genre of text out of it. For example, fiction to haiku; narrative to poem; short story to song lyrics; poem to dialogue; story or event to picture (with writing); essay to rhyming couplet.
63	Writing, learning journal	O	WR	O	O	A series of entries with or without teacher-generated starters (prompts) about an issue under discussion in a unit.
64	Writing, learning portfolio	—	WR	—	—	Student assembles representative samples of his work which shows progress during grading period or semester. Accompanied by a short table of contents and arranged into sections (units, themes, assignments by type). Accompanied by separate self-assessment.
65	Writing, letter to editor, advice column, answer to letter to advice column	O	WR	O	O	Metacognitive writing about a life issue or a text.
66	Writing, likes, dislikes	O	WR	O	—	Writing a narrative or a double-entry journal (q.v.) about a life issue, about a character, speaker of a poem, or a situation in a text.

67	Writing, literature journal	O	WR	O	—	A series of entries about a text with or without starters (prompts) given by the teacher. "What is on Lady Macbeth's mind in Act X, scene x?" "What would the character (speaker) think about. . ." "How do you feel about (issue, conflict, character, speaker). . ."
68	Writing, low stakes	O	WR	O	O	Writing which is not assessed or graded and is written because it is personally meaningful for writer. Usually only volunteers share, if at all.
69	Writing, metacognitive, strategy 1	RR	WR	RD	O	Write a letter to the speaker of a poem, a character in a story, the author of an essay (or story or poem). Tell the author what you think and, or how you feel.
70	Writing, metacognitive, strategy 2	RR	WR	RD	O	Write test questions (essay, multiple choice, or short answer) about a life issue or a text.
71	Writing, metacognitive, point of view	RR	WR	RD	O	Write or freewrite, or write a short poem (haiku, rhyming couplet, quatrain) or diallage about an ELA issue: "I am the comma, and I. . ." "I am the essay, and I. . ." "I am the short story, and I. . ." Or, write about a life issue: "I am prejudice, and I. . ." "I am "freedom, and I. . ." "I am Holden Caulfield," or "Rosencrantz and Guildenstern."

(continued)

TABLE 2.2 *(continued)*

Reference #	*Activity Name and Type*	*Reader Response*	*Writing*	*Reading*	*Speaking*	*Description*
72	Writing, peer editing	—	WR	O	O	Not peer feedback. Sharing final drafts to make suggestions as to usage, grammar, spelling. Changes are always made on a separate sheet (by line numbers), not on writer's draft (see "Writing, think sheet").
73	Writing, peer feedback	—	WR	O	O	Not peer editing. Sharing drafts with other student(s). Students must be carefully prepared how to respond without jumping to judgment (following Bloom's Taxonomy). Usually accompanied by a "think sheet" to guide response. Responder never writes on another student's paper, but on separate sheet.
74	Writing, personal, reflective	—	WR	RD	O	Write a "Dear teacher" letter about "How's it going?" May be anonymous writing (q.v.).
75	Writing, point of view	RR	WR	RD	O	Write from the viewpoint of another (or minor) character in a novel, or the speaker in a poem.
76	Writing, public	O	WR	O	O	Writing which is shared with teacher and, or other students. May be low stakes (q.v.) or high stakes (q.v.).
77	Writing, reading cards	O	WR	RD	O	Metacognitive writing, often anonymous writing (q.v.), about how the student is progressing with reading. Can be used in place of quizzes to see if students have done the reading.

78	Writing, reflective or personal journal	O	WR	O	—	A series of entries with or without teacher-generated starters, usually done each day or in x number of days per week. Can be anonymous writing, or only shared with teacher. If student does not want to share, folds over page and teacher will not read.
79	Writing, self-assessment	—	WR	RD	—	Student writes about her learning process and what she has learned. Teacher may give up to four topics (headings) for consideration based on class topic. Paired with "Writing, learning portfolio."
80	Writing, shared, strategy 1	O	WR	O	O	Two students or a small group (four or five) write one paper together.
81	Writing, shared, strategy 2	O	WR	O	—	Students each write a part of a paper, such as a four-paragraph traditional academic essay. One group writes intro, another body A, another body B, etc.
82	Writing, shared, strategy 3	O	WR	O	—	A student writes a response or original idea, and the paper goes around a circle, each person responding to the one before.
83	Writing, take a line or word, freewriting	RR	WR	RD	O	Take a word or a line from form a story, essay, poem and create another text from that line. Take a line or word from your own (free) writing and write another text based on that word for line.

(continued)

TABLE 2.2 *(continued)*

Reference #	*Activity Name and Type*	*Reader Response*	*Writing*	*Reading*	*Speaking*	*Description*
84	Writing, think sheet	—	WR	O	O	Sheet of paper, often having numbered blank lines corresponding to another student's writing. The second, reviewing student makes suggestions (editing) or corrections (proofing) go on these lines, not on the student's paper.
85	Writing, transaction, strategy 1	RR	WR	RD	O	Write as many questions as you can about a life issue or about a text.
86	Writing, transaction, strategy 2	RR	WR	RD	O	Write a case study of a character in a text or the speaker of a poem.
87	Writing, wondering	—	—	—	—	Creating a list of "wonderings" about a life issue or a text issue or character, "I wonder if . . ." May be about an Essential Question (q.v.) or about a text under consideration.

from very challenging neighborhoods, is to give students the opportunity to opt out of participating, whether it is because they are having a bad day, are feeling ill, had a fight with family or friends, or spent the night in a homeless shelter (and in New York these days one out of ten students is functionally without a permanent or stable home).

There is another rule that I have come to see as important, and this is to tell the students how the text they produce will be used. Thus, I always tell the students *before* they create a text of writing, drawing, speech, or movement how the text they produce will be *made public*, that is *published*. Before they produce a secondary text based on a primary text, student practitioners need to know:

1. How will the text be used (or not) by the teacher? Will it be seen or read by the teacher? Will it be assessed by the teacher? Is this high stakes, or low stakes writing, or somewhere in between?
2. How will the text be used by other students? Will it be shared with other students? If so, how? Will sharing be in the whole group (class), in small groups, in pairs? Or will sharing be mandatory (not recommended)? Will sharing be by volunteers (recommended)?

In the following chart of text creation activities, I have arranged activities by title and indicate by an initial essentially what type they are, whether (1) Reader Response (RR), (2) Writing (WR), (3) Reading (RD), or (4) Speaking (SP). The "O" means optional. The em-dash (—) means "does not necessarily apply, but some teachers might see an option here." The abbreviation q.v. (*quod vide*) means "which see" and refers to a related activity listed elsewhere on the chart. These activities of text creation can be done, depending on the situation, by single students, in pairs, in small groups, or by the whole class.

References

Anderson, P. M. & Rubano, G. (1991). *Enhancing aesthetic reading and response*. Theory & Research Into Practice (TRIP) series. Urbana, IL: NCTE.

Appleman, D. (2009). *Critical encounters in high school English: Teaching literary theory to adolescents* (2nd ed.). New York: Teachers College Press.

Beach, R., Thein, A. H., & Webb, A. (2016). *Teaching to exceed the English Language Arts Common State Standards: A critical inquiry approach for 6–12 classrooms* (2nd ed.). New York: Taylor & Francis.

Britzman, D. P. (1986). Cultural myths in the making of a teacher: Biography and social structure in teacher education. *Harvard Educational Review, 56*(4), 442–456.

Britzman, D. P. (2003). *Practice makes practice: A critical study of learning to teach* (revised ed.). Albany, NY: State University of New York Press.

Costigan, A. T. (2017, October 12). "I'm not teaching English, I'm teaching something else!": How new teachers create curriculum under mandates of educational reform. *Educational Studies*. Available at: www.tandfonline.com/eprint/YW6Y5F2UhED4vHVF5B3p/full.

Couperin, F. (1717/1933). *L'art de toucher le clavecin* (The art of playing the harpsichord) (A Linde, Trans.). Wiesbaden: Breitkopf & Haertel.

Dewey, J. (1971). *The child and the curriculum and the school and society*. Chicago, IL: University of Chicago Press.

Eagleton, T. (1983/2008). *Literary theory: An introduction*. Minneapolis, MN: University of Minnesota Press.

Elbow, P. (1973). *Writing without teachers*. New York: Oxford University Press.

Eliot, T. S. (1921/1998) Hamlet and his problems. In *The sacred wood: Essays on poetry and criticism*. Mineola, NY: Dover Publications.

Firbank, R. (1919). *Valmouth: A romantic novel*. In (n.d.; circa 1940s) *Ronald Firbank: Five Novels*. Great Britain: New Directions.

Gallagher, K. (2015). *In the best interest of students: Staying true to what works in the ELA classroom*. Portland, ME: Stenhouse.

Greene, M. (1995). *Releasing the imagination: Essays on education, the arts, and social change*. New York: Jossey-Bass.

Guerin, W. L., Labor, E. L., Morgan, L., Reesman, J. C., Willingham, J. R. (2005). *A handbook of critical approaches to literature* (5th ed.). New York: Oxford University Press.

Lortie, D. C. (1975). *Schoolteacher: A sociological study*. Chicago, IL: University of Chicago Press.

Macrorie, K. (1985). *Telling writing* (4th ed.). Portsmouth, NH: Heinemann,

Mayher, J. S. (1991). *Uncommon sense: Theoretical practice in language education*. Portsmouth, NH: Heinemann.

McTighe, G. & Wiggins, G. (2013). *Essential questions: Opening doors to student understanding*. Alexandria, VA: ASCD.

O'Reilley, Mary Rose. (1993). *The peaceable classroom*. Portsmouth, NH: Heinemann.

Pradl, G. M. (1996). *Literature for democracy: Reading as a social act*. Portsmouth, NH: Boynton/Cook.

Rejan, A. (2017, October). Reconciling Rosenblatt and the new critics: The quest for an "experienced understanding" of literature. *English Education, 5*(1), 10–41.

Rosenblatt, L. M. (1978). *The reader, the text, the poem: The transactional theory of the literary work*. Carbondale, IL: Southern Illinois University Press.

Rosenblatt, L. M. (1983). *Literature as exploration* (3rd ed.). New York: Modern Language Association.

Samuelson, A. (1984). *With Hemingway: A year in Key West and Cuba*. New York: Random House

Scott, W. S. (1963). *Five approaches to literary criticism: An arrangement of contemporary critical essays*. New York: The Macmillan Company.

Smith, F. (1987). *Joining the literacy club: Further essays into education*. Portsmouth, NH: Heinemann.

Smith, F. (2004). *Understanding reading: A Psycholinguistic analysis of reading and learning to read* (6th ed.). New York: Routledge.

Smith, F. (2006) *Reading without nonsense* (4th ed.). New York: Teachers College Press.

Smith, M. W., Appleman, D., & Wilhelm, J. D. (2014). *Where the authors of the standards go wrong about instruction—and how you can get it right*. Thousand Oak, CA: Corwin.

Wells, P. (2012, November 13). As not seen on TV. Restaurant review: Guy's American Kitchen & Bar in Times Square. *New York Times*. Available at: www.nytimes.com/2012/11/14/dining/reviews/restaurant-review-guys-american-kitchen-bar-in-times-square.html.

Wilhelm, J. D. (2016). *"You gotta BE the book": Teaching engaged and reflective reading with adolescents* (3rd ed.). New York: Teachers College Press.

Zeichner, B. & Tabachnik, R. (1981, May–June). Are the effects of university teacher education "washed out" by school experience? *Journal of Teacher Education, 32*(3), 7–11.

3

ENGLISH LANGUAGE ARTS

What Is It, How Is It Learned, and How Do You Teach It?

Everything Is English. Back in the 1960s, there was much debate about what English actually was, how it could be defined, and what its parameters were. Many educators came to the conclusion that English was *everything*. This sounds like hubris, but English is the system and the means we use to comprehend the world—and that covers pretty much everything. Think of it this way: Even a math problem is a problem with English, because not only is math a type of language in and of itself ($3x - 6 = 6 - 2x$ is in math language), but math problems often take the form of word problems in English. When you ask, "What is 3% of 200?" you have a language problem as much as math problem. Indeed, the reason a student fails to answer this relatively simple math problem might be more to do with English than not knowing percentages. A student who knows the formula $(3/100) \times 200$ might be stymied by that slippery preposition "of." Prepositions, by the way, are always slippery and hard to learn in any language. For instance, why do we get *on* a bus, but *in* a car? When do you say, "Different *from*," instead of "Different *than*"? If *between* refers to being between two things, and *among* refers to being among three or more things, why then is Paris *between* London, Rome, and Moscow, but not *among* them? (Bryson, 1990). Furthermore, in regard to the overall importance of the English language, as mentioned in Chapter 2, the fact that poor people, non-native English speakers, and people of color use language differently than white privileged people (the people who create textbooks and tests), may be a reason a poorer student has more difficulty answering the percentage question and any other English "word" question. This is because all tests are tests of language as much as they are tests of anything else, and they are written in the language of the privileged class, not in the language of those who are poor, or working poor, working class, non-native English speaking, from immigrant communities, or of color. This is why we've known since the 1970s that the SAT does not correlate necessarily with intelligence, or success in school, or achievement, or aptitude, or with anything except family income (Kliebard, 2004). In fact, the acronym SAT no longer includes the word "achievement, "aptitude," or "assessment," or anything else, nor is it a test of reasoning. The word SAT now stands for nothing at all (see https://en.wikipedia.org/wiki/SAT).

Here's another example. History is also English. What do historians primarily do? They read and they write. Not only does a historian have to have a good command of reading and writing, but these are the things she *does*. We can thank the followers of people like Edward Lee Thorndike, among others, that we have a situation in our schools where students do English for 42 minutes, then a bell rings and they do 42 minutes of, well, not History, but Social Studies. In any event, every subject discipline or content area not only uses English, it intimately *is* English. That's why every teacher is a teacher of reading, writing, and speaking, though they may not also teach that specialty of English Language Arts (ELA), the literature curriculum. In fact, one of the best physical education teachers I've known had his students keep a journal of their physical activities, both in class and outside. One of his written assignments was, "Design a sport." Then they attempted to play several of the designs.

The gist of this is that ELA instruction is instruction in how we perceive the world and we should always bear this fact in mind. However, an "English is everything" approach is not likely to help you teach English either tomorrow, or next week, or next semester. So, let's start with some basic ideas which seem simple, but which are essential to an understanding of the foundations of teaching English.

"Where" is English Language Arts?

As mentioned in the previous two chapters, put simply, ELA is three basic things: writing, reading, and speaking. Note that these are arranged from the most concrete to the most abstract. What this means is that writing produces a *product*, an *artifact*, or a *text*. It is a mode (or modality) of communication. The writing product is exactly that, a *product*, some-*thing* that is concrete because it is a physical artifact, which we will call a *text*. Reading produces a sort of text "in the head" as you read a physical text, but reading is not a physical text in and of itself. Speaking, on the other hand, does not produce any physical text at all. It is all sound. The text it comes from, and the text it produces is all "in the head." There is nothing you can see or touch. It is important to point out that writing, reading, and speaking all produce *texts*; that is, they produce something—some-*thing*—that can be processed by the reader or listener. However, this text may be physical, or in the imagination, or it may be aural. The text may be concrete, as in writing, or ephemeral and transitory, as in listening.

As we discussed in Chapter 2, the traditional commonsense stance toward ELA teaching and learning maintains that knowledge, information, and learning is "out there" in the world and must be transmitted to the learner, who receives it. This is why this is called the *transmissive* approach to learning (literally *trans* + *missive* = "sending across"). This is also called the *conduit* or *pipeline theory*. The learner is like an empty bucket (or blank slate) that needs to be filled (or written upon) with knowledge (information and skills) from a source (teacher, textbook, computer program) that is an expert holder of the subject discipline (Math, Science, ELA, Music, etc.). The point here is that in this traditional or commonsense view, writing, reading, and speaking exist independently from the learner. Learning, in this sense, is acquiring the correct content and skills of English, or buying into the preexisting commodity that is English Language Arts, and again this is something that preexists outside of the learner. In this sense, the learner does not add anything to the subject discipline; he can only approximate it. This is teaching and learning as product-oriented. The commonsense approach sees the learner as deficient and in need of improvement, because she is not up to snuff in acquiring the commodity of correct English; that is, she does not have enough of the "stuff" of English. This understanding of English is held by the experts (educators, text makers, textbook writers, and political entities like boards of education) who are part of the status quo. The teacher in this paradigm represents the status quo, which defines what is proper English. This is a *deficit model* in that the teacher (or textbook, or curriculum "expert," or computer program) provides instruction in "correct" English because the learner does not have it yet; she is deficient. This viewpoint is *authoritarian* as the correct definition and processes of "English" are held by the elites.

The nontraditional or uncommonsense stance of ELA teaching and learning maintains that learning is an organic process that all people do to make sense of the world (Mayher, 1991). The learner is one who is continuously making meaning of the world in more and more complex ways. The best thing a teacher can do, in this paradigm, is to assist the learner in developing what they already are doing. The idea here is that writing, reading, and speaking are not preexisting things, or *products* to be acquired, but a dynamic way of thinking, that is *processes*. The uncommonsense approach sees the learner as someone who is already engaged in rich processes of writing, reading, and speaking, even though these may not be the academically standard approaches. This approach sees the role of the ELA teacher as a coach or mentor to develop those natural and organic processes that already exist, to refine those processes, and to enhance what is already there. As in the reader response paradigm in regard to text we discussed in Chapter 2, in the uncommonsense paradigm, the learner not only adds to the ELA curriculum, by creating texts, but the learner *is* the ELA curriculum. Thus, in this paradigm, the teacher may occasionally be *authoritative* (a coach; able to be trusted as being accurate or true; reliable) but not *authoritarian* (a ruler; enforcing strict obedience to authority). This uncommonsense viewpoint is thus more democratic than the commonsense stance. Let's look at these two approaches in more detail.

The Traditional or Commonsense Approach Explained

With the traditional or commonsense approach to reading, say in a non-fiction reading passage, or poem, or essay, there is an objective message that can be agreed upon by practiced readers such as teachers, textbook publishers, computer program designers, and test makers; in other words, those who have expertise in these matters. This preexisting message can, with training and with the exercising of the discrete skills of the discipline, be adopted by the student who desires to become a more expert writer, reader, and speaker. In this light, a sonnet, or a text of fiction, or an essay, has a clear and fairly unambiguous message, which can be expressed in a preexisting, agreed-upon, summative sentence or two, sometimes called a *theme*. Students, of course, have their own thoughts, but these are not nearly as important as the official academic ones, and this is because students are seen as producing immature and erroneous interpretations in reading and have weak and error-prone skills in writing and speaking. Additionally, this immature and incorrect knowledge and skills are seen as getting in the way of the official knowledge and skills required of the discipline, and thus the learner is measured and assessed by her deficits; that is, how far she deviates from competence (as defined by the elites/experts). Furthermore, how a student *feels* about a reading passage in the classroom or on a test is relatively irrelevant, and personal expression in writing gets in the way of what is required for "correct" writing products. What matters is that they "get" the objective meaning in the text and are able to write, read, and speak in a correct and error-free manner.

In this way of looking at things, students are deficient, undereducated, or uneducated, and thus are empty receptacles waiting to be filled with the knowledge and skills of English. Therefore, there is a clear and unambiguous process to reading. Readers simply need to grasp the preexisting message or meaning about a reading passage, just like in other content areas they need to appropriate how to balance an algebraic equation in math, or define the parts of a cell in science, or conjugate verbs in French. Facts, information, interpretations, and understandings are products and commodities that can be learned as if they are acquired or "bought." They are outside of the student and not integral to him. And of course, because meaning is viewed as objective and "out there," it is easy to measure a student's understanding by testing, and then to record that understanding with a score or number.

As we have seen, in this paradigm, writing works in a similar objective and non-student-centered manner. Good writers first organize the information they need to eventually write in their head, perhaps assisted by a formal outline or a graphic organizer. In this traditional paradigm, once a writer thinks about (or outlines) a topic, then the student can write her predetermined thoughts down in that preformed order (Elbow, 1973). And, because the thoughts are already ordered before writing, the writing can be done at one sitting without multiple drafts. It is easy to see that in this conception of writing a formulaic essay is the essential focus of the writing class and ELA tests. However, I think if you have tried this yourself you will realize how difficult it is to "think first, then write" even with an artificial and formulaic essay such as a four-paragraph argumentative essay, persuasive essay, or five-paragraph theme. The reason for this is simple. This is not the way any writer in the real world ever wrote.

You can see why corporate-based educational reformers like this clear and unambiguous way of viewing writing and reading—and we'll get to speaking in a moment, below. The good students are the ones who have "grit," regardless of their low levels of education, income, nutrition, housing, neighborhood safety, and overall quality of life. They can be made to work hard, often in "no excuses" charter schools, to "get" objective meanings of reading passages, as well as to write schoolish (or examish) writing products, and to speak the standard English of the privileged classes. However, as you already suspect, and as will be explained in the next section, this book is advocating a different approach, one in which writing, reading, and speaking are not *products* to be acquired as the commodities (information) and habits (skills) of the privileged classes, but as *processes* of the human mind.

The Process or Uncommonsense Approach Explained

In the non-traditional uncommonsense tradition, writing, reading, and speaking are the organic and human processes that humans use to enhance their understanding of the world through the aesthetic appreciation and apprehension of nature, civilization, and works of art. These processes are the essentially human processes that all people use. They can be developed, enhanced, and shared.

Writing is a *process*. As noted in the previous chapter, when Hemingway wrote a short story, he often sat down for his designated three hours of writing and rewrote the short story from the beginning (Samuelson, 1984). Writing is a recursive process (recursive = *re*, again; *cursive*, writing). You write things down, but that's not the real writing. If you just correct for errors what you have written down only once, your writing probably is not very good. The real writing is when you add to, or delete from, or change, or rearrange what you've already written, what is ordinarily called *editing*. Writing is mostly a process of editing, of *re*writing as much as anything else. Writing is not "getting things correct," or being able to proofread well. For real writers in the real world, writing is more like a process of super-editing, that is editing, writing, reediting, writing, and reediting again, and so on until you can't do it anymore and need to move on to something else. A writing product is something that is never completed, so much as abandoned. There are many schemata for the writing process, but one way of looking at it is as in Figure 3.1.

In this framework, the *substance* of what you say is more important than in the *correctness* of how you say it, the process is more important than the product. Most importantly, though not reflected in Figure 3.1, writing at all stages is a collaborative act. In fact, this assistance from other writers is essential. Even Hemingway had the famous editor Maxwell Perkins, the same editor who made Thomas Wolfe cut

	Revision			
	↑↓			
(Pre)writing →	Editing →	Ending writing/letting go →	Proofing →	Publishing
	↑↓			Sharing
	Rewriting			Making public

FIGURE 3.1 A Writing Process Methodology.

90,000 words from his first novel, *Look Homeward, Angel* (1929). Anyone can help you proof your writing so that it is free from errors. But again, freedom from errors does not make it good writing. The "good" in writing is in its ability to engage the reader, not in its being technically correct, and in order to know how you are engaging your reader (or not) you can get readers to give you feedback in the re-writing/editing stage. Students, of course, have to be educated in how to do this or they will jump to immediate judgments. In fact, I don't allow any judgments at all in peer editing or readers' feedback. And if the teacher is to judge (assess or grade), this is of course the last thing that is done (following Bloom's Taxonomy). My rules for peer (and teacher) editing have become quite simple over the years—tell or ask the writer, either in speaking or in writing:

- What is "there" in the text? What does the reader "see" or "hear" in the text? (What the writer thinks he is saying is not necessarily, in whole or in part, what the reader "reads".)
- What in the text surprised the reader. What are the Ah! Moments. (The writer might not be aware of when she is being exceptional.)
- What questions arise in the reader based on the text? What does he need to know? What does he need to know more about? (The writer might not know where he is unclear or when he is transparently clear.)
- What might the reader do to the text? What changes might he make? What could be added, taken away, changed, or rearranged in the text? (The writer might not know how best to move forward with the draft.)

These comments and questions by the reader (teacher or student collaborator(s)) go in the margins and at the end of the text. And one last point: Never throw out any piece of writing. You never know when you can use it again.

How Speaking Fits in with Writing and Reading

We have begun a discussion about writing and reading in the previous chapter and summarized a bit here, but let's talk about speaking for a moment to help us frame our discussion about the uncommonsense ELA classroom. In most classes most of the time, whether they be ELA or another content area, most speaking is done by the teacher, not the students. And this is usually the teacher lecturing or using a "talk and chalk" method, and increasingly a "lecture and smart board," or a "talk and smart board" method. Most other talk in most classrooms is a teacher asking questions that have an expected "correct" answer of one word or few words. This is done either by "calling on" a particular student, or students volunteering by raising their hands. (Incidentally, I've stopped all hand raising in my class, which is a hallmark of a traditional classroom.) Thus, most student "speaking" in most classes is answering a teacher's question in a "correct" (or not) short one- or few-word answer, and if students talk to each other, it is usually for a quick "turn and talk" or "pair and share" to discuss the subject matter of the class, a sort of talking that is not done in the real world. If students talk in groups, say as they work on a project or discuss literature, they are expected to be "on task" and only discuss the matter at hand and not what happened in the cafeteria in the previous period or the latest political scandal. Student talk in most classrooms is *accountability talk*, and mostly *high stakes talk*, which risks student embarrassment when they are wrong, or which affects the individual student's grade. And, if students speak in small groups, there is often a handout to fill out or a task to do so the teacher can assess that the talk has been "on task."

The uncommonsense classroom aims to have students talk like they do in the real world, and this is—if you listen to conversations on the bus, in the supermarket, or in a restaurant—to discover, investigate, or to find out things, to work things out, to ask questions, to wonder about things, to disagree, to share thoughts and information, to share feelings, to negotiate things, to plan, and to come to mutual understandings and decisions, among a host of other objectives. For our purposes, this falls under the umbrella of *exploratory talk* (Barnes, 2008).

Exploratory talk is the opposite of just talking for your own benefit, or just to pass on information, or to get your point across, or to debate or persuade someone, or just talking for the sake of talking. It is also not necessarily talking to get the teacher's correct answer or interpretation of things. It is talking for communication, for sharing for everyone who is in on the conversation's benefit. It demands active participation of the speakers, and this involves *active listening*. This is listening that is attentive to what is said, attempts to understand what is said, remembers what is said, and shares feedback about what is said. Exploratory talk is when participants ask open-ended questions, share what they know, give reasons for what they know, build on others' knowledge, contribute actively, collaborate with each other, negotiate meanings, use democratic processes, and come to collaborative understandings and decisions (Barnes, 2008; Duckworth, 2006). In this sense, not only are reading and writing ways of thinking, but so too is exploratory talk. Thus also, *speaking is thinking*—or at least it can be if done with care. In this constructivist paradigm, speaking (like writing and reading) is both an autobiographical act and a collaborative act. Incidentally, I think this is why Socrates did not want people to write things down. He thought writing stopped the talking-thinking process of verbal dialogue.

Below are some examples of exploratory talk. These speaking activities can be used for an essential question, a general life issue (preferably one with no simple clear answer), or a line of inquiry which relates that issue to a text under consideration, either via an issue reflected in a text, or characters in a text or the speaker of a poem. I even use some of these activities for discussing the scope and nature of a unit or assignment, for discussing possibilities for completing an assignment, for discussing the central issue or key element of an assignment, for sharing or editing the assignment in the middle of completing it, or for sharing it upon completion. Additionally, many of these activities can be done in pairs, small groups, in the class divided into two or four sections (see four corners, below), or in the whole class. Furthermore, when I taught in a difficult urban school with many students who were disengaged from formal schooling, I always gave students the option of opting out of any of these activities if they were ill, just not feeling well, or had other problems and did not want to participate.

1. Carousel or speed sharing. Students create two circles, the A group facing out, the B group facing in, so that each person faces another person in a large circle of pairs. Pairs of A-B discuss the matter at hand, and after a set number of minutes, B group (outside) moves one person to right, forming a new A-B pair. The As always stay where they are, only the Bs move. The circle continues until time is up, or until all Bs have spoken to all As.
2. Believing and doubting game (Elbow, 1973). Students doubt a proposition or fact they are inclined to believe in, or believe a proposition or fact they are inclined to doubt. (Indeed, if you have ever taught the argumentative or persuasive essay, you will notice that students write better about a topic with which they disagree.) Or, they take, alternatively, a believing and then a doubting position. Or, students are doubters and/or believers as they role play, or engage in a fish bowl activity, carousel or speed sharing, in pairs, or in a four-corner activity. Students can also reverse position, from believer to doubter, and vice-versa during conversation. This can be used in writing with dialogue writing or a double-entry journal and then shared orally/aurally.
3. Role playing. Students are assigned a different role and have to present in those roles, either about an issue, a text under consideration, or a character in a story, or the speaker in a poem. Teacher may set up a problem or a scenario about a life issue, an essential question, an issue or conflict in a text, or about characters (create a dialogue between Holden Caulfield and his psychiatrist, between Gatsby and Nick).
4. Fish bowl, variation one. Two, or a small group of students are in the "fish-bowl" center of the room having a conversation; all other students are in a circle outside the fishbowl facing inward actively listening to the conversation

of the people in the fishbowl. People outside the fishbowl may not speak, only actively listen. To speak they may enter the fishbowl conversation (or not) by physically moving their chairs into the speaking fishbowl from the listening outside of the fishbowl. All fishbowls end with a metacognitive discussion about speaking and choosing not to speak, so the teacher asks the speakers and non-speakers (those outside the fishbowl) about their choices.

5. Fishbowl, variation two. Only two (or a few) people speak in the fishbowl. However, the active listeners outside the fishbowl can tap speakers in fishbowl on the shoulder and take their seat to continue the conversation, thus the number of participants in the fishbowl always remains the same. This is particularly good with role playing. For instance, I use it to demonstrate how a classroom teacher's post-observation conference works. Students get a chance to "play" teacher and supervisor. Also works with an essential question.
6. Four corners. A life issue or text is divided into four issues, characters, texts, or life issues or essential questions. A leader may be appointed for each corner of the room. Students go to the corner that they sympathize or empathize with. Variation: Students are allowed to wander from corner to corner as they see fit. At the end of the activity leaders from each corner report on the discussion.
7. The questioning game. Students can only ask questions, not make declarative statements. The teacher first makes sure that all students know each others' names. The teacher asks a question, calls on one student by name, that student asks a question, and calls on a student who has not yet been called on. Students can only be called upon if they have not yet spoken. Once everyone in the room has been called on, students summarize what came up in the questionings.
8. All talk strategy, variation one. The teacher gives each student three slips of paper or tokens or poker chips. When a student speaks, they have to put the item in a hat. When individual students use up their tokens they cannot longer speak until everyone in the class has put their tokens in the hat.
9. All talk strategy, variation two. Teacher creates a "talking stick." Only the person who holds the stick can talk.
10. Cafeteria talk/subway talk/bus stop activity. Students role play that they have just met accidentally in a public place. They discuss a text or class issue, or even an assignment, or they brainstorm an issue for an assignment. Each pair or group presents in front of the whole class.
11. Read around. Students in a circle share something of what they have written, usually after the completion of a big writing project or unit, or this could be used to share mid-process. This is low stakes speaking and is never commented on, assessed, or graded; this is not editing. Students are able to say "pass" if they do not want to share. In a read around there are no comments made (by author or listener), just a sharing of each person's writings as others in the class actively listen. The teacher may say,

"thank you" after each reading, but may not comment on the reading. If appropriate, comments can be made at the end of the read around.
12. Summarize speaking. As each person speaks, they must summarize what the person before them said. This can only work if some method is used where everyone is required to speak, though I always allow a "pass" for people having a bad day.
13. Speaking about speaking. The teacher engenders a discussion about the rules of speaking for her class. She might ask the students to come up with ten or twelve rules about how "talk" is to be conducted in class. Rules might be: Must address people by their preferred name. Must always address what the previous speaker said. Must only say things that move the conversation forward. Must disagree in a respectful manner. And so forth . . .

Here we are very far from the teacher asking fact-based one- or a few word answers. The point here is not that I am giving you just a few examples, the point is that once you become conscious of speaking in your class, you can devise ways to enhance open-ended talk. Yes, people in the real world do not use these activities, but what the activities do is make students conscious of how they are speaking, and they begin to make our classroom talk look like talk in the real world; that is, rather than just answering the teacher's questions with predetermined one- or a few word answers.

More About English Language Arts as Product and Commodity: Banking

In traditional schooling, which is the form of schooling advocated by our current corporate-based educational reformers, reading, writing, and speaking are not seen as living *processes* of thinking, but rather as preexisting *products* of information (commodities), which are thought to exist outside of the learner's mind. It is the authorities (teachers, textbook writers, politicians, computer program designers, boards of education, corporations, and governments) who determine what is writing, reading, and speaking, and the student is measured (and graded and given a number) based on how well she obtains this knowledge and these skills as defined by these authorities. This is why this type of English does not look like English in the real world. Students do multiple choice questions, write formulaic block-paragraph essays (the literature essay, the argumentative/persuasive essay, the five-paragraph theme), read non-fiction texts for facts and information, read fictional texts (or snippets of them) for one predetermined message or "theme," memorize literary devices, and do lots of multiple choice questions on tests. The result of this approach—the one beloved by educational reformers from the elite corporate and political worlds—is that writing, reading, and speaking are treated as if they were a product, a commodity, something that can be acquired or bought. This is the "banking" model of education, first expounded by Paulo Freire:

> Instead of communicating, the teacher issues communiques and makes deposits which the students patiently receive, memorize, and repeat. This is the "banking" concept of education, in which the scope of action allowed to students extends only as far as receiving, filing, and storing the deposits. . . . In the banking concept of education, knowledge is a gift bestowed by those who consider themselves knowledgeable upon those whom they consider to know nothing.
>
> *(Freire, 1970/2000, p. 71)*

Again, this is also the *deficit model* of education, and this view is represented in the Common Core State Standards (CCSS), which come from the corporate world of the Bill and Melinda Gates Foundation, as well as from reformers such David Coleman, the president of the College Board—the people who give us such tests as the SAT and a big promulgator of the CCSS (Layton, 2017; Schneider, n.d.). Again, all current educational reforms come from, or are allied to, the corporate world, and it is natural that the product-oriented, commodity-focused, banking model of education perfectly aligns with their worldview.

However, when you begin thinking of the English curriculum as a *process*, you are beginning to enter into the conversation, the discourse, or the current landscape, or ecology of teaching English *as defined by educators, as well as actual writers, readers, and speakers themselves*. When you understand that speaking in your classroom should be about using talk as open-ended discovery rather than the student getting the "right" (usually one-word or few word) predetermined fact-based "correct" answer, then you are entering into a more productive conversation. When you understand that the purpose of your student's writing is not to produce as perfect an essay as possible for their academic "level" (however that is defined), but to enhance their writing as a means of students' thinking and expression, then you also are in on the conversation. And, when you conceive of reading an essay, fiction, or a poem as a process of enhancing a student's ability to enter a lifelong development of reading acuity and aesthetic appreciation, then you also are in on the conversation.

You have a choice to make, and you will have to make this choice over and over in your teaching career: Are reading, writing, and speaking thinking processes that are natural, innate, organic, and, well, *human*—and that can be developed through classroom activities? Or, are reading writing, and speaking the exercising of discrete skills to produce artificial products that do not look like real-world writing, reading, and speaking, and that also are counterintuitive to the ways humans naturally do these things? I hope you choose the first possibility, if only because your students, no matter how much they are disengaged from formal schooling, are already *thinking*. They are expert, if nonacademic, processors of reading, writing, and speaking. They know perfectly well what "Entrance fee $25.00," and "No one under 18 permitted," and "Mets lose again," means. They know perfectly well how to tell you, the teacher, that you are putting on weight, or that you have worn the same outfit to class two days in a row, or that you are repeating yourself and are becoming boring. And they know very well how to write a note or a tweet to their friends. Isn't this what you want to build upon? My one promise is that once you begin seeing teaching and learning as process-oriented rather than product-oriented, you and your students' lives will be much, much richer.

Let's now get to how we can organize the ELA curriculum so that we can teach it in a way that our students are designed to learn.

Speaking Aligned with Writing (and Reading): The Story

As I have noted already in this book, speaking is the most difficult element to teach because it produces no physical text. But it is difficult for a second reason, namely that few teachers have specific coursework in oral English, public speaking, oralcy or storytelling, dialogue, or exploratory talk. I know of no English Education program that has a specific curriculum of *speaking*. This is a glaring omission because oral storytelling, for instance, is one of the most basic and essential ways in which we understand the world. In a sense, our consciousness is *the story we are telling ourselves*, the narrative in our head. Indeed, each of us rehearses the stories of our life to create meaning. After much rehearsal, our internal stories reach the *canonical version* (the authoritative version; *canon* = rule/ruling) which then never changes. Witness the canonical version at a gathering of family and friends when your uncle or your high school buddy tells the same story in the exact same way they always have—and they tell it the same way again and again and again. The meaning to the story, for the teller and the listener, is now in its final form after being rehearsed. It is the finalized, canonical, ruling version.

There are several "story" assignments or units I include in my classes whenever possible. When my students who are student teachers and beginning teachers try these with their classes, it's almost always a success. All of these activities ultimately involve speaking through presenting and/or dialogue:

- Autobiographical time line. This could be a time line of the student's general personal (autobiographical) history, or it could be a more specific time line of the student's *learning* history, *reading* history, *schooling* history, or any other "history" relevant to the theme of the unit in the class—the sky's the limit. Students are given few parameters on how to do this, but most produce some kind of a traditional time line; others produce a "résumé style" time line or a narrative; others get creative, and I've had students create: a video loop on a laptop, a dozen drawn-upon eggs (to suggest fragility), personal artifacts, even baked cookies decorated with events from the student's life (which we then got to eat). The time line can be accompanied with a 100–150-word explanation or abstract like you would find next to a painting in a museum, or there can be a more narrative, poetry, story, or essay writing. The time line is shared in an "art gallery walk" and or by a "show and tell," and this could include pairs or small groups going around the "art gallery" and taking notes on index cards to share later with the larger group. I usually view the time lines in two class sessions as students put a lot of time and thought into these works and are proud of them.

- Family tree. The family tree could be a traditional one, samples of which are shared with the class (and is at least one lesson), or it could be more similar to the autobiographical time line, using drawings, pictures, photographs, montage, found objects, autobiographical artifacts (see below), or whatever a student creatively comes up with. (Note that I avoid the word *parents* in my urban classes. All of my students have a *family*, and if you lose your native family, you can create another family. Not all of my students have *parents* who are present in their lives.) How about a *relationship tree* or *community tree* of those people involved in their current lives?
- Autobiographical artifact. Students bring in a personal artifact that means something to them (although I tell them not to bring something in that has great monetary value, or that can be broken, lost, or stolen). Students explain the artifact in pairs, small group, or in a "read around" large group. A writing activity may accompany the artifact.
- Autobiographical writing. Students write their own autobiographies, either a full one, or one comprising an important event, such as "an event that changed me." Or, they could write a shorter *vignette* or *anecdote*. I have few parameters for this, except to discuss the need for paragraphs and/or headings to organize it, otherwise the autobiographies tend to ramble. If the autobiography is a long narrative or essay, I have them write an anecdote or vignette (or two) that captures the essence of their life (*a time something or someone changed you, a time you realized something important about yourself*). I ask that the autobiography begins with an anecdote or vignette, much as a short story begins *in medias res*. I also discuss the need to "show, not tell" by relating events rather than just explaining. And, of course, I share my own autobiography with them, or write my own autobiography along with them (Costigan, 2013).

For those teachers who are under mandates for traditional assignments, any of the above can be turned into a four-paragraph block essay, or can accompany an autobiography reading unit.

Let us now talk about how I arrived at such "story" activities, and how you can also come up with an ELA curriculum. Let's look at an approach to ELA that can provide the basis for innumerable units and lessons, ones that are both meaningful and beneficial for your students.

Creating English Language Arts: The Points and the Wings

As we have seen at the end of Chapter 1, we can arrange English as shown in Figure 3.2.

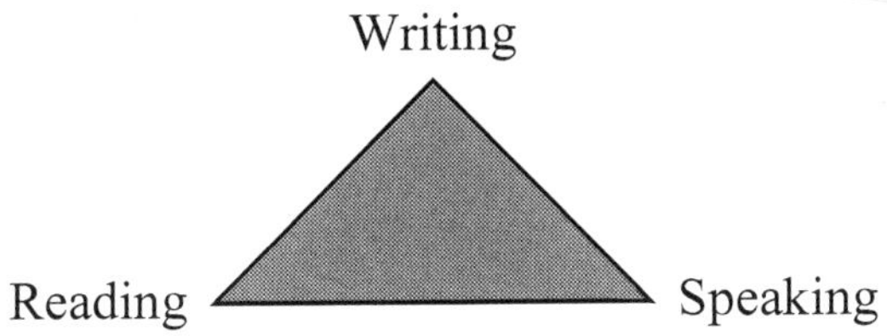

FIGURE 3.2 The Basic Intermodal Triangle.

All three are equally important. It doesn't matter which is on the top of the triangle. However, they are all not equally easy to teach. Let's summarize what we've touched upon in previous chapters, because I think these concepts are essential.

Speaking is the hardest "point" of the triangle to teach because nothing (no-*thing*) is produced, no artifact, no physical text, nothing you can hold on to, look at, rearrange and edit. The "text" of speaking by nature is ephemeral in that it can't be touched and manipulated, but it is also *final* in that once delivered, it can't be edited. You will have noticed this many times in your life as certain words, phrases, sentences, and once in a while whole pages have just "slipped out" from your mouth, usually in anger, and produced very bad effects. In other words, you've shot off your mouth and got in trouble. Speaking is also temporary and quickly lost, not necessarily going from the short-term memory to the long-term memory without specific assistance (through writing or reading). Once a person says something, it is not necessarily easy to get it permanently "in the head" unless you "get it down" somehow.

Writing is not easy to teach, of course, but it is easier than teaching speaking, first of all because every teacher likely has had at least one solid course in the teaching of writing, and secondly because, unlike speaking, the reader produces something (some-*thing*). This text is physical, it can be manipulated, added to, subtracted from, rearranged, and changed, a recursive process we call rewriting or editing. A text doesn't go away unless you tear it up or delete it from your computer, and even then, the text of what you wrote is more or less still in your head waiting to be recreated in a newly edited way (which is another form of text). The more there is a physical object produced when we teach and when students learn, the clearer it is to the student and the easier it is to teach, and writing does this.

Reading, therefore, falls in somewhere between speaking and writing in the "difficult to teach" continuum. While you are not necessarily producing a written text, you are producing a kind of text when you read. In reading you are producing a "picture in your head" or a dialogue between you and the text. In fact, all sorts of things happen when you read. You are "there" in the text, imagining it; or you are far off in a reverie of personal associations suggested by the text; or you leave the text and think of related instances in your life; or you ponder the philosophical implications of the text for living your life; or you read the same part of the text over and over and over and never "get" it; or lastly, you are completely immersed in the text so that you lose all sense of consciousness, time, and place, a phenomenon called *flow*. And flow is a good thing (Csíkszentmihályi, 1996). I need only repeat here what has been earlier discussed in this book, that if a student produces some-*thing*, that is another text, out of his writing, reading, or speaking then it is more likely to be retained, to go into the long-term memory.

The Wings and The Law of One Detailed

As noted at the end of Chapter 1, I call this interrelation of writing-reading-speaking the "wings" of the three points of the English curriculum, both terms and a process I have borrowed from the Enneagram, a theory of personality types (Riso & Hudson, 1996).

As you can see in Figure 3.3, writing has the *wings* of reading and speaking. Reading has the wings of writing and speaking. And, speaking has the wings of reading and writing. All are interrelated. So, when your lesson is a speaking lesson (the *point*), as in a debate unit or a speech unit, you might have the students write (the *wing*) and/or read (the *wing*) to support the speaking. This is the intermodal process. You will learn this when you first think that you attempt the speaking curriculum, such as in a debate unit. You naturally back this up with lots of reading and writing. Why? Well, perhaps your students asked for a debate because they think it is "fun." But a debate unit is hard work, much harder, I think, than most reading and writing units. A true debate is about as far as you can get from a Jerry Springer episode, or what politicians do on talk shows when they shout over each other. A debate unit, I certainly have found, can be done and is valuable, but it is also one of the most difficult units to teach because it is the ephemeral non-physical text of speaking. It requires of the student considerable skills in organizing, evaluating, communicating, and persuading. These concepts and skills are very high on the abstract level (see Bloom's Taxonomy). It also involves Aristotelian *class logic* (syllogisms), or *symbolic logic* (P not Q), as well as the rhetorical devices such as "straw man," "reductio ad absurdum," "no true Scotsman . . ." and "slippery slope," to name a few. So, if you do need to teach debating (point: speaking), you

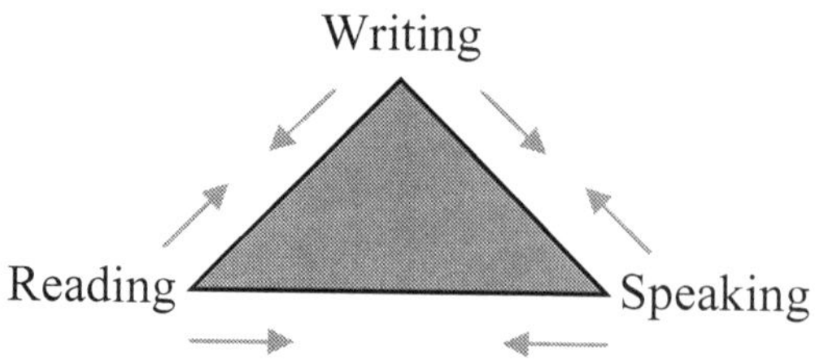

FIGURE 3.3 The Interrelation of ELA Modalities.

had better use lots and lots of the wings of reading and writing activities to support the formal, abstract, and difficult speaking skills needed.

Here are some examples of this process: So, to enhance the debate *speaking* (point) you have to do lots and lots of *writing* (primary wing), along with some *reading* (secondary wing), to enhance the modality of speaking. Similarly, when your lesson is a reading lesson (point), such as teaching a poem, you would also have them do activities that are writing and speaking—the two wings of the point of the curriculum of the reading or poetry triangle. I tell my preservice and beginning teachers that each lesson should have *one* point or focus, *either* writing, or reading, or speaking, but that that point is supported by the other wings. In fact, as writing, reading, and speaking are part of every lesson, the point is always supported by a *primary wing,* and a *secondary wing.* Let me explain further.

From here on I'm going to use *The Great Gatsby*, just because it's most likely known to all readers of this book. If a teacher is teaching a passage from *Gatsby*, the "point" or focus of the lesson is that it is clearly a reading lesson. As the novel is told from the viewpoint of Nick, the teacher may choose to have the students rewrite the selection from another character's point of view (through interior monologue or stream of consciousness). For example, the teacher might ask the students to write from the perspective of Tom who really does not get a voice in the novel and who does not come off very well (he's not only a serial cheater, but a racist and anti-Semite). Thus, the primary focus or the point of the lesson, reading *Gatsby*, is supported by the *primary wing* of writing an interior monologue in the voice and head of Tom. When students share their writings, this is the *secondary wing* of the *Gatsby* reading lesson and this is speaking. This type of lesson planning comes naturally to most teachers—and it *is* natural—but becoming conscious of the process allows for more considerations in planning such instruction. It's no longer luck or serendipitous, but focused and planned. You know the structure or scaffolding behind what you are doing.

Continuing with our *Gatsby* example, most often, given the curriculum triangle above, *reading* is the focus of the lesson (point), then it will be supported by the wing of writing. Alternatively, abandoning our *Gatsby* example, if *writing* is the focus (point) of the lesson, *reading* will be the primary wing of the lesson. In the case of most units and lessons in most ELA classrooms, speaking will usually be related to the secondary wing. However, as suggested above in this chapter, it need not be so. If a teacher had students improvise a scene from *Gatsby*, for instance, say a dialogue between Gatsby and Daisy in the car after the fight in the Plaza Hotel, the reading of a passage of Gatsby (the point) would be supported by the primary wing of *speaking*. This, then might be assisted by the secondary wing of *writing* when, at the end of class the teacher asks the students, "Write what you learned from the five improvisations of our *Imagined-Post-Plaza-Car-Scene*."

All this might seem needlessly complicated, but I think it sorts out the focus of units and lessons and gives us a way of approaching curricular design and implementation. The great difficulty I see in both new and experienced teachers is that their lessons try to do too much. As discussed below, I have found the *Law of One* a key component in curricular design and implementation (teaching). The point and the wings can be applied to both units and individual lessons. This means that the unit of several weeks, such as reading *Gatsby*, has the point or focus of reading the novel. Each lesson supports that point with a wing of reading with writing (alternative endings, character analysis, character's interior monologue, and so forth) or speaking (role playing, exploratory talk, and so forth). The point is to have one focus, one "point" at which you are aiming, if you will.

We have discussed listening and bodily movement in the previous chapter, so I need to add that there is always the possibility that our triangle turns into a pentagram, by adding listening and bodily movement (kinesthetics), as shown in Figure 3.4.

In this case, you will notice, there are still the point and the wings, but you can cross the interior. For example, in a *reading* lesson (the point, reading a scene from a play), the teacher may have the students create a silent tableau presenting the characters and their attitudes in the scene (*body*, primary wing), and this might involve students verbally interpreting the tableau (*speaking*, secondary wing). The point in curricular planning is to keep it simple. All five elements are present in every lesson, of course, but in planning, plan for only one point and only two wings.

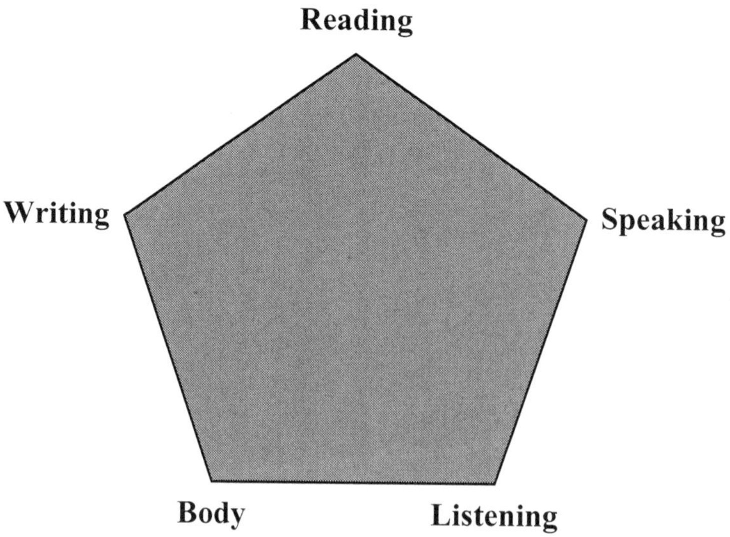

FIGURE 3.4 The Enhanced Intermodal Pentagram.

The Point and Wings in Classroom Discussions

This brings up an allied and important issue of which to be aware. Many teachers begin their careers by thinking that they will have a sort of unguided open-ended literature discussion for a full period—as indeed they did in many college literature classes. This, the new teacher finds out, almost never works. The point and the wings can help because whole group discussion is the hardest thing to do in a classroom. My rule of thumb is always to have a writing, reading, or other activity, usually in pairs or small groups, before whole group discussion. The whole group class discussion must be "set up" by the teacher so that it is "set up" in the students' heads. I think even college students need preparation for this, so I always have them at least "revisit the text" (reading), usually with some guiding focus such as a question, or I have different students in the class "revisit" different parts of the text (reading) before the classroom discussion (speaking). I have found that, even in college and graduate school, discussions need some preparation (the reading or writing wing) before a whole group discussion (speaking point) can be meaningful.

What the point and the wings overcome is the problematic ways in which many teachers go about reading, discussing, and analyzing texts of literature in their class. This is the "analysis modality" when a teacher attempts reading (or the students round robin read) and then there is a "stop and talk" where the sentence, paragraph, or line of a poem or play is "figured out" or "translated" to get its "meaning." I have found that this just doesn't work very well, simply because it is not the way people read in the real world—that is with an ongoing and continual flow. I argue that writing, reading, and speaking activities, which actively process or "work upon" the text, work much better than the "translate" or "stop and discuss" or "figure out" process, which is supposed to lead to some summative understanding or meaning of the text under consideration.

So, in summary, I don't think what I am advocating is complicated. My maxim of teaching is that each curriculum I design and attempt to implement (teach), whether it is a unit of several weeks, or a daily lesson, or even a ten-minute mini-lesson, should focus on only *one* point of the curriculum triangle. Choose to focus on writing, *or* reading, *or* speaking. Again, this is the *Law of One.* Make sure that your unit, or lesson, or activity is either a point (focus) of the writing, or reading, or speaking curriculum, but support these with the other modalities of the ELA curriculum.

Plan for doing one thing well, and *target* doing one thing well, and if you fail, you can try again. If you have trouble doing one thing well, as we teachers all do on occasion, the worst thing you can do is to try to do two or three things to replace the one thing you're having difficulty with. Adding and multiplying ways of teaching in the hope that something sticks—like throwing spaghetti on the wall—won't help and doesn't work at all. You have to work through why the *one* focus of the lesson did not work.

Again, it bears repeating, that all three aspects of the ELA curriculum are not equal: It is easier to teach *reading* a short story than *writing* a short story, which is a very complicated and detailed process. Additionally, the reading of poetry is not something in which many teachers have had much experience. Thus, the teaching of reading poetry and writing poetry is equally difficult for most teachers. Often when I observe teachers teaching poetry, they focus on the formal aspects of rhyme scheme or so-called literary devices, such as assonance, alliteration, anapest, to just mention a few of the ones beginning with "A." And, of course, these abstractions are easily forgotten because they have nothing to do with why real people in the real world write or read poetry. Or, they teach a sonnet which, unfortunately, can be reduced to a few rules about the type of information contained in the octave, sestet, and rhyming couplet at the end, all of which is a favorite for ELA test makers because it is so mechanical. But this isn't why people write or read sonnets—that usually has to do with love, or nature, or something important about being human! And of course, many teachers still use the "stop at each line and translate" methods. Teachers teach these things, and they teach this way, because they don't really know how to teach poetry. And of course, teaching *reading* sonnets is much easier than teaching *writing* sonnets, though I have sometimes done this with fairly good success. All these difficulties in poetry are not because there are bad teachers, it's just because most teachers haven't had specific instruction in poetry. I literally didn't know how to read a poem, didn't know what a poem was, despite many lessons in reading poetry, that is until I took a creative writing of poetry class with an actual working publishing poet. Then I learned something of what it was all about.

Writing, Reading, and Speaking as Text

When you write, read, or speak, you produce a *text*. "Text" ordinarily means something printed on a page, or viewed on a computer screen and saved in the computer's memory. However, in a broader way of thinking, a painting, drawing, or sculpture is also a text. In fact, my research indicates that there is no difference between the way a person reads the text of a novel and how people "read" a painting, a sculpture, or even a musical or dance performance (Asher & Costigan, 2005). A text can also be a musical performance, a dance performance, or a play because all these are "texts" that you can respond to both intellectually and emotionally, what we can call also responding aesthetically. A text is a human created product or artifact that can be experienced (read, touched, heard, viewed) by another human. It has "corners," or "edges"; that is, it is limited in size, in scope, in sequence, and in time (has a beginning and end).

Additionally, speech can also be a text, and no one can deny that a speech can be as powerful as any written text, if you think of the effects of speeches by Hitler, Churchill, Franklin Delano Roosevelt, or Martin Luther King. A story you are telling is also a text, even if it is not written down. Imagine that you are giving a speech to an audience without notes, or imagine that you are telling a story rather than reading it. There has to be some text "in your head" that keeps you progressing in some coherent order through your speech or story (even without written notes). That is, there is a text that keeps you on pathway as you are speaking. The text is somewhat flexible, of course, and you can lose your way, as people not infrequently do. In this case, you have gone "off text," that is off the text that was in your head. These texts are accessed later in your memory when you mentally revisit that painting, performance, or event. For our purposes:

> A text is the intentional human creation of a physical, visual, or oral product, artifact or text, which can be aesthetically and intellectually apprehended by a human recipient through an engagement or a transaction with it through the senses. It is thus the mode, or means, by which one human creation is apprehended by another.

Retaining Texts

As you know from your educational psychology coursework, we have a short-term memory and a long-term memory. Most things, such as your morning commute, what you ate for lunch, or last night's television show, do not remain in your mind for long because they only go as far as your short-term memory. Most of our experiences don't need to be held in our mind for any significant time, and nor do we want to. I certainly don't want my morning commute by New York City subway and bus to stay in my mind cluttering it up for the rest of the day. In fact, most of what we perceive in any given day, through sight, smell, hearing, or touch, quickly slips from our short-term memory and is lost. It is only by surprise, unfamiliarity, or effort that something goes into our long-term memory. A significant event on your morning commute—such as a near collision with a bicyclist, or some seemingly dangerous deranged person on the bus—might by its unusual nature go into the long-term memory for the rest of the day, but will soon be lost, perhaps someday to be retrieved. Indeed, when I want to, I can remember every car accident I've been in, as well at the time an obviously deranged person punched me on a sidewalk in New York City. A moving musical concert or performance might stay in my long-term memory for a long time. And of course, profound moments like a marriage proposal, a trip to Paris, or the death of a friend, stay with us all our lives.

An event that is experienced by the senses as merely ordinary needs assistance to enter into our long-term memory by becoming *extra*-ordinary (extraordinary). This is what we do when we study for an exam or remember driving directions. We have to force ourselves though effort, and perhaps some mnemonic devices or tricks, to get these things for a time into the long-term memory. You can remember the sequence of heart valves by, "Try pulling my aorta," or **Try** (tricuspid valve) **pul**ling (pulmonary valve), **my** (mitral valve)

aorta (aortic valve). And, you remember getting to Juan's house by, "Right at gas station, left at sign for Coca Cola, left at light, keep shopping mall to left, go half mile and take right into driveway." Then, once we take the test or reach our destination, we let it go—or not.

When you think of it, the teacher's job is to get the content area or subject discipline into the long-term memory, hopefully for good. A teacher wants in the long-term memory not only the information necessary to understand the subject, but the intellectual habits and thought processes used in doing that particular subject. A subject discipline such as Math, Science, History, or English are more than mere facts about quadratic equations, viruses, the Vietnam War, or *The Great Gatsby*. These subjects are *ways of thinking*. When you think about it for a moment, it is much more important that a student gets in the habit of the ways of thinking about writing, reading, and speaking than that he reads any specific piece of literature, or produces any particular form of writing.

In having your students read *The Great Gatsby*, you want them to experience this magnificent novel, and even more, you want the student to have *Gatsby* as part of her repertoire of reading lots of good literature. But additionally, reading *Gatsby* is on the path of reading other great works of art (perhaps his contemporary, Hemingway, or more contemporary fiction). And, you understand that *Gatsby* can be returned to in one year, or ten, or twenty, because it is the nature a work of art to reveal new meanings each time it is encountered. This is the primary difficulty with test- and standards-based educational reforms, because they assume that a work of art has only one agreed-upon meaning. A work of art, by definition can be revisited many times, because each time you engage with the work, it reveals new and deeper meanings. The tests and standards of current educational reforms do not want students to engage with the multiple and layered meanings of works of art. This is why educational reforms are so big on "reading for information," or reading for "plot and theme," because if a work of art has multiple meanings—and they do—then how do you teach and measure it? If a work of art has one meaning, it is a commodity and you can bank it. If it has multiple meanings, you can't. In any event, you teach a work of art such as *The Great Gatsby* because: (1) It *is* a work of art; and, (2) the habits of reading literary works in future are developed through reading *Gatsby*.

To use an example from another subject discipline, the music teacher isn't particularly interested that his keyboard student "masters" playing a two-part invention by J. S. Bach. Indeed, for the novice a level of mastery is probably an impossible and unrealistic goal. What the teacher wants is for the student to experience Bach's counterpoint—that is separate melodies working together in two separate hands—as an essential ability for any competent keyboardist. What the teacher is more interested in is that *in addition* to experiencing a magnificent example of counterpoint, playing the piece enhances the skill or competence in playing the keyboard. After the music student has experienced this work and increased his competency *to the extent that he is able*, then the teacher might give another two-part invention, or move on to a three-part invention, or perhaps to an early Mozart sonata. And because a two-part invention is a work of art, when the same keyboardist returns to it in 20 years, he will see it differently and play it differently, and of course with more competence. The same goes with reading literature. What the music teacher does *not* do is to try to have the music student perfect a two-part invention before moving on to another two-part invention. As with reading *Gatsby*, the music teacher only wants the novice keyboardist to move ahead *just enough* in the processes of playing. Again, the test- and accountability- educational reform movement believes incorrectly that there is one "mastery" level of interpretation of a work of art, and that each individual falling short of mastery (the deficit model) can be measured and given a number.

In ELA and in all content areas, the purpose of education is to move the student ahead *just enough* to develop the skills, habits, and processes used in how people read, write, and speak, *in addition to* experiencing particular works of art. However, in order to develop these skills and processes, the learner has to get the text under consideration into the long-term memory, what I call more colloquially *getting it in the head.* The literature that you teach, along with the writing that you wish your students to do, is not to them at first *extra*-ordinary (extraordinary) and will not necessarily get into their long-term memory without your explicit assistance to make it extra-ordinary. This is why teachers hear "this is boring" all the time. Students have not yet acquired the competence to see the extra-ordinariness in the work of art under consideration. Again, as Maxine Greene said, "In many respects, teaching and learning are matters of breaking through barriers—of expectation, of boredom, of predefinition" (Greene, 1995, p. 14).

Getting The Text In the Head: More on Intermodality

Writing, reading, and speaking are modalities that are applied to texts (works of art) under consideration. So, to apprehend a text, both intellectually and aesthetically, the process I advocate is intermodal, that is the learner uses one mode of apprehension (for instance, writing) to understand another mode (for instance, reading a novel). In the discussion of intermodal lessons that follows, note that I am using the term *pericope* (per-***i***-co-pee, emphasis on the second syllable) to refer to an extract from a larger text, or for any text under consideration. A mnemonic device for this is the word "periscope," which is a device to concentrate on a specific focused area on the larger horizon. So, the pericope is limited in scope, what you could engage with in one class: a poem, a page, several paragraphs, a scene or two from a play. The term comes from the *hermeneutic* critical tradition, which we need not go into here except to say that hermeneutic comes from the word Hermes, who is of course the Greek demigod who carries the messages of the gods—he's usually pictured with a winged helmet and sometimes winged heels. The general idea is that a selected passage "carries" a meaning to the reader. I use the term pericope in unit planning of novels, plays, and longer works of art because I strongly advocate that a teacher does not attempt to "cover" the entire text in a step by step, chapter following chapter, or act following act way, as many teachers attempt to do. The reasons for selecting a specific pericope as the focus of study in a lesson is that, first of all, it is often impossible to read in its entirety a large work of art in a three-week unit (which is about the limit students can pay attention to a topic before becoming burnt out and bored). Second, and more positively, I advocate that the teacher's responsibility in each lesson is to focus on those passages of text that she thinks are important for her students because they "carry meaning" based on the particular theme, focus, or line of inquiry of the unit. The use of the term pericope indicates that the selection of the reading passages for each lesson in a unit of a larger work are not random, but are purposeful chosen specifically because they are important for the students in their transaction or engagement with the larger work of art.

Thinking About Learning and Doing Teaching

Again, let me give an example from *The Great Gatsby*. And again, I am using this work of art because it's one we're probably all familiar with. In this work of art, a teacher is somewhat challenged when she comes to the complicated confrontation in the Plaza Hotel between Tom, Gatsby, Daisy, Nick, and Jordan. The Plaza Hotel confrontation leads up to the death of Myrtle, Tom's mistress, who is run over by Daisy, for which Gatsby takes the blame—and gets the punishment. What takes place in the Plaza is an emotional and implication-rich conversation between the characters, which is very adult in nature as it reveals the characters' desires and the deceptions each is making to the others and to themselves. These subtleties, revealed by narrator Nick, may easily be missed by young or inexperienced readers, who, after all, have little experience with marriage, adultery, longstanding unrequited longing, and elaborate self-deception. In the conversation among the characters, Tom reveals that he has cheated on Daisy but that, paradoxically, their relationship bond is stronger than anything she can have with Gatsby. Daisy confesses her love for Gatsby but shows no willingness to leave Tom. Jordan is embarrassed, unhelpful, and silent. And Nick reveals his status as someone who feels he is only an outsider, an isolated observer to life.

Lesson One: A Common Gatsby

The teacher starts the class by announcing that they are going to cover "the next part of the book," which takes place in the Plaza Hotel. Without giving any more background, the teacher then has the students read the selection in what is called *unrehearsed public reading*. The purpose of this approach is to have the student reader figure out what is happening (plot), which will lead them to the inferences the novel implies about the characters' development, all of which should touch upon the overall message or point of the book (theme). In this traditional class, the passage is read out loud in a round robin fashion, that is, each student taking turn in the order in which they are seated.

During the reading, the teacher often stops and asks plot-based questions, such as those that follow immediately below. The idea of asking plot-based questions is so that the teacher can assist the students in reading the more subtle implications of the text, where the author is showing something about the character rather than just stating it outright. Her goal is to assist students in (1) understanding the facts of the text, the plot, and (2) assuring that students are making inferences from what is implied in the text. I am numbering these questions for a reason that will be clear later on in this chapter:

1. When Tom criticizes Daisy's complaining about the heat by saying, "You make it ten times worse by crabbing about it," what does Gatsby's interjection, "Why not let her alone, old sport," reveal about his attitude toward Daisy, or toward Tom?
2. Why is the symbolism of, "The telephone book slipped from its nail and splashed to the floor, whereupon Jordan whispered, 'Excuse me'—but this time no one laughed"?
3. What does the following reveal about Daisy's attitude toward her husband, "Open the whiskey Tom . . . and I'll make you a mint julep. Then you won't seem so stupid to yourself."
4. What does the following reveal about Tom's character, "And what's more I love Daisy too. Once in a while I go off on a spree and make a fool of myself, but I always come back, and I love her all the time"?
5. What does the following reveal about Jordan's participation in the scene when Nick says, "I glanced at Jordan . . . who had begun to balance an invisible but absorbing object on the tip of her chin"?
6. What does the following reveal about the narrator Nick as he is reflecting on his birthday, "Thirty—the promise of a decade of loneliness, a thinning list of single men to know, a thinning briefcase of enthusiasm, thinning hair"?
7. Why did Tom suggest that Gatsby and Daisy drive together back to Long Island, stating to Daisy, "Go on. He won't annoy you. I think he realizes that his presumptuous little flirtation is over"?

After reading several pages with frequent stops for students to infer more about the characters, the teacher then initiates a whole group discussion about the idea that Tom believes that he and Daisy have a relationship that Gatsby can never understand. By the end of the class, this leads back to the theme of the teaching unit about "privilege and or/responsibility" and to the Hemingway-Fitzgerald difference about "the rich are different from you and me" ("Yes, they have more money"). As the bell is about to ring a student states about Gatsby, "And I now think he's really sad because he is not going to get Daisy."

A Greater Gatsby

Referring again to our writing-reading-speaking triangle, the "point" of this lesson is *reading*, and the teacher uses writing as the *primary wing* and speaking as the *secondary wing* to assist the students in being engaged with the reading. The teacher begins the class with having the students write in their ongoing literature journals about (as he states), *A time when you—or a person you know—got into an argument. What was said and done? How did it end? Write about what you saw or heard. Write about how you felt.*

An important note and a digression here: As this is early in the semester and the teacher is trying to build a community of learners, which is a safe place for them to explore important human issues, he is careful to add, "This is personal writing and I won't collect it or read it. You will be asked to share your writing with a partner, and you can share by letting your partner read what you wrote, or you can read some of what you wrote to your partner, or you can explain what you wrote to your partner and just summarize it. And, of course if it's really personal, you don't have to share it at all. When I review your journals this weekend, you may fold over the page as usual, and I won't read this page." Note also that when this teacher has students write about a potentially difficult, personal, or "trigger" topic, he gives the students the option of writing about "yourself *or a person/other student/acquaintance you know.*" As these are young adolescents in the ninth grade and have not fully developed their self-understanding, this technique often lets the students distance themselves from events and experiences that are difficult to share, by writing about "another person," or *themselves* as another person.

After the students write, they take a few moments to share with each other in what the teacher calls "pair and share" or "turn and talk." The teacher then asks for some students to "report back to the whole group about what they heard." Many hands go up and five students are called on to read "your arguments in whole or in part." This teacher knows that his goal is to have the students *read what they actually wrote* rather than *summarize what they wrote*, the latter being something that unsure and novice writers tend to do. One reports about an argument about money that he heard from "his friend's" parents. Several students report arguments about they have with their friends, and several others report arguments about sports and arguments with their parents about their household responsibilities, curfews, and the like. One student reports an argument she got into in a store when she felt that the security guard was following her unfairly. This reminded another student of the argument he got in yesterday with the security guard at the entrance to the school because he was disrespectful to the student.

The teacher then states to the class, "OK, I'm handing out some quotations and I would like you to rate them on a scale of one to seven. A "7" means that these are "fighting words" and will lead to a serious argument or physical action. A "1" means that these are simply words that any reasonable person should ignore. A "4" is the middle, which means that it may lead to an argument or not, it just depends. The sheet has the following statements:

1. You make it ten times worse by complaining about it.
2. Why not leave her alone?
3. She said, "Excuse me," but no one laughed.
4. I'll make you a drink. Then you won't seem so stupid to yourself.
5. I love her all the time. But once in a while I go off and make a fool of myself, but I always come back to her.
6. The promise of a decade of loneliness.
7. She looked like she was balancing an invisible but fascinating object on the tip of her chin.
8. He won't bother you.

Or, rather than rating each phrase with a number from one to seven, the teacher could also have the students arrange the statement numbering them from "1" (most fighting words) to "8" (least fighting words), with each statement having only one number and no number repeated. Alternatively the students could physically arrange the phrases, which were cut out each on their own slip of paper. The students could also do any of this in groups or in pairs rather than individually.

After arranging the phrases, the students have a lively discussion about what these phrases mean and which is the most argument producing. A general consensus seems to be "Why don't you leave her alone," followed closely by, "He won't bother you." This was followed by calling someone "stupid" as leading to an argument. The rest of the phrases were fairly argumentative, but the students were surprised by the "balancing on the chin" statement, so the teacher had the students actually do this gesture. (Try this yourself now.) Several students noted that this made them feel like they might be "choosing whether or not to fight." The phrase "the promise of a decade of loneliness" was found generally to be the least argumentative, and there was no consensus about what this meant.

In contrast to the first example where the teacher gave no background information, this teacher next gives the students some background to the pericope they will be reading. He even passes a few pictures of the Plaza's exterior and interior around the room. He says, "This next part of the novel takes place at a luxurious suite of rooms at the Plaza Hotel, a very fancy hotel in Manhattan, where the four characters go to spend the afternoon on what is a very hot and steamy day. Tom has brought a bottle of whiskey to make a drink called 'mint julep'."

Note that in contrast to the traditional teacher in the commonsense lesson, this teacher is very willing to share the plot with his students. This teacher does not believe that "figuring out the plot" plays an important part in literature lessons. In fact, most of us read novels, watch TV shows, or go to movies, when we pretty much know who the main characters are and what is going to happen. It bears repeating what was mentioned earlier in this book: The joy of reading is not in having to figure out what happens (the plot), but in engaging with the way the writer "plays with" what happens (the plot). This is why novels get turned into movies, movies are remade into new movies, and plays and movies are remade into each other: It's the variations that engage us, not the basic plot. I am always surprised when I visit a classroom dealing with a Shakespeare play when the main focus is for students to do unrehearsed public reading to figure out "what happens." No actor or director ever read any Shakespeare play this way.

At this point in the lesson, the teacher reads the pericope out loud while the students read along. There are many ways he could choose to read this pericope, but he has chosen this because he believes that this story works *as a story* and he wants the students to experience it as if he were a storyteller, which Fitzgerald certainly is. After a page or two, the teacher then instructs the students to continue to read silently on their own. The teacher then asks the students to quickly write a word or two—no more—about how they feel or what they think now. A moment is given student to state their responses, which are: "Confused," "dislike," "cheater," "hate," "soap opera," "bad scene," "distressing," "nasty."

This follows with a whole group discussion of the passage; again, there is the mantra: *Whole group discussion is the hardest thing to do in a classroom, so prepare for it with an activity (or two).* The students are interested if Daisy and Gatsby were cheating on Tom, even though it is pretty clear that no physical cheating was involved. The discussion revolved around the unpleasantness of Tom, how Gatsby doesn't fight enough, how Daisy doesn't take a stand and is confused, how Jordan "does nothing," and "what does Nick turning thirty have to do with anything?" After all, the students point out, relationship or marital infidelity is a serious thing. All students are interested in relationships, in faithfulness, and in the dangers of cheating, and in betrayal. More importantly, they have begun to see that all the characters are complex. They do feel Tom is a brute and that Daisy is confused and irresponsible, but they are beginning to see that Jordan, by her silence and reserve, doesn't help the matter. They give the teacher an idea that he didn't have before, namely that she may be one of the careless and irresponsible rich that Nick talks about. He plans to develop this over future lessons. And Nick is getting more and more problematic for the students. One student wonders, what is it with the "thinning list of single men"?

Before the bell at the end of class rings, the teacher has the students do two things. First, below the initial "argument" writing assignment, he asks the students to write one sentence which they will continue that evening for homework. They are to use the usual prompts or "starters": *I think, I see, I notice, I understand, I don't understand, I like, I don't like,* or *A question I have is . . .* The final activity of the class, right before the bell rings, is for the teacher to have the students write an "exit ticket" by stating either "What I learned today," or, "A question I have is . . ."

No lesson is perfect—ever—but I think that you will realize that the second lesson is much more engaging for the students. First of all, whatever the teacher did, she got this part of the novel "in the head" of her students. Second, the "not on grade level" students in the class "read" this text in the same way as, and with as much care as, the "on track" students. I think that the second lesson helps the students get *Gatsby* pretty much "in the head." They are, I believe, more likely to do well on a typical question, such as:

> In literature as in life, people (characters) make choices that can lead to their eventual success and fulfillment or eventual failure and frustration. From your reading, choose *two* works of literature and *two* characters and explain how specific thoughts, attitudes, and actions lead to their success and fulfillment as a person, or to failure and frustration as a person.

How the Aesthetic Works

Every lesson should only have three elements. That is what you plan for—the point and two wings. The Greater Gatsby lesson has only three elements, and what is essential is that the planning is simple.

- Point: Reading. The Plaza Scene—getting it "in the head," into the long-term memory
- Primary wing: Writing. Unarticulated response statement rating sheet
- Secondary wing: Speaking. Whole class discussion after reading the pericope.

But, once you do that, in practice, things become more complex. You should not *plan* for complications, but they stem from the simple planning. So, simple planning allows for complex learning. Looking at the lesson as it would appear in a chronologically ordered lesson plan, the lesson would look like:

Gatsby "Plaza scene" reading lesson (point, or focus modality = reading)

1. Freewriting about arguments (wing = writing).
2. Brief sharing of freewriting (wing = speaking).
3. Unarticulated response activity rating argumentative statements from text (wing = writing).
4. Teacher "story reading," and student silent reading (wing = reading/listening).
5. Students writing literature journal entry (wing = writing).
6. Whole group discussion (wing = speaking).
7. Beginning homework starter to be completed that night (wing = writing).
8. Exit ticket assessment of lesson to be read by teacher at home (wing = writing).

Looking at this lesson more schematically from our original writing-reading-speaking triangle, it might look like Figure 3.5.

Journal writing about arguments

One work reader response writing about the passage

Exit ticket

One sentence journal writing to start homework

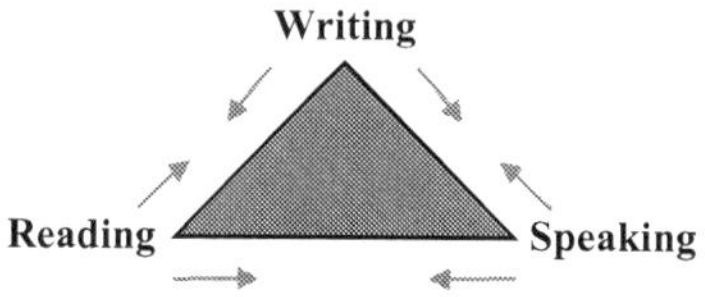

The Plaza Argument	Sharing what causes arguments
Reading along with teacher	Sharing thoughts/feelings about text
Individual silent reading	Teacher storytelling reading
Reading of student journal entry	Student whole group discussion

FIGURE 3.5 An Intermodal Triangle for The Great Gatsby Lesson.

There is a lot going on, but I think you will agree that that what is missing from the above is the action of tilting their heads like Jordan, something that came up accidentally in the lesson as a teachable moment. So, I'm going to add to our original triangle and make it a pentagon:

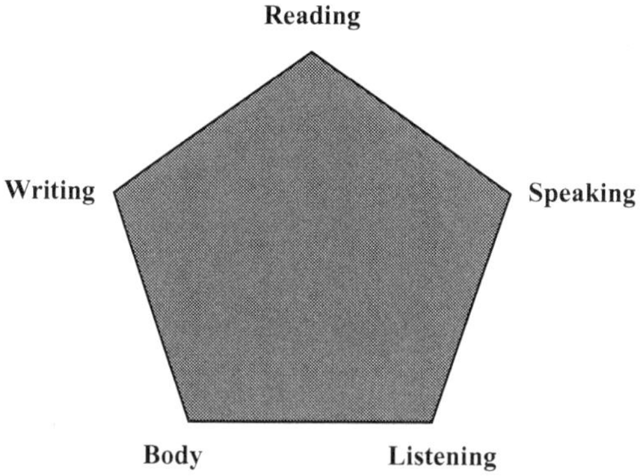

Turn and talk	Student active listening of teacher's reading
The Jordan movement	Listening in turn and talk/pair share
	Listening in whole group discussion

FIGURE 3.6 An Enhanced Intermodal Pentagram for The Great Gatsby Lesson.

I do want to point out that many ELA examinations now have a listening section where exam takers must listen to a passage, usually of non-fiction, with or without taking notes, and then answer multiple choice questions. In a more expansive sense, however, why should listening not be an upfront and important part of the ELA curriculum? Now that we have seen some of the basics in considering the ELA curriculum, our next chapter will take us further into how to design and implement curricula through considering intermodality.

References

Asher, R. & Costigan, A. (2005, July). Art and the city: A case of collaboration in Art and English teacher education. In M. Hotzler (Ed.), *Community in the making: Lincoln Center Institute, the arts and, teacher education*. New York: Teachers College Press.

Barnes, D. (2008). Exploratory talk for learning. In N. Mercer & S. Hodgkinson, (Eds.), *Exploring talk in school* (pp. 1–16). Thousand Oaks, CA: SAGE Publications, Inc.

Bryson, B. (1990). *The mother tongue: English and how it got that way*. New York: William Morrow.

Costigan, A. T. (2008). *Teaching authentic English Language Arts in a test-driven era*. New York: Taylor and Francis.

Costigan, A. T. (2013). Gaying up the teacher: From ungay teaching to a gay curriculum. In H. Endo & P. C. Miller (Eds.). *Queer Voices in the Classroom* (pp. 27–36). Charlotte, NC: Information Age Publishing.

Csíkszentmihályi, M. (1996). *Creativity: Flow and the psychology of discovery and invention*. New York: HarperCollins.

Duckworth, E. (2006). The having of wonderful ideas. In E. Duckworth (Ed.), *"The having of wonderful ideas" and other essays on teaching and learning* (3rd ed., pp. 1–14). New York: Teachers College Press.

Elbow, P. (1973). *Writing without teachers*. New York: Oxford University Press.

Freire, P. (1970/2000). Chapter Two. In P. Freire, *Pedagogy of the oppressed* (30th anniversary edition, p. 71). New York: Bloomsbury Academic.

Greene, M. (1995). *Releasing the imagination: Essays on education, the arts, and social change*. San Francisco, CA: Jossey-Bass.

Kliebard, H. M. (2004). *The struggle for the American curriculum, 1893–1958* (3rd ed.). New York: Routledge/Taylor & Francis.

Layton, L. (2017, June 7). How Bill Gates pulled off the swift Common Core revolution. *The Washington Post*. Available at: www.washingtonpost.com/politics/how-bill-gates-pulled-off-the-swift-common-core-revolution/2014/06/07/a830e32e-ec34–11e3–9f5c-9075d5508f0a_story.html?utm_term=.e0568e4fcf88.

Mayher, J. S. (1991). *Uncommon sense: Theoretical practice in language education*. Portsmouth, NH: Heinemann.

Riso, D. R. & Hudson, R. (1996) *Personality types: Using the Enneagram for self-discovery*. New York: Houghton Mifflin.

Samuelson, A. (1984). *With Hemingway: A year in Key West and Cuba*. New York: Random House.

Schneider, M. (undated). A Brief Audit of Bill Gates' Common Core Spending. *deutsch29* (blog). Available at: https://deutsch29.wordpress.com/2013/08/27/a-brief-audit-of-bill-gates-common-core-spending/.

4

EXPANDING OUR UNDERSTANDING OF INTERMODALITY

This chapter builds on the foundations of the concepts and terms we covered in the previous chapter, namely the intermodal triangle of writing, reading, speaking, where there is a *point* modality (for instance, reading a text) as supported by a *primary wing modality* (for instance, writing a stream of conscious narrative for the main character of a novel), and an informal or *secondary wing modality* (for instance, students reading all or part of their narratives in a *read around*). By the end of the previous chapter we saw that there are other modalities that stem from the foundational three. The *speaking* curriculum, for instance, implies that there is a *listening* curriculum. In other words, the organic process of listening is something that can be developed through *active listening* or *exploratory talk*. Another way teachers can make *speaking* or *talk* a point or wing of the curriculum is in small groups, such as *literature circles*, to assign roles, such as Facilitator, Recorder (secretary), Arbiter (decision maker), Summarizer, Note Taker, Reporter (to whole class), and so forth—your choice is dependent on your students and the situation. If a teacher has students role play to enhance students' transaction with a text (for instance role playing an encounter between two characters in the story, or role playing something that took place outside of the story), then the teacher is enhancing the students' understanding of speaking. In other words, *hearing* is something most of us find natural, but that does not mean that we really *listen*. Similarly, the reading curriculum can be enhanced by *movement*, or what we call *kinesthetics* (small case "k"), which is tactile learning using the body and movement. When you engage your students (and yourself as teacher) in kin*esthetic* activities—note the [a]*esthetic* in the word—you are probably also engaging your students in activities that are *aesthetic education*. Note also that kinesthetics is not to be confused with *Kinesiology* (capital "K"), which is the scientific study of the mechanics of movement in human bodies. There are other modalities of learning out there, of course, which individual readers of this book can supply, but our discussion here needsto limit our discussion of the ELA curriculum to: Writing, reading, speaking, listening, movement. Therefore, let us continue to speak of how we can expand our understanding of curriculum design (curriculum conception and planning) and implementation (curriculum teaching).

The Body and Movement (Kinesthetics)

I am always amazed when I observe ELA classes in middle school, which are frequently extended periods of one hour and 30 minutes. For almost all classes I observe, the preadolescents are basically sitting in their seats receiving direct instruction and then working in groups. The only movement they do, if at all, is to move into groups. But more often than not they simply sit in groups with their desks pulled together for the full period. I usually observe from the back of the class. I find that about 20 to 30 minutes into the class that I can't stand it anymore, and I have to stand up and move around. I can't wait until the students begin their group work because then I can move about the room observing the groups. I don't understand how a 13-year-old can sit for one and a half hours in an uncomfortable school chair. In fact, I don't understand how young people can sit for five 42-minute periods a day spending their time primarily listening to a teacher talk. We ELA teachers need to create a curriculum of "doing" rather than listening.

John Dewey tells the story of going to a school supply store and looking for work stations for students. He writes, "And finally, one dealer, more intelligent than the rest, made this remark: 'I am afraid we have not what you want. You want something at which the children may *work*; these are for *listening*'." (Dewey, 1900/1971, emphasis added). In fact, if you observe many 7–12 ELA classrooms, it is as if young people don't have bodies at all. All they do is sit. And listen. It is a hallmark of the uncommonsense constructivist classroom that the teacher creates a place where the students engage in activities, where they *do*. When I teach my ELA methods course, I always ask students to account in their lesson plans for, "What are your students doing with their bodies?" This usually is confusing to my novice English teachers. I think this is an essential consideration.

The reason for this is, first, that an *activity* should be the center of each lesson. Listening to a teacher lecture or "talk and chalk" (or smart board and talk) is not an activity. This activity, whether acknowledged or not, takes place with *bodies*. The second reason for considering what students do with their bodies is that much of our learning takes place in the body. In fact, when you think of it, learning and all knowledge comes to us through the body, and not just through the eyes and ears—the primary senses used in traditional school learning—but also through all the senses of touch, smell, and taste (Boal, 1995). You have memory *in the body*. I've used the image of eating a hamburger before (or a veggie burger if you prefer). To do this is a complex task requiring thousands of steps stored in the mind, yes, but it is stored in the mind *as body*. That is, something seemingly as simple as eating a hamburger is a series of complex steps, which you have stored in your body memory. Even how to dip a french fry in ketchup is a complex procedure when you think about it—I mean how do you get enough ketchup on it and not your clothes and get it to your mouth? If you doubt this, try to write out logically the steps involved in eating a hamburger or dipping a french fry in ketchup and getting it into your mouth.

If you want to realize the power of body knowledge, think of the time you were in a bodily position and what you did. Think of when you proposed marriage, or a sports-playing position, or something else: If you put your body in that position, you're recalling a powerful moment; and if you even think about putting yourself in the position you were when you did it, you've recreated that moment. Alternatively, put yourself in the position of a time you asked someone for something important, received a surprise (pleasant or not), the time you were "caught," the time you were embarrassed, the time you were happy. If you get your body into that same position, you are "there," you've recalled the moment, and more importantly recalled what it means.

Similarly to having the students balance something on their chin as Jordan did in the Plaza Hotel scene in *Gatsby*, mentioned in the previous chapter, I sometimes have pairs or small groups of students create a *tableau moment* of a key scene of a story, such as creating the Plaza Hotel scene with the four characters. Or, I have the student's role play the scene, perhaps in a *fish bowl activity*, and then ask them to "freeze," and then have the observers outside the fish bowl describe and discuss the attitudes and/or thoughts of the characters. As a writing activity, you can place your coat at the front of the classroom. Ask the students to write the directions about how to put on the coat. Then have yourself or a student follow these directions as a student reads them out loud. The directions will be perfectly inadequate for getting on the coat. If you are really daring, bring an éclair or cream puff and have a student eat it, with the other students writing down all the steps he takes. Or, ask the students to write the directions for eating a serving of spaghetti or a slice of pizza—it's very hard to do. One of the greatest writing activities you can do to enhance a student's organizational skills is to have them write recipes, not something easy to do. Without considering the steps the cook must take with her body, no recipe can work. This activity is also a great means of getting students' writing organized, as well as creating a writing workshop environment, and the recipe workshop can result in the creation of a class recipe book. "In body" memory is much more powerful and complex than we give it credit for in school.

I suggest that when knowledge is "in the body" it is in the long-term memory. That's why kinesthetic "in body" activities work, such as the "Jordan chin activity," or a tableau moment from a story, or role playing a scene from a story and freezing it. Going from short-term memory to long-term memory is not easy to do with hearing and seeing, but it is easy with "doing." You never forget how to ride a bicycle, or to "touch type" on a keyboard, or to play a C-scale on the piano, or the guitar fingering for a G-sharp diminished chord, or how to skip rope. The list is endless. All I am suggesting is the very important fact that body knowledge is the most powerful knowledge you have. It is also the rarest type of learning occurring in classrooms today, where seeing and hearing are the primary modalities of learning.

Additionally, a word needs to be said about resistance to movement and kinesthetic education. When I introduce this in my ELA methods class, I hear the typical—and understandable—chorus of:

- But *They* won't let me.
- Well, this would be good for advanced courses, but my not-on-grade level freshman would get out of hand.
- This might be good in the lower grades, but my advanced placement students would never put up with these seemingly childish activities because they won't see this as getting them ready for college.
- Well, I can't do this in my current school, but once I have tenure I can try such creative things. (This is the only one I don't believe. If you don't try it now, you never will.)

The only answer to these objections is to test it out. I have found that when my ELA methods and curriculum students try these things, they work and all the hesitation and worry about what might be was unfounded. I do the same things in my university-level courses that I did when I taught ninth grade, that is I use the same intermodal activities. The *quantity* of how intensely I do them and for how long is different, but the *quality* or kinds of things that I do stays the same.

I do understand that kinesthetic learning is about as uncommonsense as you can get. After all, in the traditional commonsense classroom almost all students do is sit and listen and take notes. I do understand that getting students to move and to position their bodies in the attitudes and expressions of characters is atypical and unusual. But I urge you to try it. You can see in the *Gatsby* Plaza Hotel scene that the "Jordan expression" just came up accidentally because it is there in the novel. I think if you look at your lessons, such kinesthetic movements do come up regularly and you can begin incorporating them into your teaching. As we will see in Chapter 5, curricular mandates are built on the foundation that teachers are weak. If I were an administrator and saw some of the above activities actually working in your classroom, producing enganged students, I'd probably begin to trust you and support your innovations even if you were even untenured and a novice teacher, giving you more space to be innovative and to try new ways to engage your students with writing, reading, speaking, movement, and listening. I know, I've seen this happen a lot.

More on Intermodality

Let's review the way intermodality works as discussed in the previous chapters. It's rather simple:

Learning. When a person (a student) creates a text out of a text, or a personal text based on an existing "objective" text, deep meaning and long-term learning is created for and in the person (learner). In other words, when a student relates one mode of knowing (writing, reading, speaking, listening, bodily movement) to another modality of knowing (reading a novel), a *transaction* with the text takes place and long-term learning is enhanced. This is because this is an aesthetic process that engages the whole person, physically, intellectually, and affectively.

Teaching. A coherent and clear way to approach curriculum design and implementation (teaching) is to focus on one point (modality) of the ELA curriculum, either writing, reading, or speaking. This is following the *Law of One*; that is, teachers should create *either* a writing, *or* a reading, *or* a speaking lesson, and to back it up with an activity which is a primary wing (modality) of writing, reading, speaking, listening, or movement. This will also engage an informal or secondary wing (modality) of the ELA pentagram.

Aesthetic Education. Intermodality is a type of constructivist approach to the ELA curriculum and is *aesthetic education* because this type of learning engages the senses, engages students' autobiographical selves, and engages students through collaboration with each other. This is related to *reader response* theories and practices because the intermodality process enhances students' *aesthetic transactions* with the text (Rosenblatt, 1978, 1983).

Chances are, you are doing the above already, or you have seen this done. This is because intermodality is the natural way people learn in the real world. Now might be the time to make it intentional.

Even in a traditional transmissive, information-based lesson, for instance, when a teacher has her students briefly *turn and talk*, or *pair and share*, she is having them create the text of moving, speaking, and listening out of the text she is presenting in class. And, if this occurred during a largely traditional "talk and chalk" lesson, this simple activity would be where the class came alive simply because students were engaged in autobiographical and social learning. In other words, good teachers are probably already doing intermodality already, if not all the time. For instance, if you are teaching how to write an argumentative essay or persuasive essay because of the perceived mandates of the CCSS—about as traditional, schoolish, and non-real world task as can be—you might present a controversial article from a newspaper or newsletter. You announce, "Turn to a partner and discuss why you agree or disagree with the point that this article is trying to make." This is a simple example where you, as a teacher, naturally assist your students in creating the modality of "speaking text" out of the written text of the article under consideration.

In elementary and middle school, teachers often have students respond to a story by having them draw a picture based on an incident in that story and write an explanation underneath; for instance, this explanation could be about the central conflict, or about the climax of the story, or to predict what will happen next in the story, or an alternative ending of the story, or an event from another character's viewpoint. Note that the teacher is having the students do what experienced readers do when they read, but what inexperienced readers need help doing: Predict and imagine. So, many teachers do intermodality, reader response practices, and constructivist learning naturally and serendipitously in classrooms. However, once you are aware of the principle, you can begin to use intermodality not accidentally, serendipitously, or occasionally, but as the core of designing your lessons. My attempt in this book is only to make that process conscious and an active part of curricular design and implementation.

Here are my notes from a subway encounter activity when I had my students discuss intermodality. If you live in a place that doesn't have a subway, it could be a food court, or cafeteria, or parking lot, or supermarket encounter activity. In my class the role-players pretended to hang on to subway poles and imitate straphangers, as well as mimic the bumpy, jostling ride on the subway tracks. Let's call our two students Steve and Maria:

Steve: You know, I was in Arthur's class and we read about intermodality.

Maria: Really, what's that?

Steve: That's when you create a written, oral, visual, or kinesthetic text based on a written or other text under consideration in the class.

Maria: So, that's sort of like what we're doing now?

Steve: Yeah, we're creating a subway conversation using talking to summarize a key concept in the chapter.

Maria: Can you give me an example of this process, I'm still not totally sure of it?

Steve: Why, sure, let's say I'm teaching Michael Barakiva's *One Man Guy* [2014]. At the climax of the book Alex's parents don't allow him to see his boyfriend, Ethan, not because of the gay thing, but because they think he's a bad influence on their son because they've been cutting school and sneaking off to New York City—once to a Rufus Wainwright concert, of all things. Because of this, Alex and Ethan have a fight. Well, if I were teaching this book, by the time we come to the fight and break-up, I'd have half my students write what is going on in Alex's mind, and the other hand write what is going on in Ethan's, then they'd share. . . .

Maria: [Interrupting] . . . Or, you could have them write the two characters' thoughts in a double-entry journal . . .

Steve: . . . Yeah, that would be a great intermodal activity, too. Or they (students) could role play . . .

Maria: . . . OK, oops, that's my stop. Gotta go.

Steve: OK, bye.

Getting Back To *Gatsby*

I need to repeat that I'm using *The Great Gatsby* in the following narrative because it is a common text used in ELA classrooms, and preservice and beginning teachers tell me that they consider it one of "the classics." Let's return to the "Plaza scene" argument given in Chapter 3 and earlier in this chapter to see some examples of how intermodality can be the basis of a lesson for this pericope (see Sample 4.1 on pp. 99–100).

Once you understand that intermodality presents many different ways of engaging with a text, you will see that the above are only the most essential suggestions, which range from the most typical (the reader response journal entry) to the most atypical (positioning bodies and facial expressions in light of the characters).

I could just as well have used other so-called classic texts such as *Catcher in the Rye*, or *Of Mice and Men*, or *The Color Purple,* or dozens upon dozens of other novels typically found in ELA bookrooms. I need to mention that I do advocate using contemporary texts, and in particular young adult literature (YAL), particularly those which deal with characters who represent the incredibly diverse population in the United States today. YAL includes stories about people of color, females, those with exceptionalities, the disabled, the LGBTQ community, those who are marginalized in some way, and those who are transgendered or gender non-conforming. The activities described below can be used for texts with these various focuses. Here are the young adult novels I used the year I wrote this book in my ELA methods courses. This list is, of course, personal to me and not exhaustive at all, and there are hundreds of other books focusing on the experiences of our diverse population of young people. These, however, I know engage readers both on the 7–12 grade level, as well as undergraduate and graduate students, and, well, I've read them and simply like them, and if you know of them (or others), imagine using contemporary texts when I'm talking about *Gatsby*.

- Alexie, Sherman (2007). *The absolutely true diary of a part-time Indian.* Boston, MA: Little Brown. (A young man on a Native American Reservation has to choose whether to attend an all-white school off the reservation to get ahead in the world.)
- Barakiva, Michael. (2014). *One man guy.* New York: Farrar Straus Giroux. (A young man deals with his first relationship with another young man who is not approved by his family.)
- Beam, Chris. (2012). *I am J.* New York: Little Brown and Company. (A young person who was born a girl struggles with the reality that he feels that he is a boy.)
- Cofer, Judith Ortiz. (2006). *Call me Maria.* New York: Scholastic. (A young girl is caught between two worlds: Puerto Rico where she was born, and New York where she now lives.)

SAMPLE 4.1 Sample Writing, Reading, and Speaking Activities

Pericope = Reading "Point"	*ELA "Wings"*	*Activity*
The Plaza Scene: Gatsby and Tom bicker about whom Daisy loves. Tom admits loving Daisy despite his serial cheating on her. Daisy does not seem to commit to Gatsby and does not seem to reject Tom. It is unclear if Gatsby realizes this and we wonder if he still has hope for his relationship with Daisy. At Tom's suggestion, Gatsby and Daisy leave the hotel resulting in the death of Myrtle, which eventually causes the death of Gatsby. Jordan and Nick are observers, but Nick muses on his outsider status here, and about his life in general	Writing	Students write a classic reader response entry to this pericope choosing using a starter or prompt such as: *I notice, I see/I don't see, I like/I don't like, I understand/I don't understand; a question I have is*, among other starters. Students write a stream of consciousness narrative about the pericope from the viewpoint of Gatsby, Daisy, Jordan, or Tom. Students may choose a character to write about, or the teacher may assign a specific character. The teacher has the students stop reading at a point before the characters choose to leave the hotel. They write their own ending to the chapter. After sharing their endings, they compare their endings with the novel's. With only a synopsis or summary of the scene, students write their own dialogue. Or, after reading the chapter, students write the dialogue which takes place between Gatsby and Daisy in the car, or between Jordan and Nick when Tom leaves, or between Nick and Tom after Gatsby and Daisy leave the hotel suite.
	Speaking	Rather than writing the above, students present their conversations between these characters in a short spoken dialogue in class, either ad lib or based on what they have written. After reading the pericope, and from their memory and without writing, several pairs or groups of students represent the scene. After each pair or group has presented, the class discusses the differences in interpretation about this passage, eventually comparing it with the novel's account.

(continued)

SAMPLE 4.1 *(continued)*

Pericope = Reading "Point"	*ELA "Wings"*	*Activity*
	Body	Without speaking, groups of students place themselves in positions analogous to the way in which they envision the scene. The other observing students relate (writing and/or speaking) what the bodily positions and facial expressions reveal about the characters.
		Students choose a character, or are given cards and assigned a character. They must place themselves in a bodily position of a character. The other students must interpret which character they represent.
	Reading	The teacher arranges sentences taken from the chapter and numbers them. The sentences can be about all five characters or only one or two characters (e.g. Tom/Gatsby, Jordan/Nick, Daisy/Gatsby). Students rate each sentence from (1) confusing and not revealing much about the character, (4) somewhat revealing about the character, to (7) revealing a great deal about the character.
		Students rate several paragraphs (or it could be chosen sentences) in this section on a scale determined by the teacher. The scales could be "pleasant/unpleasant," "I like/I dislike," or "confusing/understandable," or any other binary the teacher wishes.

- De La Pena, Matt. (2010). *Mexican whiteboy*. New York: Random House. (A half-Mexican, half-white young man going to a "good" white school spends the summer with his father's family in a Mexican neighborhood.)
- Myers, Walter Dean. (1999). *Monster*. New York: HarperCollins. (A teenage boy in juvenile detention and on trial presents his life in the format of a screenplay and journal entries.)
- Orr, Wendy. (1982/2007). *Peeling the onion*. New York: Farrar, Straus & Giroux. (An athletic, popular, and "normal" young woman is severely hurt in a car accident and has to reconfigure her life.)
- Palacio, R. J. (2012). *Wonder*. New York: Random House. (A young man with a severe facial disfigurement begins going to a public school.)
- Pung, Alice, *Lucy and Linh*. New York: Alfred A Knopf. (A disadvantaged young woman gets a scholarship to a good school and struggles in her relationship with a friend.)
- Sanchez, A. (2010). *The God box*. New York: Simon & Schuster. (A religious young man in a small conservative town meets a new student in his school who claims he is both Christian and gay.)
- Woodson, Jacqueline. (2014). *Brown girl dreaming*. New York: Nancy Paulsen Books/Penguin Group. (Written in poetry, this novel is a reflection on a childhood as an African American growing up in the 1960s in South Carolina and New York.)

As I discussed in the beginning of this book, what I am attempting to do here is not to give pedagogical gimmicks and tricks about teaching this scene from *Gatsby*, or indeed any other scene from any other novel. Rather, I am attempting to illustrate *a way of thinking* about teaching works of art. I suggest that once you have the intermodal mindset, or *orientation*, once you are in the intermodal *environment*, landscape, or ecology, then you will come up with your own reading and writing activities, ones that are much more innovative than the basic ones I have presented in this section of this book.

A Short Digression About Recording Class Activities

Let me digress for a moment and comment that I no longer understand why students should sit in a class and all take similar notes when the teacher lectures or "talks and chalks." When you consider it, isn't this a waste of time and effort? The only way it makes sense is if students in the class are all competing against each other to get the most correct information from the teacher, and this is a traditional commonsense strategy that is not recommended in this book. If your class is cooperative rather than competitive, and if notes must be taken, why not simply have one student (or two for accuracy's sake) take notes for everyone and then publish those notes to the whole class (after review by the teacher of course). I think this is much better than everyone taking similar notes on the same thing. As I seldom lecture in my classes, and then never for more than five or ten minutes (and I have someone time it for me!), often I appoint a note taker to record my lecture, or our discussion, or an activity, or whatever needs to be documented, and then they send it to me electronically and I publish it for the class. I know an excellent teacher who records what happens in his class on big sheets of newsprint on an easel.

Learning as Imitation and Play

Intermodality and aesthetic practices are what we can call *grounded theory* and *grounded practice*. That is, this concept is grounded in a praxis (practice) or way of doing things that mirrors the way people learn in the real world. For instance, children learn by imitation and play and figuring things out on their own rather than explicit "telling" or direct instruction. Children are born imitators of adults, and they are expert "figurers out" of the actions that adults are doing, and they are hardwired to want to know what adults are doing and how those actions bring on results (Gopnik, 2016). They learn best by not being told what to do, but by being presented with opportunities to physically, intellectually, and affectively (aesthetically) work out on their own how the world works. While direct instruction is often important to use with children—for instance, "don't play with fire," "stay away from snakes," "don't play near the cliff"—such directives should be rare because children primarily learn by manipulating reality. This manipulation is most often called *play*, and this is the way all youngsters learn, whether they be feline, canine, our primate cousins, or human. And of course, I don't see any *qualitative* difference between the way children and adolescents and adults learn. Incidentally, this is one of reasons why the test- and accountability-driven educational reform movement is failing, and that it *must* fail, is simply that it necessitates conceiving of learning as a fact- and skill-based endeavour, which looks nothing like the active and engaged ways in which actual children learn in the real world.

For the preadolescents and adolescents in our 7–12 ELA classroom, intermodality, like play, is taking one text (and one modality of the text) and creating another text (through another modality) that mimics or mirrors it. In a sense, the mimicry *reflects* the text, and at the same time is in itself another text, which is different and separate from it. This is, when you think of it, a type of play. It is taking the text of the author or creator, and in turn making the receiver of that text into another creator who makes a new text out of the original text. In ELA, the text is usually a work of art we call literature, or it could be the text of narrative, non-fictional, journalistic, or expository writing. In this sense, intermodality and aesthetic practices are both play and *re*-creation because they re-create the original text under consideration through manipulation.

These are also play because they are enjoyable. It needs to be said, however, that the "fun" or "play" aspect of intermodal activities, is not an end in itself. In fact, if a teacher sets out to design a lesson that is simply enjoyable or fun, two things are certain to happen. First, it is not a given that anything fun is necessarily true learning. Second, when a teacher sets out to design a fun lesson, it never seems to result in actual "fun." What we are talking about here is that intermodal theory and practice *result* in enjoyable learning activities. The byproduct is enjoyment simply because learning is—and should be—enjoyable. It is enjoyable because the learner is actively engaged in creating her own text in light of the text under consideration. For classrooms with transmissive learning, using pedagogies such as lectures, talking and chalking (or talking and smart boarding), and quizzes and examinations—there is seldom much fun at all. Testing, by the way, is always painful because it is the least like imitation and play.

This is not to deny that authentic learning is not often challenging, difficult, and creates resistances in the learner. If you think of learning to play the position of shortstop in baseball, or the playing the guitar, or writing short stories, it is fair to say that there will be many challenges, frustrations, and resistances to learning these activities. As Dorothy Parker said, "I hate writing, I love having written" (Meade, 1989). However, writing and reading, on the whole, are engaged in because they *are* enjoyable and rewarding, if challenging. Human learning, as it exists in the real world outside of school, is overwhelmingly enjoyable despite the inevitable frustrations and resistances, which the learner must work through.

In fact, a good test of how authentic learning is in your classroom is to assess how overtly painful it is. It is a contradiction in terms, I know, but when students don't *feel* in the classroom (anesthetic learning), the classroom is a painful place. Aesthetic learning, though often challenging, frustrating, and creating resistances in the learner, always tips the scale on the enjoyable and rewarding side, because—like Dorothy Parker—that is its end for the learner. Lack of feeling in a classroom is, conversely, painful learning. This is because this type of learning is what the human mind is not designed to do. Humans by their very nature are learning machines. Humans *like* learning; it's what we do—at least learning as it is found in the real world, if not in traditional schooling. Note also that you *play* shortstop and *play* the guitar. Learning is playing.

Designing Curriculum: The Big Picture

So far, this book has addressed how a teacher can engage students with a particular pericope in a reading class, or with a particular part of the writing process. The question now arises of how do you fit all the lessons together? How do you choose which particular pericope to focus on in your two or three weeks with *The Great Gatsby*? How to you choose which elements of essay writing to focus on in your two-week unit on a literary essay? Which poems for your poetry unit? The answer is both simple and complex, so let me explain. The one thing you do not want to do, which is something unfortunately many teachers do, is to string along random sections of a text without something coherent to relate them all to each other. I think this is why "covering" is so prevalent. Teachers just don't know how to select what is important. Actually, this is asking the question in reverse. The question should not be how you string lessons together coherently, but rather, how you have a coherent plan in the first place which organizes the scope and sequence of your lessons. You don't assemble your lessons into a unit, rather your unit assembles your lessons based on some overall plan. What you want to avoid in your unit is *not* having a coherence, *not* having a plan or a design, and *not* having something to pull all the lessons together.

Therefore, your unit should have a "way in" for your students. It also should deal with some big human issue that your students are interested in. This concept is nothing new. Smagorinsky calls these "conceptual units" (Smagorinsky, 2007; see Wiggins & McTighe, 2005). The Lincoln Center Institute for Arts Education calls this the *Line of Inquiry* (LOI), which is the big question that relates the work of art under consideration to a question that students and inquirers might have about some issue that is relative to their lives. I call it the Big Human Issue (BHI), and, as I argue time and time again, students, no matter how disengaged from formal schooling, are interested in (in no particular order) justice, gender, sexuality, fairness, love, friendship, betrayal, religion—and a host of "big" human issues that affect us all. This is similar to essential questions (EQ), which were introduced back in Chapter 2 (McTighe & Wiggins, 2013). However, the difference between what I'm talking about and an essential question is that this is a big human issue *as presented in the work of art itself*; it is the big human issue as intrinsically and integrally linked to the substance of the text of the work of art.

One BHI that I use time and time again is the question of whether human nature is intrinsically good or evil. That is, left on our own, are humans inclined to be selfish, greedy, and self-serving, or are we by nature generous, helpful, and caring toward others. The jury is out on this. When I teach one particular novel (I'll get to the title in a moment), I used to begin by "accidentally" dropping a twenty-dollar bill on the floor, or leaving it on the desk—and don't do this unless you've built up a positive relationship and trust with your students! I then left the room for a few seconds (or walked away, or turned my back), and when I came back usually the twenty was where I left it, or someone had taken it, usually in humor. (Let me point out that in most districts a licensed teacher must be present at all times in the classroom when students are present.) I then asked them why the twenty was still there or why was it "stolen." Was it only because we fear punishment or have other's eyes on us that we behave ourselves? If laws and rules were removed from our lives, would we behave reasonably, or begin acting selfishly and committing crimes? What would happen if we didn't have laws and the police, would people still behave as they do? It is surprising that this conversation could fill up the entire period if I let it.

In case you haven't figured it out, the novel I was introducing was *Lord of the Flies*, which precisely sets out to show how a group of privileged boys behave when they are removed from social constraints. Of course, the class doesn't have to agree with William Golding's presentation of human depravity. Students could believe that human nature really is basically good and that the novel's presentation is wrong. That's the point of LOIs and BHIs and the "Way In" (WI); they are the big questions and issues that can't be answered. In my curriculum class I use BHI, WI, or LOI interchangeably because it is hard for my preservice teachers, none of whom has ever designed curriculum before, to arrive at *conceptual units*, that is, units that have a theme, focus, purpose so that the individual lessons are not random (Smagorinsky, 2007; Wiggins & McTighe, 2005). Here's a BHI or LOI, or WI:

- How does Golding's Lord of the Flies allow us to question whether our human nature is basically inclined to good or inclined to evil?

I was once very much surprised at the effectiveness of this kind of curriculum design when I was teaching a Social Studies American History and ELA American Literature combined class. We processed the Puritan era and Edward's Sermon, *Sinners in the Hands of an Angry God.* As part of this class, we visited a colonial era church near the school. I was extremely pleased that my urban kids asked the minister giving the tour if he believed in predestination. (He did.) These urban kids from a tough neighborhood cared if humans were actually evil beings deserving of punishment or basically good beings who would do good things without fear of punishment or promise of reward. This was a question that was really important to them, not only in the novel, but in their daily lives.

I want to stress that the BHI is not an inherently complex concept. However, BHIs are hard to arrive at and get into a workable form. Developing BHIs takes time and effort and is never easy. When I work with a Lincoln Center teaching artist designing a lesson to aesthetically engage with a painting or photograph, or a concert, play, or dance performance, we're allotted a one-hour planning session to arrive at the Line of Inquiry (LOI is their version of the BHI) and decide how to implement it in our lesson. That's one hour with two people (teacher and teaching artist) who have been practicing this for a long time. When you start doing this, it takes much time and practice, but once you get the concept it gets easier and easier. However, without the BHI or some "way in" for your students and you as the teacher, what do you have? At best, you have a succession of somewhat related lessons without any overarching "way in" to get the unit "in the head" and in the long-term memory. However, if you do have a BHI or some bigger cohesion to the lessons in your unit, it is much more likely the unit will get "in the heads" of your students and enter their long-term memory. As it is never a good idea to attempt to read an entire novel in a class—though many teachers attempt to do this—the BHI (or LOI or WI) is a way to organize the pericope that you choose to investigate in the context of classroom time (the lesson), whether the students are asked to read the entire novel at home, or not.

You might use the following formula to begin practicing this:

- How does [the work of art] show us/tell us/make us/allow us to question the [big human issue]?
- How does [the writing/speaking technique] allow us through [the writing genre] to express the [big human issue]?

This might look like:

- How does the use of logic and the Aristotelian syllogism assist us in developing arguments for and against capital punishment (or legalizing marijuana, or school choice, or whether or not we should have school uniforms)?
- How does *The Great Gatsby* help us question the difference between realistic and unrealistic dreams (or if "the rich are different than you and me")?
- How does the use of anecdote or vignette allow us in writing (narratives, or descriptive essays) to link our autobiographies to the general human problems and issues?

The BHI, The Unit, The Pericope, and Lesson Activities

To explain how the BHI, the unit, the lessons of the unit, and the reading selections (the pericope) fit together, I am using *Annie on My Mind* by Nancy Garden because it is a classic Young Adult (YA) novel (originally published in 1982). There are several reasons why I use this longstanding book. First, it's a great read. Like *Gatsby*, it's well-known and is likely to be familiar to most readers of this book. Second, I don't feel that the issues it presents are very much out of date. Third, I have evidence of the ways in which my preservice and student teaching students struggle with this book and curricular design when I assign it. Fourth, and most importantly, when I teach LGBTQ young adult novels, I ask the students at the end of the class if they would teach this novel or one like it. This brings up a fifth issue with this book of whether or not things have improved in LGBTQ issues in the past 36 years. Unfortunately, I find very often my students say that they would not use such a book, or any LGBTQ-focused book because it might cause problems with the administration or parents. I find this troubling as many educators believe that real-world issues present in our contemporary society should not only be brought into the classroom, but should be the core of our classroom (see Ayres & Ayres, 2014; Darvin, 2015; Gaughan, 2001). I also acknowledge the high levels of censorship in our schools. I was astounded, during the writing of this book, that one young teacher in one of my classes was not allowed to teach Orwell's *1984*!

This young adult novel is the story of two adolescent females who come from different worlds, one from the gentrified upscale brownstone neighborhood of Park Slope, in Brooklyn, New York, and the other from the diverse working class and working poor neighborhood of Washington Heights in Manhattan, New York. The two girls develop a relationship, and once that relationship is discovered, they run into trouble in their private school. They are befriended by two of their teachers, who it turns out are in a same sex relationship, and an incident happens in which the two girls are discovered to have more than just a simple friendship. The young women come to understand that there are various levels of, and intensities of, relationships, and that these complex relationships have rewards as well as dangers.

As in almost all young adult literature (YAL), the theme is that of a young person (prot*agon*ist) struggling with the passage from the simple clear-cut, on-off, black-white, good-bad world of childhood to the complex, ambiguous, and gray areas of adulthood. (*Agon* is classical Greek for "struggle" or "contest," as in a wrestling match, horse race, or in athletic competition; add *pro*- and *ant*[*i*]- to the root word *agon* and you get the idea). In all YAL, the protagonist discovers that friends, or family, or social institutions such as school, and ultimately their whole world, is a much more complex place than they had thought as children. In short, YAL is all about the transition between the clear-cut but simple world of childhood to ambiguous but far richer (and, yes, sadder and happier) world of adulthood.

Getting back to *Annie on My Mind* in specific, below is a unit plan outline guided by a BHI, WI, or LOI. I have made the unit plan as a 15-day of the three-week unit, which is usually what is required for full engagement with a novel. The unit plan presented here is in an essentially traditional form, which will be understood by teachers and supervisors from the commonsense, transmissive, or traditional approach, while at the same time it allows for student-centered, inquiry-based, aesthetic practices. Note also that the final lesson plans in the unit are when students present their own lessons about the book. This "presentation option" does make teaching the unit more complicated, but richer, as students get to present and demonstrate their transaction or engagement with the novel. Presentations are optional in curricular design, and something you may or may not want to do with any particular novel, text, or work of art.

Please also note also that in the BHI when I use the phrase *special relationships* I am not saying that LGBTQ relationships are in any way unusual or non-ordinary! I am not implying that the relationship of the two main characters, which is between two young women and touches on LGBTQ themes, is any more special or less special or qualitatively different than a heterosexual relationship. Rather, deep friendships and romantic relationships (of all sorts) are a type of special relationship which needs to be differentiated from our more ordinary relationships, and treated accordingly. What I am saying in the LOI or BHI or WI, below, is that I believe that adolescent students need to think about how we have all sorts of relationships in our lives, casual ones (buying a soda from a clerk at the store), ordinary ones (with teachers and acquaintances), and special ones with people who are special to us (family, close friends, and loved ones). I say this because preadolescents and adolescents often don't understand that there a level of engagement we have with different people. One of the things about our 7–12 students is that they most often have not fully developed the sense of self and its separateness from the world around them, and they tend to treat all relationships as somewhat similar. The "diss" by the clerk in the store becomes of earth shattering importance, or one treats one's close friend as carelessly as if it were the same as a causal relationship. Reflecting on the various intensities is, I think, something 7–12 students need to give some time to.

The *Annie on My Mind* Unit: Developing Special and Ordinary Relationships

Name of text: *Annie on My Mind* (AOMM)

Author: Nancy Garden

Date of Publication: 1982

LOI/BHI/WI: How does *Annie on My Mind* allow us to consider how our special relationships differ from our ordinary relationships and that this understanding has an impact about how we reflect upon the degrees of intensity of the relationships in our own lives?

Rationale for unit: While presenting LGBTQ issues is an important focus of this novel, it is also about two teenagers learning to deal with the complexities of relationships, separations, and aspirations (e.g. college) in the real world. The book is highly interesting to teenagers, has never been out of print, and has been banned in Kansas and is number 48 on the most frequently banned book list of the American Library Association—so it's obviously a book that we want to read!

Venue: New York City, Brooklyn Heights, Washington Heights, the Foster Academy

Prot***agon***ist: Liza Winthrop, lives in Brooklyn Heights, privileged

Other main character: Annie Kenyon, lives in Washington Heights, poor, immigrant family background (Italian American)

Ant***agon***ist(s): Social rules, family, the headmistress

Agon (struggle/conflict): Liza and Annie's growing relationship must be hidden from the conservative world of the Foster Academy, their parents, and society at large: Fear

Climax: Discovery by the headmistress, the "trial" in front of the parents

Pericope #1: Liza Winthrop first meets Annie Kenyon at the Metropolitan Museum of Art on a rainy day

Pericope #2: A poorly conceived program: ear piercing in the school basement

Pericope #3: Thanksgiving break and the first kiss

Pericope #4: The two girls house sit for two female teachers: Discovery

Pericope #5: The "dismissal of the two teachers" and "it's OK" discussion

Pericope #6: Annie writes "the letter"

Pericope #7: The girls finally meet again

Pericope #8: TBA Student presentations

Pericope #9: TBA Student presentations

Pericope #10: TBA Student presentations

Authentic project: "Relationship and Life Paper." Students will engage in an ethnographic and qualitative research project and interview three people about "relationships which changed their lives." Using three examples from real life and two examples from the book, students will answer the question: "How do special relationships differ from ordinary relationships and open up wider possibilities for our lives?"

School project: After the unit is finished, students will practice a literature essay as defined by state high school exit examinations using comparison and contrast of two works of literature dealing with a human issue of "plot events and/or characters attitudes (stances, behaviors) changing people (characters) for better or worse."

Presentations: Groups of students will present scenarios (role playing, not "acting out") of relationships students may encounter in their high school years. A discussion will follow of what makes relationships "ordinary" or "special" and how we can differentiate between the two. What are the benefits and dangers of relationships will also be discussed, as well as how we need to act differently in special relationships than we do in ordinary relationships.

I think the above unit plan covers a great deal of what would be necessary to present to administrators and parents about why this would be an important unit for a secondary level classroom, and would address those who might unfortunately have reservations about teaching young adult literature with overtly positive LGBTQ themes.

A Kinesthetic Lesson

Here are some kinesthetic activities related to *Annie on My Mind*. What follows is then a suggestion of various pericopes to be used in class. The point of this lesson is a pericope from *Annie on My Mind*. The primary wing of the lesson is kinesthetic learning. The secondary wing, depending on the lesson, is writing or speaking.

1. **Freewriting**. The class begins with a writing activity about "a special relationship you have with someone who is important to you (or someone you know, or a typical person your age). Why is this relationship important to you? What does it look like? What challenges and opportunities does it present in your life?" Important: The teacher explains how this writing will be used and how it will be published (made public). She tells the students that only volunteers may share if they wish; it is perfectly fine if students do not wish to share their writing as it might be personal.
2. **Metacognitive writing**. Since Elbow's seminal work (1973), freewriting is usually followed by *postwriting*. This is where the writer briefly reflects on how her freewriting (or other writing) went in this particular writing session. This acknowledges that anytime a writer writes, she may have a productive, creative, positive, focused writing experience, or one that is somehow unproductive, uncreative, negative, or unfocused—or anywhere in between. Usually the post writing is a sentence or a few sentences, such as, "Write a sentence or two about how your writing went today. Why did your writing go well or have challenges today?" Or as a prompt such as, "My writing today went xxxxx because yyyyy." I've also varied it with starters such as, "What color was your writing today? Why did you give it that color?" or, "Everyone loves a slice of pizza. Was your writing today as good as a slice of pizza, or not? Why was that?"
3. **Sharing through student talk**. Teacher asks students to share their writing in some fashion with one or two other students in pairs or triads. If they wish they can only share the post writing, or they can explain their freewriting, or they can read it to each other, or they can exchange papers. Any form of sharing is fine.
4. **Kinesthetic activity warm-up, "handshake"** (optional). The teacher has the students pass a gentle slap handshake from person to person to unify the group physically. This is attempted twice so that the class gets into a solid steady rhythm passing the handshake slap. The teacher then asks them to pass the handshake slap with "some kind of an emotion attached." This is practiced twice. Then the students are instructed to pass the handshake slap as quickly as possible around the room.
5. **Kinesthetic activity warm-up, "Metamorphosis"** (optional). With the students in the circle the teacher explains that she is going to pick up an object in the center of the circle and, without speaking, they will know what the object is. The teacher will then pass this object on to the first person in the circle and it will change (metamorphose) into another object, which will be apparent from the way it is carried and passed on to the next person. The teacher goes to the center of the room and picks up an imaginary heavy object, probably a rock, and passes this on to the first student. The rock becomes a ping pong ball, which is paddled to the next person. This becomes a kitten, which is stroked and passed on to the next

person, and so forth. After the "object" has changed from person to person and returns to the teacher, the teacher changes it again to a rock and puts it in the center of the room.

6. **Kinesthetic activity warm-up, "Naming"** (optional, but recommended). The teacher has the class get into a circle. They are asked to present one word from their writing that represents how they feel about the relationship they described. Students are to take a step forward into the dramatic space (Boal, 1995) and state the word with a tone and expressions that reflect the word.
7. **Activity preparation**. Students are instructed to go into groups of four or five. They are to review from their writing their concepts of a special relationship and to pick one scenario that represents this. They are to choose two students to present it (not "act out") in the center of the circle when it re-forms. The other students are to assist them in presenting the scenario. The scenario should present the relationship so that the students can infer its nature (e.g. parent-child, friends making up or quarreling, and so forth). (The instructor walks around to groups and urges them to stop talking about what they will present and actually practice it.)
8. **Active observation**. The students again arrange in a circle and observe the presentations. The instructor is careful to explain that those who are observing have as valuable a role as those who are presenting. They are *active observers* who will be called upon to relate what they have observed.
9. **Whole class discussion**. The teacher and the students *unpack* the presentations. The general consensus is that we have varied and rich special relationships which we value very much as an important part of our lives.
10. **Next step**. The teacher instructs the students that they will be now reading (perhaps for homework) a selection of the text (pericope) that shows that Liza and Annie have a special relationship. Their literature log writing will be to compare their special relationship with the types of special relationships presented in class.

The pericope assigned (from the unit plan) could be any of the following:

- Pericope #1 Liza Winthrop first meets Annie Kenyon at the Metropolitan Museum of Art on a rainy day
- Pericope #3 Thanksgiving break and the first kiss
- Pericope #4 The two girls house sit for two female teachers: Discovery
- Pericope #5 The "dismissal of the two teachers" and "it's OK" discussion
- Pericope #7 The girls finally meet again

If you want to do kinesthetic activities such as the handshake slap and "metamorphosis," you will have to prepare yourself further than this book. There are many excellent texts available that allow you to bring dramatic or theater activities into the classroom; just search for drama + learning/education/ELA, and so forth. However, I need to point out that you are not a theater teacher, nor are you a drama teacher, thus I avoid the word, *act out* and rather have students *present*. What you are doing is "presentations," not acting activities.

I certainly understand that many readers of this book may hesitate about beginning the kinesthetic process—that is, getting the students out of their chairs and having them physically (and verbally) present a text based on the text of fiction, or even non-fiction. I clearly understand that a teacher might think that the handshake slap will get out of control. What I can tell you is that it doesn't. You simply have to try it out to see if this can work, and I assure you it can.

Of course, commonsense applies here. I've had some really difficult classes in my career where I wouldn't try this activity. But you can try activities like this in many classes. You build slowly. One thing I do is to have students write about "How I'm doing" as the class beginning freewrite, and similar to activity 5 above, "Naming," I just have them choose a word. Then if I can't yet trust them to form a circle, they can speak the word "with feeling" from their seats, though a circle is preferable. With any class, you begin new things slowly and build them up.

Let me give a personal anecdote: When transferred to a new school near the end of my secondary teaching career as I was completing doctoral studies, I knew that I had to prove myself both to my students (as they talk to each other) and the other faculty and administration. It took me the first half of my first semester at this school to even get the students out of rows of chairs and into a circle for whole group discussions (which always occur after an activity, usually a writing activity). But once they got used to getting into a circle they never wanted to go back to rows; after all, who wants to spend their time looking at the back of someone's head. A "good circle" is where everyone can see each other's faces. That's far more humane.

And, of course, when you begin kinesthetic activities, you have to have a fallback position in case the students begin getting out of hand. In fact, you have to have this fallback position in something as simple as small group discussions. In my classes I used an old-fashioned seating plan to begin the class, with the students in traditional rows which I assign. (By the way, always have the students sit where they want the first day or two; then you assign them seats based on who is sitting with their friends and who may be disrupting the class!) The idea is that in group discussions, in various activities, and certainly in presentations that involve kinesthetic movement, the students can get overexcited and out of hand—though I assure you this is surprisingly rare—and then you state, "OK, back to your assigned seats, open up your books to page . . ."—that's the fallback plan.

What you will find, however, when you bring the body and kinesthetic learning into your class, is that the students most often don't get out of hand. In fact, your most difficult and/or disengaged students, those who don't do well sitting for long periods of time just listening and watching a teacher talk and chalk, are the ones who you will find blossom when they are allowed to move, to express, and to use the body, voice, and movement. I think you will be very, very, surprised at how relieved your students will be to do learning like it occurs in the real world, and how your most disengaged and academically disinclined love learning in the new world you are creating in your classroom.

Good Teaching or Bad? Graphic Organizers

When I observe ELA classrooms, very often I see some kind of a graphic organizer in use. It seems as if graphic organizers have replaced the old fill-in-the-blank worksheets. You can do a simple internet search and come up with hundreds and hundreds of different forms of this same tool. Graphic organizers are seen as particularly useful in reading so-called informational texts, which people assume is the focus of the CCSS. They are also used in organizing writing, particularly the schoolish and artificially constructed block essay (introduction + one, two, or three body paragraph(s) + conclusion). I need only point out here what I have said earlier in the book: This is not the way people read or write in the real world. You don't use a graphic organizer when you are reading a novel on the beach, in your bed, or in your armchair. You don't use a graphic organizer when you are writing in your diary, writing a poem, or even a blog entry, text message, or email. Rather, graphic organizers are for schoolish and artificial activities, where students fill in boxes, bubbles, or spaces with information garnered from reading a text, or in writing for organizing a "block" style essay. A four-paragraph block persuasive or augmentative essay would have the following paragraphs:

- Paragraph 1—Introduction—Outlining the issue and taking one of two sides of the issue.
- Paragraph 2—Body A—one reason or fact to support your side of the issue. Or, textual evidence A.
- Paragraph 3—Body B—a second separate reason or fact to support one side of the issue for a four-paragraph essay. Or, textual evidence B.
- Paragraph 4—Conclusion—summing up the argument made in the Introduction.

Similarly, a five-paragraph theme would have three body paragraphs instead of two, sandwiched between the introductory paragraph and conclusion paragraph. I've even seen this organized in the form of a cheeseburger. The top bun was the introduction with a space for "state my opinion." The cheese, lettuce, and pickle layer were the "first reason for my argument." Then came the hamburger for the "second reason for my argument." And, of course the bottom layer was the "restate the reason for my opinion" bun of the burger.

When I observe a class with graphic organizers, I typically ask the teacher, "Why did you choose to use a graphic organizer?" or, "How is that graphic organizer effective for engaging your students' understanding of the text?" or, "How do you *know* that the graphic organizer you used actually helped your students?" The teacher's answer is always vague. Graphic organizers are just something that "is done." Everyone says it is supposed to work. Administrators like it and the students are used to filling in the boxes (or bubbles), so it keeps them busy and quiet. After I direct a few more questions at the teacher, it becomes clear that he usually doesn't know: (1) When and how a graphic organizer can be effective; (2) why it is the best tool to use in this specific class with this specific reading assignment (informational texts) or writing assignment (argumentative essay); or, (3) how it is supposed to work in theory and practice. I don't do this to play a game of "gotcha" with the teacher, who is after all struggling with a difficult workload. I do it to try to get the teacher to think about why they use the tools and pedagogies that they do, to assist them to become more reflective practitioners.

In the post observation conference, the teacher usually acknowledges that the graphic organizer really didn't do a very good job of enhancing their students' understanding of the text, that is, except for the handful of school-smart students who would understand the material anyway. These are the students who already have the habits and instincts and craft knowledge of readers and writers. More importantly, the teachers can't explain how the graphic organizer is *supposed* to work. This is because the type of text of an organizer, the modality used, is not a text or a mode that is natural and used in the real world. While humans use maps and diagrams, the graphic organizer is an artificial text or modality when related to the organic process of reading and writing.

Good Teaching or Bad? Whole Group Unrehearsed Public Reading

When I observe a class that has a strong reading component, I ask teachers why they have the students read in the particular way. Again, I'm not playing "gotcha" here. I just want teachers in my educational program to be aware that how reading is done in a class should be a conscious and informed decision. In fact, there is no perfect way to read in class at all (see Table 4.1 on p. 115).

You can identify a dozen or so other ways in which teachers have students read in class and you can identify that each reading modality has both benefits and drawbacks.

What we do know is that having students read something they haven't seen, that they are reading for the first time (unrehearsed), out loud in front of others/the class (public) is a technique that has the most problems of all. You need only briefly reflect to see that this type of reading disadvantages in experienced, novice, and non-native English speakers.

In fact, while there is no perfect way to read in a class, the good news is that each reading modality has at least one distinct benefit for the students, so good

TABLE 4.1 Reading Strategies and Reading Issues

Reading strategy	*Problematic issue*
Teacher reads out loud, students follow text in book.	Students get confused by hearing and reading at the same time and at different speeds with different cognitive process.
Teacher reads out loud, students only listen.	Harder to pay attention and easily distracted.
Students read out loud in turn.	Student can anticipate what they have to read, disengage from what they do not personally read.
Teacher calls on students to read a paragraph or defined amount of text.	Inexperienced readers and non-native speakers of English disadvantaged and embarrassed.
Volunteer students read out loud.	Only self-assured readers volunteer.
Teacher calls on (picks on) students to read.	Potential for shaming of bad readers, distracted students, daydreamers.
Popcorn reading 1. Volunteers just read as much as they want and other volunteers follow.	Only experienced readers volunteer. Teacher has difficulty assessing individual's reading abilities.
Popcorn reading 2. Readers read in order, as much as they like or just one word, or can say "pass."	Teacher can assess who wants to read and who is hesitant, can judge reading ability. Overall comprehension is reduced.

teachers use a variety. And, as this book suggests, whichever reading process is used, what is important is what the students *do* with that text, the modality by which they process it. This takes the reading from the verbal and aural short-term memory to long-term storage.

Good Teaching and Bad? Contextual Information, The Third Factor

Many teachers, particularly novice teachers, are faced with the fact that their students are not engaged with the text they are reading, perhaps because they have been labeled poor readers or are inexperienced readers, perhaps because they have been made to hate reading by the way they have experienced it (or been taught it) in school, or perhaps just because they don't see why they should be interested in this particular text. In the last case, the teacher has not made the case for engagement (transaction) with the text through a LOI, BHI, or WI. Even when a teacher has experienced and able readers—who, again, may be reading for a good grade and not for an authentic transaction with a work of art—there is the belief by many teachers that somehow contextual information about the Globe Theater, the Great Depression and Dustbowl, the Roaring

Twenties and Prohibition, or the challenges to LGBTQ equality today, somehow aid in engaging with *Romeo and Juliet*, *Of Mice and Men*, *The Great Gatsby*, or Alex Sanchez's *Rainbow Boys* (Sanchez, 2001). It is as if confronted by the difficulty of the student reader (factor one) transacting with the written text on the page (factor two), that reading can be enhanced by adding contextual information (factor three). The issue is that factor three (contextual information) does not automatically, or even very often, enhance the transaction between factor one (the reader) and factor two (the text).

Now contextual information should be a part of the ELA literature curriculum. Students should know something about the treatment of African-Americans in the rural South when they read *The Color Purple*, but that context should come up organically during the unit. I simply have never seen a teacher who can get readers engaged with a text *primarily* by adding contextual information (the third factor) into the mix. By quantitatively adding to the curriculum, the teacher has not solved the basic challenge of getting the students engaged with the text. Once they are transacting with the text, however, the students will want to know about the background and context of the text under consideration.

Let me give an example that occurs often in ELA classrooms. This is when a teacher uses Breughel's painting of Icarus to assist in explaining W. H. Auden's poem "Musée des Beaux Arts." In the minds of many teachers, the use of the painting should assist the student in understanding the story of Icarus getting too close to the sun, as well as the irony of great tragedies like this happening while the world goes along with its daily routine. After all, the poem is a direct reference to the painting. But the fact is that the painting, which is the subject of the poem, doesn't really assist students with their engagement (or not) with the poem. Sure, the painting is integral to the poem, but before Breughel is brought in the students need to start the transaction with the poem, and that difficulty cannot be alleviated by showing pictures on a screen. What then can be done? Well, in the case of Auden's poem, it is first to set up the work of art with a Line of Inquiry (LOI) about a big human issue (BHI) in the poem as a way into (WI) the poem to start the readers' transaction with it. I think this would begin by having the students consider the very "ordinariness" of suffering (perhaps something students saw on the way to school). This would lead to a LOI: "How does Auden's poem MDBA, allow us to examine how our experiences and our suffering is both ordinary and extraordinary?"

Thinking about Learning, and Doing Teaching: Reality and Curriculum

Let me give a further example from my own teaching. Many years ago, I was trying to teach a unit on editing as an integral part of the writing process. Specifically, in the lessons of the unit, I was trying to establish that the editing of a draft could be done by (1) adding to, (2) subtracting from, (2) changing (altering), and (3) rearranging the original draft. The point of one particular lesson was #2, "subtracting from" the draft to improve it. Why did I do this? Because I simply thought it was good, if not essential, for students to know. I had seen the following lesson in a workshop and decided to try it. Up on the board in front of the room I put up photocopies of Picasso's succession of drawings of a bull in which he begins with something that looks very much like a bull, and is gradually reduced to just a few representational lines. [You can obtain it by a simple internet search for the images.]

I asked the students what the drawings were about. One student eagerly raised his hand and announced, "A dog." I was dumbfounded. There went the editing lesson into the dustbin. After some gentle prodding, I found that in the class of 25 students, only two or three had ever left New York City, and then this was to see families who live primarily in South or North Carolina. Incredibly to me at the time, none of the students had ever been to a zoo—and the five boroughs of New York City contain five zoos and one aquarium. As someone from a working class to white-collar family (me) who did go to museums and zoos, I was amazed. However, reflecting later that night, I wondered what real opportunities did my students have to visit museums and zoos and other cultural institutions. In fact, I was teaching New York City students in a magnet school from three separate poor or working poor neighborhoods (none with easy access to a zoo). Furthermore, these students were attending a school under review for low test scores. The school was ranked low in the city's rating system of high schools, and its enrollment contained 97 percent minority (non-white) students, with 87 percent of students being economically disadvantaged; of these, 81 percent were eligible for a free lunch, and 6 percent were eligible for a reduced price lunch. As measure by the state mandated ELA exam, the school was one of the lowest performing schools in the state.

I am not looking down upon my students, I liked them very much and wanted to be in that school and wanted to teach them as best I could. Indeed what I was representing was an issue in the United States today; namely, teachers nationwide are predominantly white, urban or suburban, female, working class, and they differ from a population of students who are increasingly self-identified as non-white, poor or working poor, non-native English speaking, immigrant, or of color (Feistritzer, 2011; Wideen, Mayer-Smith, & Moon, 1998).

Yet, it became very clear to me that I was not teaching the students I actually had before me, but some imaginary "student" who would benefit from some generalized "editing" lesson. The same is true very often when I observe teachers. They are teaching solid lessons, which are seen as beneficial for the (ultimately imaginary) general student, or are reflections of what the state or the CCSS or some other standards see as beneficial for "the students," but which are not lessons that relate to the specific students in the teacher's classroom. Often, we teach as if there were some kind of generalized absolute lessons that are suitable for generalized standardized students. However, a brief reflection reveals this not to be true. Who your students are matters very much.

I need to say that the teachers of the privileged have similar but different problems. One of my colleagues from a wealthy area told me of a troubled student. Every weekend his lawyer father and medical doctor mother went to the summer house and left him at home in the suburbs apartment with credit cards and the Mercedes—a recipe, you can agree, for disaster. You can bet this school had quantitatively equal but qualitatively opposite student issues than my urban school. Indeed, when you teach in a school where the student parking lot has much better automobiles than in the teachers' parking lot, there are student issues—very different issues, but issues nonetheless—than I was experiencing in urban schools with no parking lots for anyone.

For those of us who are city teachers, and to put this phenomenon into perspective, when I observe classes, and when I read educational mandates from the state, it is as if the following were irrelevant: At least 30 percent of students in New York City never graduate from high school at all (Stringer, 2016), and I think it is closer to 50 percent who never graduate, once, that is, you tweak the numbers which are provided in hard to interpret ways, such as not including students who simply disappear during the school year (Costigan, 2000). And then, there is the fact that one out of seven students is functionally homeless during the school year (Harris, 2017). This does not mean that these young people are necessarily living on the street or in shelters—though some or many might be—it means that they have *housing insecurity*; they might be staying with different family members different nights of the week, or they move to different housing and are transferred to another school at least two times a year, or they miss on average 88 school days per year, or they are likely to live in overcrowded apartments due to a severe shortage of affordable housing (ICPH, 2017). I say all this because, given these tragic demographics, it is unlikely that many of my students had the opportunity to go to a museum or farm (there is one in NYC), or indeed to go to boroughs other than their own. Neither these students, nor privileged students, are young people who will be engaged by standardized and generalized lessons aimed at The Universal Student.

Some General Rules for Teaching and Learning

So, given the unique demographics of the students we have, there are some lessons or rules, and again, I think this is the case if you are teaching working class or privileged suburban students or any type of rural students:

- **Rule #1:** Teach the students you have, not the ones you think you have—and certainly never, ever teach the students you want or think you deserve. Base your curriculum on the personal autobiographies and experiences of your students, something John Dewey pointed out almost 120 years ago (Dewey, 1900/1971).

Additionally:

- **Rule #2:** A terrific "sexy" lesson, with all the bells and whistles, is not a successful lesson unless it's relevant to your students' experiences, needs, and understandings. No great lesson can move any student forward in knowledge and abilities (skills) unless they can relate to the text or modality of the knowledge with which they are presented.

The other essential difficulty with my Picasso "Bull Lesson" is that, even with those who "get" the comparison of Picasso's drawings with editing by subtraction, the fact remains that the modalities (the different texts) are too dissimilar, too unrelated. What, after all, is the purpose of this seemingly excellent and relevant lesson if students are not able to associate or link one modality (the text of Picasso's bull drawings) to another text (the student-written draft and editing by elimination or subtraction). This bring us to:

- **Rule #3.** In intermodality, the students must see the relationship of the text (most often a work of art) to the text they produce out of it. Conversely if they are producing a type of writing, they must see the relationship of their writing to the text used to enhance it. The modality of both the text and the student must be relatable and associative. For instance, even speaking texts (modalities) of students, using a carousel, or fish bowl, or four corners activity, or even small group or whole class discussion, can be related to the text or modality of a work of art (novel, poem, scene from a play) because the modalities are natural and related. Students cannot necessarily and automatically relate the textual modality of a succession of physical drawings (of a bull) to a process of editing by subtraction. The texts and the modalities are too dissimilar.

Contextual Information and Lines of Inquiry

This brings us to an issue discussed above, contextual evidence. I also call this the *third curriculum* or *the third factor*. As discussed above, the first curriculum, at least according to Dewey (1900/1971) is the student, the second curriculum would be the text under consideration, and the third curriculum is the contextual information assist. To the discussion above, I can add:

- **Rule #4:** Contextual information and a related curriculum should be brought into the discussion about the work of art. Students could find Picasso's drawings of value in light of editing; they should know about the Roaring Twenties and The Volstead Act (seems Gatsby was a bootlegger), but this must arise during the unit (or lesson) when the students are engaged by the work of art, after they have begun the transaction with the work of art; after they are able to care about the work of art text in light of the Line of Inquiry, Big Human Question, and after they have a Way In to the work of art.

SAMPLE 4.2 Sample Works of Art and Sample Contextual Information

Sample Works of Art (Units)	*Sample Contextual Information (Only when the intermodal transaction has been established)*
The Grapes of Wrath / Of Mice and Men	The Dust Bowl, Great Depression.
One Flew Over the Cuckoo's Nest	Beat Writers, The Beat Generation, counter culturalism of the mid-20th century, the anti-hero, social changes in mid-20th century, authoritarianism as a political philosophy.
James Joyce, Virginia Woolf, early 20th-century, non-linear novels	Cubist or abstract paintings.
The Great Gatsby	The Jazz Age, Roaring Twenties/ Prohibition, personal responsibility and decision making.
The Color Purple / I Know Why the Caged Bird sings / Harlem Renaissance poetry / texts by James Baldwin, James Weldon Johnson, Langston Hughes	The blues (music), African-American History, the Great Migration, Harlem Renaissance, the blues (music), jazz.
The Catcher in the Rye	Psychoanalytic theory.
1984 / Animal Farm	Socialism, communism, contrasting political theories.
YAL	Background information on the exceptionality of the main character: Physical dualities (*Wonder*), emotional and psychological issues, such as hyperactivity (*Joey Pigza Swallowed the Key*), the normal family is not really normal (*Jack*), dual cultures (*Call Me Maria*), African-American (and other) identities (*Brown Girl Dreaming*), radical life changes (*Peeling the Onion*), LGBTQ issues (*I am J*).
LBGTQ YAL	LBGTQ issues and facts in an era of retrenchment since marriage equality (due to Trump, Sessions, Pence, among others). Journalism about transgendered issues (serving in army, "bathroom" issues), rights of LGBTQ people, such as the "cake" cases.
The Color Purple	Traditional subservience of women; rural South; African-American women; the blues, jazz.
The Crucible, The Children's Hour	Mid-20th-century McCarthyism, communism (and other) "scares."

Sample Works of Art (Units)	*Sample LOI, BHI, or WI*
General. All works of art, text-based formula	How does [name work of art] show us that [human value] can [do. . . .]?
General. All works of art, (main) character-based formula	How does [character in works of art] show us that [human value]?
General. YAL by theme	How does [name of work of art] show us how people move from the simple and clear-cut understandings of [issue in novel] to the more complex, more difficult, but richer realities of adult life?
General. YAL by character	How does [the character N. in the work of art] show us how people move [we can move] from the simple and clear-cut understatings of [issue in novel] to the more complex, more difficult, but richer adult realities of adult life?
Example. *One Man Guy*, by Michael Barakiva (YAL)	How does *One Man Guy* show us that becoming aware of one's gay identity allows one to make friendships and choices that challenge self and family, but also allows a person to enter into richer self understandings and relationships with family and friends?
Example. *Wonder* by R J Palacio (YAL)	How does Auggie show us that both the serious difficulties and disabilities a person has, as well as the great abilities and promise he or she has, can be a foundation for building a rich sense of self though those disabilities and abilities?
Example. The Great Gatsby	How does *The Great Gatsby* allow us to reflect on human wishes and desires to understand these desires on a continuum from realistic to unobtainable?
Example. The Glass Menagerie	How does *The Glass Menagerie* show us how people come to terms (or not) with their sense of self in the light of the demands of family and self actualization? How does TGM show us the dangers of individuation or self actualization?
Example. Animal Farm, 1984	How does *Animal Farm*, or *1984* inform our understanding of what makes a just and equitable society that is beneficial for all members, as well as what hinders the creation of a just and equitable society and makes it not beneficial for all?

The above "rules" deal with reading, or transacting with, a work of art. In writing, however, where the central focus or point is student-produced writing (narrative, essay, poem, and so forth) the central problem with all writers—even experienced ones—is that they think they know what they write, that they've got all the necessary material on the page for the reader to understand. But when the reader gives feedback, it becomes clear that the reader is not "getting" what the writer thought he wrote. The practiced writer then realizes that she is not coming across clearly in the original draft and has to revise by editing.

This issue is shown in very young people's writings, when they write something like, "My grandmother died a few months ago. I was very sad." And the writer stops. Young and inexperienced writers don't know how to write relevant details. The issue—his grandmother's death—is all too present in the writer's head, it's *there* for him; and because it is present in the head, and it is assumed that it's somehow got on the page and that the reader sees and experiences it in the same way the writer does. Not so, of course. Even experienced writers face the primary issue that the reader most often needs to know more about what she is trying to say; it's "there" for you, the writer, and you have to work hard to make it transparently clear for your reader. In the 14 or so peer-reviewed scholarly research articles I've written in my college teaching career, in every case have I been asked to add clarification to the original draft; I have never been asked to take something out. And in all cases, the published draft has had to be longer than the original draft. Subtracting is not the editing issue that usually needs to be addressed, and certainly not first.

That said, once students are engaged and transacting with the text of the work of art, a teacher should bring in contextual information and outside sources (see Sample 4.2 on pp. 120–121).

The above are not comprehensive, of course; they are only meant to be examples of contextual information.

As we have seen, while contextual information is important, it can only be relevant to the student once the student has found a way in (WI), or a Line of Inquiry (LOI), or a Big Human Issue (BHI) in the work of art. A work of art, or literature if you will, must have a human value, related to a big essential question about life. Every student, even if he is greatly disengaged with schooling, is very much interested in these questions. Getting the students to transact with these issues is to get them to transact with the text of the work of art under consideration (see Sample 4.2 on pp. 120–121).

References

Ayres, R. & Ayres, W. (2014). *Teaching the taboo: Courage and imagination in the classroom* (2nd ed.). New York: Teachers College Press.

Barakiva, M. (2016). *One man guy*. New York: Macmillan.

Boal, A. (1995). *The rainbow of desire: The Boal method of theory and therapy*. (A. Jackson, Trans.). New York: Routledge.

Costigan, A. T. (2000). A study of how English Education students view their learning histories (Unpublished doctoral dissertation). New York: New York University.

Darvin, J. (2015). *Teaching the tough issues: Problem solving from multiple perspectives in middle and high school humanities classes*. New York: Teachers College Press.

Dewey, J. (1900/1971). *The child and the curriculum and the school and society*. Chicago, IL: University of Chicago Press.

Elbow, P. (1973). *Writing without teachers*. New York: Oxford University Press.

Feistritzer, C. E. (2011). *Profiles of teachers in the United States, 2011*. Washington, DC: National Center for Educational Information.

Gaughan, J. (2001). *Reinventing English: Teaching in the contact zone*. Portsmouth, NH; Heinemann.

Gopnik, A. (2016). What babies know about physics and foreign languages. *New York Times*, p. R4. Available at: www.nytimes.com/2016/07/31/opinion/sunday/what-babies-know-about-physics-and-foreign-languages.html?_r=0

Harris, E. A. (2017, August 15). 1 in 7 New York City elementary students will be homeless, report says. *New York Times*. Available at: www.nytimes.com/. . ./report-says-elementary-students-homeless-new-york.html.

[ICPH] The Institute for Children, Poverty, and Homelessness. (2017). *On the Map: The Atlas of Student Homelessness in New York City 2017*. New York: ICPH. Available at: www.icphusa.org/new_york_city/map-atlas-student-homelessness-new-york-city-2017/.

McTighe, G. & Wiggins, G. (2013). *Essential questions: Opening doors to student understanding*. Alexandria, VA: Association for Supervisors and Curriculum Development [ASCD].

Meade, M. (1989). *Dorothy Parker: What fresh Hell is this?* New York: Penguin Books.

Rosenblatt, L. M. (1978). *The reader, the text, the poem: The transactional theory of the literary work*. Carbondale, IL: Southern Illinois University Press.

Rosenblatt, L. M. (1983). *Reading as exploration* (3rd ed.). New York: Modern Language Association.

Sanchez, A. (2001). *Rainbow boys*. New York: Simon Pulse/Simon & Schuster.

Smagorinsky, P. (2007). *Teaching by design: How to create and carry out instructional units*. Portsmouth, NH: Heinemann.

Stringer, S. (2016, September 22). Diploma disparities: High school graduation rates in New York City. New York: (Office of the) New York City Comptroller, Scott B. Stringer. Available at: https://comptroller.nyc.gov/reports/diploma-disparities-high-school-graduation-rates-in-new-york-city/#Graduation_Rates_in_New_York_City.

Wideen, M., Mayer-Smith, J., & Moon, B. (1998). A critical analysis of the research on learning to teach: Making the case for an ecological perspective on inquiry. *Review of Educational Research, 68*(2), 130–178.

Wiggins, G. & McTighe, J. (2005). *Understanding by design* (2nd ed.). Alexandria, VA: Association for Supervisors and Curriculum Development [ASCD].

5

THE ELA CLASSROOM IN THE CONTEXT OF CONTEMPORARY SCHOOLING

Educational Reform, Standards, and Assessment

The previous chapters in this book have examined: (1) The composition of the English Language Arts (ELA) curriculum; (2) how those individual elements of the curriculum are related to each other through intermodality; and, (3) how students are best able to learn, and how teachers can best teach and reach, those students. But this teaching is not done in isolation. Even when we close the classroom door, there are influences that squeeze through windows and doors and affect the way in which we can teach, the way we actually do teach, and what we are able to teach. This chapter looks at how we create and teach the ELA curriculum in light of three realities: (1) The neoliberal educational reform movement; (2) the allied standards-driven, high stakes testing-driven, and accountability-driven movement; and lastly, (3) how these phenomena affect not only the curriculum taught, but how students' learning is assessed.

How We Got Here

It is a fact that teachers now teach in an era of educational reform, high stakes testing, and increased and intensified accountability systems. This began way back in 1983 with the publication of *A Nation at Risk: The Imperative for Educational Reform* (The acronym used is usually ANAR, but I'll refer to it as *A Nation*) by the National Commission on Excellence in Education, a group handpicked by the Reagan administration of educational policy makers and politicians (NCEE, 1983). Absent from the document were the many voices of the educational research community (those who present at national conferences such as American Educational Research Association (AERA), the American Education Studies Association (AESA), the Modern Language Association (MLA), and the National Council of Teachers of English (NCTE), among many other professional groups.

And, certainly missing were the voices of actual teachers, local school communities, students' families, and of course the students themselves. After all, the very point of the study was that schools, teachers, and students are themselves deficient and defective and in need of reform, so why listen to them? Here again is the *deficit model* of education. The message of *A Nation was* simple and alarmist: Students are unchallenged, the curriculum is watered down, and schools are failing. This quote gives the flavor of the overall document:

> Our nation is at risk. Our once unchallenged preeminence in commerce, industry, science, and technological innovation is being overtaken by competitors throughout the world . . . If an unfriendly foreign power had attempted to impose on America the mediocre educational performance that exists today, we might well have viewed it as an act of war. As it stands, we have allowed this to happen to ourselves. We have even squandered the gains in student achievement made in the wake of the Sputnik challenge. Moreover, we have dismantled essential support systems which helped make those gains possible. We have, in effect, been committing an act of unthinking, unilateral educational disarmament.
>
> *(NCEE, 1983, p. 1)*

Since then, there have been many critical analyses of this document (Berliner & Biddle, 1995; Berliner & Glass, 2014; Costigan & Grey, 2014; Gabbard, 2008; Hursh, 2007). Contrary to the report, there is strong evidence that, despite the great poverty and manifest social inequities present in the United States today, more students are finishing high school, more students are going to college, and more students are doing better on tests, particularly the highly reliable National Assessment of Educational Progress test (NAEP) (Ravitch, 2000, 2013; Ravitch & Maris, 1995). I always wonder at the alarmist "these days are terrible" jeremiad. When, I wonder, were students doing better than they are today? In the Civil War era? Back in the Great Depression? In the 1890s? After World War II? Read *The Blackboard Jungle* (Hunter, 1953), *To Sir, With Love* (Braithwaite, 1959), *Up the Down Staircase* (Kaufman, 1964), *Teacher Man* (McCourt, 2005), and ask yourself if things then were better than they are now, or if we've suffered some grave decline. We haven't. I also don't think the types of young people represented in *West Side Story* (1961) were great students. The word for disengaged young people in the 1950s and 1960s was *delinquent*. And all those hippies from the sixties, were *turning on, tuning in, and dropping out*. This is not to say that there are not serious problems with schooling in the United States today, particularly in the deficient education offered in communities that are poor or working poor, immigrant, non-native speaking, or of color. The educations in these communities are to be contrasted with the educations available to privileged communities. After all, families buy homes based on how good the local schools are, which begs the questions of why all local schools are not equally "good." However, it is quite another thing to say that education is worse than, say, mid-19th-century rural or urban America, or during the social upheavals of the 1960s and 1970s.

A Nation set the reformist trend of completely ignoring social realities and pretending that education exists in a vacuum in the United States. In fact, our education system is not nationalized as in other postindustrial societies; rather, it is local, and based largely on real estate taxes, which in turn are based on property values. So, we have some of the best schools in the world and some of the worst. In my home "city" of the Bronx (it is 42 square miles of dense urban landscape), you can bet there is the world-famous Bronx High School of Science, which has eight Nobel Prizes from former students, more than from any other school in the world; but we also have great schools in the Bronx neighborhoods of Riverdale and Fieldstone, as does the neighborhood aptly named Country Club. However, Mott Haven, located in the poorest congressional district in the United States, has failing schools, while the good solid working class areas of Parkchester and Pelham Bay Park have pretty solid schools. It's all where you live and how much money you have. The writers of *A Nation*, like all educational reformers, ignore these geographical and economic inequities.

Neoconservative and Neoliberal Educational Reforms

A Nation at Risk came during the conservative revival of the Reagan years, and while the document did not have much effect at first, it built up steam through the two Bush presidencies. More than a conservative revival, or a *neoconservative* movement, the attitude toward education was *neoliberal,* which is a term that refers to an economic, political, and social worldview. Let me take a minute and explain how politics invades what you are allowed to do in the ELA classroom. There are three terms about the educational (and social, economic, and cultural) worldviews which you need to know: (1) *classical liberalism*, (2) *neoliberalism*; and, (3) *social democratic liberalism*. Stay with me for a bit, for these terms explain why you are teaching for that high stakes test, or why you might be working with particular curricular mandates, or even with scripted lessons, and this explains why you are probably adapting your lessons to the Common Core State Standards (CCSS) or other standards.

To oversimplify, classical liberalism (or continental/European liberalism) is the liberalism of Adam Smith (1723–1790) and many of our nation's founders. Get rid of the hereditary rights of the monarchy, the aristocracy, and the church, and let the "invisible hand" guide the market; that is, an open, unrestricted market free from interventions of church, state, and even government—known as a *laissez faire* system. The cream will automatically rise to the top, and those with initiative, intelligence, and will to success *will* succeed. (For a perfect example of a parable of classic liberalism, read the Parable of the Talents in Matthew 25: 14–30.) If you build a better mousetrap the world will beat a path to your door. If you don't bother to build anything, well, you don't get rewarded with anything at all. It's your own fault. Education is to be *meritocratic*, to let the most able rise as high as they can regardless of high or humble origins. Jefferson saw education and his University of Virginia (UVA) as a *meritocratic* institution (it's even called *Jeffersonian meritocracy*); that is, identify those (men, of course in those days) with the best capabilities and develop them to their fullest ability. (Of course, this does not address the issue of who can afford to go to such a university.) Indeed, the problem with classical liberalism is that nowhere in the world does there actually exist a level playing field, and those from rich communities with privileged families have every advantage to get ahead, whereas those who live in poverty do not. The people with the right parents are the ones who usually get ahead.

Neoliberalism is a current adaptation and extension of classical laissez faire free market liberalism and is reflected in policies since Reagan and through Trump. Even Carter and Obama had some neoliberal tendencies, certainly in education with the ideas of competition (as a good), vouchers, charter schools, and the CCSS. To put it simply, neoliberalism is the unregulated lassiez faire free market *as assisted by the state, as maintained by the state, and as corrected by the state*. The state gives the free market a helping hand. The state actively tries to privatize social security, the educational system (school "choice," vouchers for private schools, establishing non-public charter schools), health care, and all social services, because without privatization there is no free market competition. And competition is good because (supposedly) the best will survive and thrive and the unworthy and unable will not. This explains some of the current Republican contempt for the Affordable Care Act (ACA, or "Obamacare"), social security, food stamps, free lunches in schools, and many other social safety nets. In the neoliberal view, you have to undo the systems that are overregulated or "owned" by the government because this prevents personal initiative and responsibility and encourages laziness and entitlement. Neoliberalism is liberalism on steroids, not afraid to use politics to force competition on organizations (and groups of people) which are seen as being too regulated; to make governmental organizations private, where they can compete so that the best and fittest survive. Environmental regulations, workers' rights, unions, work safety regulations—all these need positive action by the government to weaken or destroy them, all because protections weaken free market competition. As for health care, social security, and education: Privatize it all! As Reagan said, "The government is not part of the problem, the government *is* the problem." In the neoliberal worldview, private is always better than public. Competition is always good in business and politics, and by extension in education. And schools should be run like competitive corporations. You will note the taint of Social Darwinism here where the fittest survive, and, "A drunkard in the gutter is exactly where he out to be" (W. G. Sumner). Many accuse neoliberals of cruelty. As the saying goes, "A neoliberal is someone who can't enjoy his dinner unless he knows someone else who is going hungry." Whether this is actually true or not, you, the readers of this book, will have to decide for yourselves.

Social democratic liberalism, what we usually mean colloquially by just the word "liberal," is quite different from classical liberalism, and is almost the opposite of neoliberalism (and hence the terminology gets confusing). Social democratic liberalism maintains that there really never is a free market, there never is a level playing field. Some people are born poor, are forced into bad schools, live in crowded apartments, or are homeless, are food insecure, or live in communities overrun with gang and drug violence, or live in urban or rural, and increasingly suburban poverty. The early childhood program called Head Start says it all about the social democratic liberal agenda: Level the playing field, give the disadvantaged a leg up, a head start. There are a vast number of families that can't send their children to a $40,000 a year Montessori school to begin the journey on to Harvard and Yale (or UVA) and thence on to being a CEO of some corporation, or to a partnership in a white shoe law firm. So, the government gives the disadvantaged some positive and active assistance. That "leg up" to the disadvantaged is, in fact, in the democratic liberal perspective the specific duty of the government. Teddy Roosevelt's Progressive Era and reforms (e.g. the Pure Food Act), Franklin Roosevelt's New Deal and social security**,** Lyndon B. Johnson's Great Society, Obama's Affordable Care Act (ACA, or Obama care), food stamps (WIC, SNAP, EBT), affordable housing initiatives, and much more, are all examples of social democratic liberal politics. These are seen from this perspective not only to benefit individuals and their families, but benefit the general health of society at large—after all in Keynesian economics (liberal economics) the more people you have who can afford to buy commodities, the richer is the overall society. Additionally, social democratic liberals would be in favor of actively increasing diversity with underrepresented minorities in schools and colleges.

OK, So What Does All This Have to Do with Teaching ELA?

Up until the first decade of the twenty-first century, most teachers were pretty much free to teach the ELA curriculum as they saw fit, and ironically, despite this, most classrooms across the country witnessed ELA teachers teaching the same texts in pretty much the same way (Cuban, 1984). Teachers taught *Julius Caesar* in the ninth grade, *Macbeth* in the tenth, and such standards as *The Great Gatsby, Of Mice and Men, The Glass Menagerie* were typically taught from Alaska to Miami and from Bangor Maine to San Diego. And they were taught in the same close reading New Critical way. I witnessed this on an international level in 1994 when I was on a study program for my doctorate. I visited a school in rural Yorkshire in England for three days. One teacher I followed was teaching *The Crucible* in the same way a teacher would in any New York City high school. And the students acted *exactly* the same. This sameness, however, was to change.

While *A Nation* started things rolling in seeing schooling as defective, it took some time for neoliberal policies to be legislated, and this happened with a 2001 revision of an original law of 1965 called the Elementary and Secondary Education Act (ESEA), called the *No Child Left Behind Act* (NCLB) (US Congress, 2001), and this was followed by the Race to the Top Initiative (RTTT) (US Department of Education, 2009). Then there was another revision of the ESEA through Every Student Succeeds Act (ESSA) (US Department of Education, 2015) which is currently in effect. And of course, ideologically related to this is the imposition in many states of the Common Core State Standards (CCSS) (Common Core Standards Initiative, 2014). (Are you getting the idea that the succession of reforms indicates that each individual reform wasn't quite working as expected?)

There are several points to make about the phenomenon of the educational reform movement, all of which are colored with the hue of neoliberalism, all of which directly affect the ELA classroom:

1. All these initiatives want all students to have a "mastery" level of the curriculum. This is the equivalent of wanting the *Lake Wobegone effect*; namely, that *all children are above average*—an impossibility. Many educators feel that the idea of all students mastering all of the curriculum is an unreal goal. This unreal expectation may be to destroy public schools as teachers, students, and schools are set to fail, and then "failing" public schools can be privatized through vouchers and charter schools, which replace public schools.
2. These laws and movements as a phenomenon rely on various myths about education, in particular the *deficit model*; namely, that our students are underchallenged, that our teachers are deficient or lazy, that our schools are failing, and that our students know less than students in other postindustrial countries. In fact, given our social and economic realities, we have some of the best schools in the world, our graduation rates are rising yearly, and scores on the NAEP have risen steadily (Berliner & Biddle, 1995; Berliner & Glass, 2014; Costigan, 2014; Costigan & Grey, 2014; Ravitch, 2000).
3. These laws and initiatives come from national, state, and local governments, not educators. They also come from for profit and non-profit foundations, in other words these are reforms imposed by elites on teachers and students and communities. The Bill and Melinda Gates Foundation, for instance, is the leading force behind the CCSS (Layton, 2014). As teachers, students, schools, and presumably the families and communities they come from, are deficient and defective, the reformers don't want to listen to families, teachers, or students, because it is obvious—given the test scores—that they are deficient or defective. They are doing something wrong, or they are unable to do the right things. The political and economic elites are the ones who tell the teachers, students, schools, their families, and their communities what to do.

4. These imposed laws and mandates have very much influence on what *happens*, what can happen, and especially what is *thought possible to happen*, in the ELA classroom. How any individual teacher conceives of the ELA curriculum, how possibilities of instruction are directed and restricted, are a direct result of these policies (Costigan & Grey, 2014; Hursh, 2007, 2008). There is evidence that the reformist mandates in the ELA classroom actually destroy the traditional writing and literature curriculum (Costigan, 2017). This is why "reading for textural evidence" and "the argumentative essay" is such a focus in many classrooms, and not the literature and writing curriculum as taught in college classrooms where NCLB, RTTT, ESSA, and the CCSS do not have much influence (at least not yet).
5. The reform mandates are imposed by non-teaching authorities without consideration of the actual situations of teachers and their understanding of the craft of teaching. The mandates are hard to understand, hard to interpret; they are easily misunderstood because they are counterintuitive and disruptive of teachers' craft knowledge; and the mandates themselves may be impossible to implement given the actual needs and situation of the ELA classroom (Fleischer & Fox, 2004; Kaufman, et al., 2002; Smagorinsky, Lakly, & Johnson, 2002; Smagorinsky, et al., 2004).
6. As quickly as educational reforms come, and as they are regularly imposed by non-teaching authorities and corporations, they just as quickly disappear. This has been happening for over a century in education in the United States where we have a history of a neverending succession of failed educational reforms (Ravitch, 2000, 2013; Ravitch & Maris, 1995). There are signs that the CCSS and ESSA are slowly dissolving away and being replaced with mandates on the state level. In New York State, for instance, the CCSS have been replaced with state standards, and there is evidence in Massachusetts that they are returning to their original high standards and abandoning the less rigorous and more confusing CCSS standards.
7. Most importantly, as borne out in a seven-semester research study I recently conducted, when even when the reform mandates (such as the CCSS) are partly understood, they seem to contradict what teachers know of the study of English from their secondary, college, and university-level classes. As one young teacher put it, "I'm not teaching English, I'm teaching something else. It's like teaching kids like the foundations of reading, or something. It's not English!" (Costigan, 2017, p. 18). Another preservice teacher wrote of her observations of local classrooms:

   > I witnessed a lot of fake reading and writing. English wasn't really taught in the classrooms I've observed, sadly. This led to many bored, disinterested students. All of the reading and writing that was done had an analytical approach to it . . . and it certainly wasn't English. There was no realness to

> it, and students weren't encouraged to feel. Rather, students were encouraged to pull facts and evidence to support their arguments. To be honest, even without understanding many teaching theories or practices, it was easy for me to learn that I don't support that type of teaching . . . After observing so many fake English lessons, I became disheartened. That's not the type of teacher I want to become.
>
> *(Costigan, 2017, p. 1)*

The reason for all this confusion is quite simple. ELA teachers spend many hours in classrooms studying *literature,* and this is essentially what comprises the post-secondary English curriculum. But the CCSS and all educational reforms are about "college and career readiness." That is, ELA is (supposedly) for the purpose of the individual's social and economic advancement. The writing, reading, and speaking of English has no intrinsic value for reformers, it has only extrinsic value for economic advancement (of the individual and the state). Teachers—at least the ones I talk to—go into ELA teaching because they love literature, and they love talking about it and writing about it (see Kaufman, 1964). They are also frequently people who love writing. They keep diaries, write stories and poems and narratives. This is not what any educational reform is concerned with. To them, ELA has only a utilitarian value. It is a product that can be acquired, like cash; it is a capital that can be banked (Freire, 1970/2000).

We have seen from the beginning of the educational reform movement in Texas in the 1980s, that strict mandates and high stakes testing actually water down the curriculum. Teachers need to teach simpler things that can be measured on the tests (McNeil, 1988, 2000). What I have found is that when teachers are teaching under high levels of mandates, accountability systems, and high stakes tests, they really aren't teaching English at all. They are teaching snippets of vocabulary, reading for "textural evidence," and writing an artificial "argumentative essay" under the perceived mandates of the CCSS. When I visit schools, and when I ask students to report on what they are teaching, they explain that they are "lost at sea" and are just teaching the random things they can find that might fit the bill of the CCSS and other requirements (see Fleischer & Fox, 2004; Kaufman, et al., 2002; Ravitch, 2000; Smagorinsky, Lakly, & Johnson, 2002). I have come to call this the *idiosyncratic curriculum* (Costigan, 2017). (The tables at the end of the Preface contain lists of the varied curricula ELA students use, arranged by topics, instructional techniques, ELA themes taught, and literature taught.) In seven semesters of research, I could find no common ground in what was taught, how it was taught, or what the benefit was supposed to be for the students. All this is because the teachers and their administrators really don't understand what CCSS is supposedly asking them to do. So, they throw the ELA spaghetti at the wall of reformist demands, and hope something sticks.

Teaching from the Human Heart versus Teaching to Standards

In the previous chapter, I explained that when we teach a novel, for instance, we have a Line of Inquiry (LOI) or a Way In (WI), or a Big Human Question (BHQ) to guide us in exploring and transacting with the work of art. *Lord of the Flies* allows us to ponder the very basic nature of what makes us human (and inhuman) and if our basic human nature is good or evil. Palacio's *Wonder* allows us to ponder how our very identity is not wrapped up in things beyond our control, including how we look, how other people perceive us, and how other people relate to us. Walker's *The Color Purple* shows us an insight into how a severely oppressed person can come to understand and celebrate her true human nature, including her womanhood and even her sexuality. Ira Kaminsky's poem "We Lived Happily During the War" (see Chapter 1) allows us to question our complicity in our contemporary culture where constant warfare is the norm—if you think of the US's involvement in the Near East since the first president Bush in 1989. Shelley's "Ozymandias" lets us wonder about the ultimate status of the politicians and leaders who we think control our lives. As Maxine Greene says, "Part of teaching is helping people create themselves" (Gentry, 2011). It is the nature of the work of art to help young people (and us teachers) continue to create ourselves in deeper and richer ways of self-understanding. When we write, read, and speak, we are *thinking*. If we do this as a conscious part of the ELA curriculum, we are also growing as human beings.

I think, that there is a reason, by the way, that the English classroom has been the focus of reform when you would think that STEM subjects (Science, Technology, Engineering, and Math) should be the way to go for the future-oriented pro-USA educational reformers. The reason is that English is a very dangerous curriculum to the political, economic, and corporate elite, because it's about critical thinking. By its very nature, literature challenges uncritical thinking, something that the elite and politicians need very much to maintain control. The Modern Language Association (MLA) defines English as, among other things: (1) To engage with artistic creation and expression imaginatively; (2) to work both independently and collaboratively; (3) to develop historical and comparative perspectives by studying the development of societies, cultures, literatures, and philosophies; (4) to become informed global citizens; (5) to engage with people across a range of languages, histories, traditions, and ways of seeing; (6) to experience people and places that are different and distant from those of their families or home communities; (7) to apply moral reasoning to ethical problems; and, (8) to understand environmental challenges (MLA, 2008, p. 2). This is not the kind of thinking that corporate and political elites (often the same people) want young people to do. The MLA's heartwarming, expansive, and positive conception of the ELA curriculum is quite at odds with CCSS conception of English as a utilitarian tool for "college and career readiness" (CCSSI, 2014).

In fact, the MLA definition of English is almost completely the opposite of how the CCSS conceives it, with the emphasis for "reading for information":

> The Common Core asks students to read stories and literature, as well as *more complex texts* that provide facts and background knowledge in areas such as science and social studies . . . This stresses critical-thinking, problem-solving, and analytical skills that are required for success in college, career, and life.
>
> *(CCSSI, 2014, emphasis added)*

It seems clear to the creators of the CCSS that reading for information is seen as more complex than reading works of art or literature. This is something I think most readers of this book would find not only incorrect, but perverse. Imaginative thinking—the thinking we do when we engage with works of art—is the most politically dangerous form of thinking at all. Walt Whitman is dangerous, Ernest Hemingway is dangerous, Anne Sexton and Sylvia Plath are dangerous, James Baldwin is dangerous. Reading for a predetermined message or theme is not dangerous, nor is reading for textual evidence dangerous. This is why the corporate elite of the CCSS want this type of reading instead of reading works of art.

I should like to point out that this is precisely what *A Nation*, NCLB, RTTT, ESSA, or the CCSS do not want us to do, that is to read for the human values and critical thinking abilities that the MLA enunciates clearly. They take no notice of aesthetic appreciation of works of art. As neoliberal entities, these are about the curriculum as a *product*. In all of these reform movements, the work of art has a "set" predetermined "theme," determined by authorities. The educational reform movement does not care about the individual's transaction or engagement with a work of art. They do not care about writing, reading, and speaking as explorations into our sense of self, our very awareness. To the reformers, all of a neoliberal bent, the ELA curriculum is all about acquiring (buying) the commodity just because it's something you need to get into a good college to get a good job. You acquire knowledge like you do money, so it can be banked and expended at another time; the matter of intrinsic value to the individual is irrelevant (Freire, 1970/2000, p. 71).

Your best bet to stay abreast of the ever-changing mandates and responses to them is to get on several blogs, such as that of Diane Ravitch (https://dianeravitch.net/), the leading education historian in the United States, or the organization she founded Network for Public Education (NPE) (https://networkforpubliceducation.org/), or Fair Test (www.fairtest.org/) Not to mention reading the proceedings of conferences such as the American Education Research Association (AERA), American Educational Studies Association (AESA) and The National Council of Teachers of English (NCTE).

Remember that educational reforms, including the CCSS, have little to do with the reason many, if not most, of us are teaching writing, reading, or speaking, namely that the study of these things has an inherent aesthetic value and this has social, ethical, and political implications. As the historian Michael Katz (1968) explained half a century ago:

> We still have to see a [educational reform] movement driven by a desire to bring a joy to the life of the individual, to enrich experience solely for the purpose of making life more full and lovely. The goals of [educational reform] movements, quite to the contrary has been extrinsic; they have stressed the needs of society and the economy. They have also been utilitarian, stressing the concrete value of schooling to the individual . . . Goals have been formulated with scant regard to the indigenous culture, even the aspirations, of the working-class groups to be reformed . . . The reformers have determined to foist their innovations on the community, if necessary by force.
>
> *(Katz, 1968, p. 214).*

An Intermodal Interlude

Before dealing with the Common Core State Standards (CCSS) in specific ways, arguably the standards most teachers now work under, let's just recap how a human engaged curriculum can work by creating a *text* from the "text" of a work of art, creating a *mode* of the reader's (or writer's or speaker's) understanding from the authors "mode" of presenting the work of art.

Activity One: Look up Jamaica Kincaid's short story (or prose poem, if you will), "Girl" which is a very long sentence a Caribbean mother is giving her daughter (available at: www.newyorker.com/magazine/1978/06/26/girl). As a response to the short story or prose poem, have your students write a series of instructions for a role they have in their lives, such as: student, teenager, babysitter, high schooler, sibling, family member, job holder, and so forth.

This could be part of a unit with the Line of Inquiry (or Big Human Question, or Way in) on the roles we assume or are given in our lives, and how such roles are given to us and are self-determined. This could be part of a literature unit where a character is dealing with preconceived roles imposed upon him. Or, it could be part of a writing unit where students are asked to write a personal essay about a person's own development in the light of expectations placed upon her entering an urban school:

> Enter through the green paint peeling door; stand in line; and stand in line; and stand in line; put your book bag on the belt; see it go through on conveyer; through the square black mouth; walk through the metal detector; listen to the yelling guards; enter the school; smell the school smell again . . .

I think this fits in with what preadolescence and adolescence is really about: The discovery of self, and one's emerging individuation or self-actualization; that is, making decisions to become a "self" rather than the self one is expected to be. And, as "Girl" is one long sentence separated by semicolons, you can have a mini grammar lesson along with the writing activity.

Activity two Look up the review of Guy Fieri's Times Square restaurant which appeared in the *New York Times*, "As Not Seen on TV, Restaurant Review: Guy's American Kitchen & Bar in Times Square" (Wells, 2012). This celebrated (and criticized) review is composed entirely of a series of snarky questions about the weirdness of the food and the inefficiency of the service (don't miss the several references to "donkey sauce," the nuclear waste cocktail, and the cooling tunnel the french fries go through). Several times I've had my students write a response to it, not necessarily about a restaurant (though some do), but rather about other institutions they deal with in their lives, such as school, their education program, the Department of Education, the DMV. Bureaucracies make a great subject for this type of reader response activity. Here's one young man reflecting on his college experience:

> Have you ever had the displeasure of having to register for classes at Hortense College? Have you ever tried to get on to the Elmhurst-computex only to see that there is "maintenance on the site?" Have you ever stared at the spinning circle on the corner of your screen for what felt like hours? Possibly experienced the pain when you think your wait is finally over, and you're met with, "Error: Please Choose a Specific Subject!"? Have you ever felt the anguish of finally filing your shopping cart, only to be told, "Permission Denied: Please Choose a Course that Fits Career Path!"? How many people did you have to email? One? Two? Three? Four? Why is it so hard to register? Do they not want our money? Do they not want us to learn?

I'm trying to make several points in these two example activities. First, they are ways of creating a text out of a text, but doing so with a similar modality of text (the modality of instructions and the modality of questions; see also Chapter 2 where I discuss the speaking "call upon" question activity). Second, these examples could be a simple freewrite at the beginning of a class, or as a part of a larger reading or writing unit on (in the first example) expectations, demands, autobiography, and (in the second example) on analyzing something with satire, or even sarcasm through the use of questions. Anyway, these two examples can be part of a writing, reading, or speaking unit (e.g. time line, personal speech, or presentation) with an overarching Line of Inquiry (LOI) about the Big Human Issues (BHI), which could be Way In (WI) to a larger unit focused on reading or writing allied with a work of art (literature). Or, imagine a student or groups of students writing questions about a work of art. Think of a succession of questions a student could come up with halfway through *The Great Gatsby* or *I Know Why the Caged Bird Sings* or a challenging poem by William Carlos Williams or Wallace Stephens or Sylvia Plath. I am giving these two simple examples to frame my (hopefully short) discussion on the Common Core State Standards (CCSS) in specific, and the standards movement, in general. This is because, there is an *alive curriculum*, an aesthetic one—which is, I hope readily apparent in the two examples I've given here—and there is a *deadly curriculum*, an *an*esthetic one, which is a danger in standards movements such as the CCSS (Applebee, 1996, p. 21). Let's see which category the CCSS and other standards fall into.

The Common Core State Standards and the Standards Movement

My colleagues, reviewers, and readers who have helped me with this book have various ideas about how much, if any, attention I should place on the Common Core State Standards (CCSS) in particular, or the standards movement in general. ELA researchers and writers are of many minds about the standards movement. Some hold that they are beneficial, some hold that they are tolerable, some hold that they are an ugly necessity that can be used to raise the level of ELA instruction, and some (like me) hold that they are an infringement on beneficial teaching and healthy learning (for these issues, see Beach, Thein, & Webb, 2016; Gallagher, 2015; Smith, et al., 2014). Of course, every teacher wants high standards in instruction (or they should), and every teacher must have specific objectives (a goal, a purpose) to her units and lessons. Teaching doesn't make sense without standards and objectives. I am just not sure that I need to have imposed on my classroom standards that have not been tested and found trustworthy (as the CCSS have not) or standards that come from corporations and not teachers (as do the CCSS) (Layton, 2014).

An activity that I usually do in my methods of teaching English classes is to have the students search out and pick for homework some CCSS standards. Then we bring them to class and put them up on the overhead projector or board and do a sort of close reading. Here's one eighth grade standard, which I defy any student or teacher of English to make any sense of (Cronin, 2014; Schmoker, 2014):

> Analyze how the points of view of the characters and audience or reader (e.g. created through the use of dramatic irony) create effects like suspense or humor.

If your eyes have not glazed over, on the surface this might look reasonable and clear. But it is not. Look at the number of variables or terms in this one standard, all of which need clarification and clear definitions: (1) Analyze, (2) point(s) of view, (3) character, (4) audience, (5) reader, (6) dramatic irony, (7) effects, (8) suspense, and (9) humor. Each of these nine terms is complicated and needs careful clarification. For instance, I ask any one reader of this book to tell me in simple, clear language what is the art (or science) of *analyzing,* or, what is *dramatic irony*, and how *suspense* is related to *humor*. And, more importantly, how are any of these variables and terms—none of which seem to be related to each other—able to help a student to transect with a text so that he is making meaning of it and getting it "in the head," that is, in the long-term memory?

I don't want to belabor the point, but when you examine CSSS they are full of terms that don't bear examination and don't make any coherent sense. For instance, you often see the words *author's intent*, or *author's purpose*, as some kind of a legitimate goal in making meaning of a work of art. The New Critics did away with *author's intent* almost a hundred years ago. See any classic textbook on literary theory on this (Eagleton, 2008; Guerin, et al., 2005; Richards, 1929; Scott, 1963) and they will explain that in a New Criticism literary theory we don't know the *intent* of Shakespeare or Tennessee Williams, we only have the work of art. That's the principle of a classic *close reading*. We don't need to know the background of the author to appreciate *Hamlet* or *A Streetcar Named Desire*. In New Criticism's way of thinking, the *author's intent* is a fallacy. In Reader Response critical theory and practice, it doesn't matter at all. Again, what Christopher Marlowe thought about his "The Passionate Shepherd to His Love" would be interesting (and might make one blush), but the poem nonetheless stands on its own. At least Walter Raleigh, John Donne, and Ben Jonson and a few dozen other poets thought so with their variations on it.

It bears repeating that you also will see the term "analyze" constantly in CCSS. What does that mean? There are books and books of literary theory from all sorts of perspectives—new criticism, reader response, Marxist, gender studies, structuralism, poststructuralist, deconstructuralism, semiotics, and so on, which all are attempts to deal with the "analysis" question, or better, how texts are to be "read," interpreted, understood, or cognitively and affectively processed. This is the very substance of literary theory; how readers make meaning of texts (Eagleton, 2008). As we have seen New Critics "analyze" through close reading, Reader Response people analyze the "aesthetic transaction," and there are dozens of other literary theories out there (semiotics, anyone?). Yet, it is as if the authors of CCSS have never read a book of literary theory. Take any CCSS standards from any level and try to figure out what it is they actually want you to do. Chances are, this has nothing to do with why anyone on the planet reads any work of literature. Here is one that a student of mine picked when we did this activity in class. I've added in parentheses the number of variables (and sub-variables) a teacher has to consider in applying this standard:

> CCSS.ELA-Literacy.RL.9-10.2. (1) Determine a (2a) theme or (2b) central idea of a (3) text and (4a) analyze (4b) in detail its (5) development (6) over the course of the text, including (7) how it emerges and is (8) shaped and (9) refined by (10a) specific (10b) details; (11) provide an (12a) objective (12b) summary of the (3, repeated) text.

I don't mean to belabor the point, but I have spent over 30 years teaching English, and have several degrees in the subject discipline, and I can't tell you what is an "objective summary" of a text. I mean, can there be a summary that is "objective"? And why summarize in the first place? As Maxine Greene and Louise Rosenblatt point out again and again in their writings: Great works of art defy predetermined expectations; that is, they by their very nature defy one simple explanation or interpretation. That is what makes a work of art a *work of art*. And the more a work of art *is* a work of art, the more it is open to differing interpretations (Greene, 2001; Rosenblatt, 1978, 1983).

I have seen dozens of presentations at national and local conferences about how to "meet" standards (CCSS or others), and I have had to align my education programs assessments with NCTE standards (twice, as they have changed) and I can say that when you do good teaching, you meet standards. Indeed, the standards are always *less* than what you are trying to do in your ELA classes. Conversely, if you try to design units and lessons to meet specific standards, whether CCSS, NCTE, or various state or local standards, you will drive yourself crazy. This is because you don't teach writing or reading primarily to meet standards, but to teach these things *as a process using high standards*. Standards are a *process*, a means, not a product or a goal. In any event, I urge you to read the CCSS's self-defense of their standards, available at: www.corestandards.org/about-the-standards/myths-vs-facts/. I don't think they really address the following questions, which, if answered in the affirmative, might make the standards relevant, do-able, practical and beneficial. Furthermore, these questions, directed as they are to the CCSS, could be applied to other standards imposed on the ELA classroom on the national or local levels:

1. What is the evidence or data that these standards have been tested in the real world or in an actual classroom or with actual readers and learners for accuracy, effectiveness, trustworthiness (reliability or validity). How are these standards based on research?
2. What is the evidence that ELA teachers have any significant input into these standards?
3. Where is the evidence that the creators of the standards have any expertise in the subject discipline of ELA? In regards to the CCSS, why should (1) Bill Gates (bankroller of the CCSS) (Layton, 2014), David Coleman (president of the College Board), (2) the National Governors Association, and (3) the Council of Chief State School Officers, tell teachers what to do?
4. Where is there any evidence that the CCSS standards have increased graduation rates since 2010 when ELA standards were implemented?
5. Similarly, what is the evidence that any set of standards have increased student ELA competencies?

6. How do the standards enhance student engagement with literature? How do the standards create better writers, readers, listeners and speakers? How do the standards create lifetime learners of English who regularly enjoy writing, reading, and speaking?
7. In the CCSS, where can teachers find a clear definition of what is college and career readiness; that is, what it looks like, how anyone would recognize it when they saw it, or what elements constitute the necessary knowledge and skills for such academic and/or personal competencies, attitudes, or dispositions? Where can teachers find how college readiness compares and contrasts to career or workplace readiness?
8. How are the standards aligned with, or how do they relate to, standards coming from professional organizations of teachers and educational researchers, such as MLA and/or NCTE?
9. In what ways do the standards reflect the common professional understandings and experiences of the English curriculum held by most teachers in the United States today, or reflect the traditions of curricular understandings as they have developed over the past century or so?
10. How do the standards embrace various literary theories; or, which specific literary theories are they engaged with, or in conversation with, such as New Critical, Reader Response, gender, women's, LGBTQ, Marxist, semiotic, constructivist, formalist, deconstructivist, or any other literary theories.
11. How do the standards allow deep investigations into the multiple and complex meanings of works of art? How do the standards reduce the tendency for simplistic summative understandings of great literature with multiple perspectives and multiple meanings?
12. How do the standards, through the enhancement of the ELA curriculum, create people who are better at critically thinking using the modalities of writing, reading, and speaking? How do the standards create thinkers who are prepared to participate in a democracy, and who can understand issues of ethics, equity, and social justice?
13. How do the standards enhance the reading of texts on the full continuum from aesthetic readings of works of art (literature) to efferent or informational reading of non-fiction or journalistic texts (Rosenblatt, 1978, 1983)? How do the standards enhance readers' consciousness of the varying kinds, qualities, and genres of texts, and how best to respond to these differencing forms of texts?
14. How are the standards reflective of what is known about human cognitive and affective development in writing, reading, speaking, and thinking from childhood, through preadolescence and adolescence, and into adulthood?
15. How can the CCSS and other standards assist teachers in implementing the multitude of elements in each standard "system." For instance, there are 42 English Language Arts standards and 200 different skills teachers are expected to implement or teach per year (Cronin, 2014; Schmoker, 2014).

16. How have the CCSS or any other national or state standards been proven to be better ways to assess learning than state-generated tests from the two highest academically performing states with the two highest high school graduation rates: Connecticut and Massachusetts?
17. How do the standards assist teachers in engaging students with the ELA curriculum in today's incredibly diverse population of students, including the gifted, English language learners, non-native English speakers, those with reading and writing disabilities, those from poor or working poor, immigrant communities, or communities of color, among others?
18. How do the standards level the playing field between privileged students in well-funded, well maintained, and well-resourced schools with experienced teachers, while also equally benefiting those students who are disadvantaged in underfunded, ill-maintained, underresourced schools with inexperienced and out of license teachers?
19. And how is time allotted in schools so that teachers can develop professionally in light of the demands of standards?

And lastly, and most importantly:

20. What specific assistance does the standards handbook, guidelines, or directives give to teachers to assist in the implementation or teaching of the standards? How are the standards not just prescribing standards without describing, explaining, and showing how they can be implemented in the complex realities of classrooms?

I think you will realize that the CCSS answer very few of these questions in the positive.

This brings us to the fact that standards—the CCSS or any others—ultimately are used by authorities as *assessment tools*, the means by which teachers, students, and schools are assessed, if not actually judged. Some have argued that the CCSS and other standards are part of the "test and punish" educational reform movement, which ultimately is designed to close "failing" public schools (who can't meet the standards as presented on standardized high stakes examinations), and thus must be replaced with vouchers for private and religious charter schools.

Assessment: Good and Bad

For most students, assessment is a bad word. The word is equated with judgment, with finding out one's deficits and defects, with not measuring up to an objective standard, with not measuring up to other students, with being classified, with not succeeding, and falling short. Most often assessments mean a symbol, a grade, and this grade is often no longer what it should be—an indicator of achievement—but it becomes something of an absolute value in itself (think of your SAT grades).

The grade becomes the god, not the knowledge and skills it's supposed to represent, and schooling becomes essentially a *grade chase* (Mowrer, 1996).

For teachers, assessment is also a bad word. First of all, it's very hard to do well, even if the teacher is given the autonomy to create his own curriculum and his own tests. It shows a teacher's shortcomings when her students don't do well. Often mandated high stakes tests effectively guide the curriculum, and the teacher is assessed on how well his student do on these tests—tests over which the teacher has no control. Often the standardized and/or high stakes tests are not available for review or change year to year so the teacher can't properly prepare her students. Or, if the texts are coherent from year to year, the teacher finds that she has to teach to the text because student assessment has come to equal a score on a test. Often a teacher's tenure, yearly rating, and even keeping a job are based on standardized test scores, sometimes on students she has not actually taught!

I would also like to point out that, particularly in the ELA classroom, assessment does not need to be a "test" at all. I taught for almost 14 years in New York City public high schools, and most of that time was in urban schools which had students of whom many were seriously disengaged from formal schooling. Daily attendance rates were from 60 to 80 percent and we had some of the lowest scores on the state ELA exit exam. Our young people were from communities which were poor or working poor, recent immigrant, often non-native English speaking, or of color. These were communities which had food and housing insecurity, homelessness, and gang and drug violence. Nevertheless, I think we teachers did a pretty good job with the students we had. Almost all of us cared. We liked our students. And we tried to do our best for them. Unfortunately, we and the school were assessed—as always happens—as if the social context of our students didn't matter at all. The belief was then, and is still, that if the teachers were just doing their jobs, all the social and economic disadvantages that impinge on our students' ability to do well in school simply wouldn't matter. This is the great myth of *A Nation*, NCLB, RTTT, ESSA, and the CCSS, and all educational reforms. In fact, I have come to believe, that the real reason the elites in this world—the Gates, the Waltons, the Koch Brothers, the College Board, Betsy Devos—love educational reform is that it allows these privileged people to ignore the gross social inequities in the United States and ignore the fact that based on the 2016 census, 2 to 14 percent, or 43.1 million, Americans live in poverty, and that those poor people are located in specific communities who fund underresourced schools.

A specific teacher knows that she has to assess her students, so she knows what they need to be taught (general assessment), and in turn this indicates that she should teach, say, Curriculum X. So, the teacher then has to assess what the student knows about Curriculum X (pre-assessment). She asks the student to write, "what have your experiences been in reading Shakespeare?" (or novels? or short stories? or writing essays?). Or she might give a short questionnaire about what the students know about Curriculum X. Then, during the teaching of Curriculum X, she has to continually check to see the students are learning as the unit goes along (*formative assessment*, think *formation*). Then, when she has finished teaching Curriculum X, she has to know what the student have learned about Curriculum X (*summative assessment*), and this tells her how she needs to adjust the curriculum looking forward, whether more of Curriculum X needs to be taught, or if she should go on to teach Curriculum Y or Z. The final assessment (which need not be a test) is a *formal assessment* (it is in a "form" of a product, artifact, or text). (It could also be in the form of a presentation, but note that if the student gives a presentation, I recommend a writing assignment to go along with the presentation. This firms up the "text" of the speaking presentation with a concrete written text to assist in evaluation.) And, along with the formal assessment product (artifact, text, presentation), is an *assessment instrument*, which has the standards or rubrics that would let the student know what is a (1) Target, (2) Acceptable, (3) Emerging, or (4) Unacceptable product. However, during the unit, the teacher has also used a lot of *informal assessments*—something as simple as watching how much antsy-ness, side-talk, and foot jiggling, or pen dropping, there is in a class, or asking the student to answer the "aim" (if the lesson has one), or students writing a sentence or two or an exit ticket asking "what did you learn today?" I often end my class by having my college students stand in a circle and state something that they are "taking away from today's class." Either we go around the group and everyone says something, or I just say, "Let's hear from five people." Or, when they are sitting in their seats in a circle they stand up when they state what they learned. When everyone has stood up, the class is ended and we all can leave.

Nevertheless, the word assessment is usually an unpleasant and negative word to teachers and students. To teachers it has little to do with why they came into the profession (a positive love of literature and writing), and to students it implies finding out where they fall short, among others (*norm referenced*) and according to what she should know (*criterion referenced*). I would like to suggest that there are beneficial ways to look at assessment and "bad" ways to look at assessment. You might want to check and see how your local state high stakes tests fit into this schema:

Note that the last box has praise as both a good and bad thing to do. Alfie Kohn argues that extrinsic rewards (the A+ and gold stars) destroy the fact that students learn best when they knowwhat they learn has an intrinsic value, not for an extrinsic reward or grade (Kohn, 1999). If a teacher can create a curriculum where doing the activity and producing the artifact, text, or academic product is its own reward (*intrinsic motivation*), then *extrinsic motivation* is not only not needed, but impedes the organic rewards found in writing, reading, and speaking. I will tell you, however, from my experience, that few of my education students, preservice teachers, and beginning teachers agree with Kohn's concept that we are actually "punished by rewards," "gold stars," "A+ good job!" or any other extrinsic praise by the teacher (Kohn, 1999).

TABLE 5.1 Authentic Assessment Versus Common Assessment Errors

Good Assessment	*Bad Assessment*
Immediate feedback for curricular adaptation	Too late feedback for curriculum adaptation
Tells student what was "there" or present in assignment	Does not tell what was "there" or "seen" in assignment
Provides an informative narrative about assignment about what was actually done by the student	Provides only a symbol, e.g. "A+ very good"; or, "B- "needs improvement"
Focuses on a few errors that have been specifically taught in context of the particular unit of instruction in the light of the many positive things present	Redlines all errors, even those that have not specifically been taught in context of the particular unit of instruction and does not present in context of positive things present
Based on standards or rubrics given at outset of assignment or curriculum	Based on rubrics that have not been clearly defined or not given to student at outset of assignment or curriculum
Based on elements of assignment which have been specifically taught	Based on elements of assignment which have not been taught or have been presumed to have been taught
Emphasizes students' progress and growth in process of composition of assignment	Emphasizes students' final product and ignores process of growth
Makes student feel good about progress, competencies, and successes	Makes student feel bad about deficits, errors, falling short from "mastery"
Shows student how to improve rather than judges	Judges and does not show student how to improve
Gives feedback for improvement before final assessment (product, artifact, text, presentation) is due	Assesses or judges only final assessment (product, artifact, text, presentation) without feedback for improvement
Student knows specific elements of a target / acceptable / emerging / unacceptable assignment	Student never told specific elements of an target / acceptable / emerging / unacceptable assignment
If student repeated assignment, she would know what to do to excel next time	If student repeated assignment, she what not not know more than at the outset of the first assignment
Is competing only with self	Is competing with other students
Student knows how important the assignment is in the context of the class. Student knows where this assignment is on a continuum from high stakes assignment to low stakes assignment in the course	Student might not know how important the assignment is in the context of the class. Student does not know where this assignment is on the continuum from high stakes assignment to low stakes assignment in the course

(continued)

TABLE 5.1 *(continued)*

Good Assessment	*Bad Assessment*
Student knows who will read assignment, how it will be made public, how it will be published	Student does not know who will read assignment, how it will be made public, how it will be published
Safety. Student knows level of personal versus impersonal discourse; student knows the degree to which he can revel personal information, or not	Safety. Student does not know the level of personal versus impersonal discourse; student does not know the degree to which he can revel personal information, or not
Assignment has intrinsic value for student, is personally meaningful	Assignment is only valuable for the extrinsic goal of a grade, and is not personally meaningful
Student has a personal interest in doing the assignment well	Student has no personal interest in doing assignment well; does it well only for grade or status in class
Is praised for what student does well	Is praised for what student does well.

I can't go into all the aspects of assessment in the ELA classroom. And there are books that cover this area in a comprehensive way. Barry Raebeck's *The Teacher's Gradebook: Strategies for Student Success* (2002) is really more about assessment than simply grading, for instance, and he provides a host of matrices by which students can be fairly and humanely assessed—and feel good about it. Most reputable curriculum books have a great deal about assessment matrices. Previous chapters of this book (particularly Chapter 2) have also covered how to respond to students' writing (and this bears repeating): both in text, in the margins, and at the end by: (1) Repeating back to the student what you "see" in the writing, what is "there"; (2) asking questions of the text; (3) relating back to the writer what surprised you in the text (if anything); (4) offering suggestions for improvement by adding to, taking out, changing, or rearranging the written text; and, (5) optional (very!) providing as summative evaluation or judgement with a symbol called a grade. If a grade must be provided, then an assessment instrument must be provided to the student at the outset of the unit. This would be a list of objectives, standards, or rubrics to be met in the assignment. However, many ELA writing researchers argue that giving verbal and written feedback in a narrative style can be enough feedback for the student and the summative judgement of a grade and the assessment instrument may not be needed. I don't think the editor Maxwell Perkins, when faced with a manuscript of Hemingway or Thomas Wolfe gave grades and used a list of rubrics in an assessment instrument. Not needed!

We do know what is harmful in commenting on students' written work; and, let's face it, student written work is often the bulk of the type of material to be assessed in the ELA classroom. But what does a beneficial ELA classroom look like? Well, most of the writing your students should do in the classroom would be anonymous (only for their own eyes) and not public (published to teacher and/or other students); it should also be low stakes (not graded). However, during the semester a teacher wants to move students from personal writing to writing which is published or shared with other student collaborators. Tennessee Williams, like all good writers, constantly shared even imperfect drafts of his works with readers and writers and friends whose opinions he valued (Lahr, 2014). Unfortunately, most writing in most ELA classrooms I observe are high stakes and public. I think, instead, that to create people who love writing, you need to give them anonymity, freedom, and the opportunity to experiment and make mistakes. However, there is the need for some high stakes, public writing in the classroom. And there are things that I have seen teachers do that I do not think are helpful:

1. Redlining or red inking every error on a student's paper does not help him develop as a writer. This is only confusing to writers, not to mention disheartening. Rather, you need to be selective and focus on a discreet number of writing objectives that your student needs *at the place where they are at in their writing now*. Limit the number of usage or grammar elements required in the test to ten at most, teach these as part of the lesson (e.g. subject-verb agreement, use of semicolon, when to use commas, whatever the students need to know now) and limit your grading to those specific five or ten usage or grammar elements specifically taught. Writers need a few discreet positive writing objectives to work towards, not punishment for putting themselves "out there" on paper.
2. If you correct any error in a student's writing, she should have the opportunity to change it based on your suggestions (Raebeck, 2002). And, if the suggestion is a matter of style or preference—rather than a simple matter of correct usage—the writer always has the right not to choose to follow your suggestion.
3. *Editing* writing is much more important than *proofreading* writing, which is done last of all in the writing process. Writers aim for more than mere "correctness," they aim for richness of expression and meaning.
4. Writing something like "A-plus," or "Excellent paper!" (or both comments together) tells a student absolutely nothing at all if there is no explanation why it is an excellent paper. Same goes for any "needs improvement" comment.
5. Every comment on a student's writing must encourage him to become a better writer, and enhance his membership in *The Writers' Club* or *The Literacy Club* (Smith, 1987).
6. Beware of pseudo advice that helps students avoid errors, such as writing "sentence fragments" Which is not correct at all (!). I once sat in a bus behind a teacher who was correcting by redlining her students' papers. Not one of her suggestions was correct or true, from "not beginning a sentence with a preposition" (But, you can!), to not splitting infinitives (I just did), to ending a sentence with a preposition (as Winston Churchill purportedly said, "That is something up with which I will not put."). There are hundreds of pseudo grammatical errors which *just ain't true*.

Authentic Assessment

I am not going into explanations and explications of various "grid" type of assessments, checklist types of assessments, or assessments where students are assessed by a list of rubrics. These can be found in many books and online (again, I recommend Raebeck, 2002). But what I do want to advocate is something called Authentic Assessment. This is in line with a recurring theme of this book, namely that what we do in the ELA classroom (or any classroom for that matter) should look as much as possible like how we do these things (writing, reading, and speaking) in the real world. Two components of authentic assessment are (1) the Portfolio of student works, and (2) the Self-Assessment.

The Portfolio is a representative sample of the student's work by which he shows his progress through the semester or marking period. The Portfolio usually is organized into sections, which correspond to the units taught. For example: (1) The descriptive essay section; (2) the state exam preparation section; (3) the *To Kill a Mockingbird* section; and, (4) the creative writing section, and so forth. As an artist carries a portfolio to an interview to show *representative samples* of his work, so too the authentic assessment Portfolio is an attempt not to show perfect products the student has completed, but the student's progress, her growth. The Portfolio usually contains a simple road map or Table of Contents, and is arranged in tabbed or labeled sections. No idea is too good in education to be misused or perverted, and I've seen in some schools that the Portfolio is used to show the best or perfect samples of student work. That is not the metacognitive purpose of the Portfolio; it is to show the *process* of the students' progress in learning, not simply to show off *products*.

The Self-Assessment, which is an authentic document that replaces the schoolish and artificial exam, is a metacognitive tool accompanying the Portfolio. It is a personal essay where the student tells the teacher (and other stakeholders) the progress of her learning through the semester or learning unit. It is not "anything goes." Rather, it must be organized into sections with themes, and I find that one section must deal with readings (literature, works of art) assigned in the class. Without dividing the Self-Assessment into sectional themes of focus, I find they ramble. Because this is a personal, but organized, account of the student's personal learning, I've had Self-Assessments of 36 or more pages! I usually tell them at first, I need just six pages (double spaced, Times New Roman 12 point font, one-inch margins all around) to make them less apprehensive when I give the assignment. They almost always write more—a hallmark of a good writing assignment. The sections can be adapted for your class needs, but again, one should cover the required readings. Here are some ideas:

1. **Personal Development**. What did I know at the beginning of the course, what have I learned during the course, and what do I know now? What changes have I noticed in the development of my knowledge in the subject area and my skills in being engaged with the subject area? How has what I

have learned in the course changed my views about myself, other people, about nature and the world? What challenges did this course present me with? What resistances did I have to the material presented in this course? What specific parts of this course have most influenced me? What have I come to agree with or disagree with based on what was presented in course?

2. **Development as a Student**. What have I learned about myself during this course as a student? How have the activities in the class influenced my understanding of how I go about learning? What have I learned about myself as someone who is continuing to learn how to learn? What are my resistances to learning? What challenges do I face as a learner? What have I learned about my fellow learners? How have other learners helped me, and how have I helped them?
3. **Works of Art/Literature/Critical Texts**. How have the readings and texts in the course influenced me? What have I learned about English literature (or media, non-print media, or electronic media) in the course? What examples from the texts can I give that show my growth as a reader and as a critical thinker? What texts have most engaged me and which ones have I been resistant to?
4. **Development of Skills, Abilities, and Competencies**. What have I learned about writing, reading, and speaking in this course? How has the course developed my communication skills and/or thinking skills? How has the course helped me become a better thinker? What resistances and challenges have I faced during this course?

Students, of course, can use the above headings, or they could be allowed to develop their own. In one memorable Self-Assessment, a student arranged his paper "green light," "red light," "yellow light" to show his learning, the challenges he faced, and things he was still struggling with. Another student used quotes from Dr Seuss, her favorite author, to describe her learning. And another simply arranged it: Past, Present, Looking Ahead.

The Self-Assessment can be rubricated or given an assessment instrument, if needed, and here is an example based on what I give my students. Below is the most holistic way of rubricating an authentic learning activity, artifact, or product. These are very complex examples, but they can easily be simplified for your students—pick and choose:

4.0 **A target paper** will address all the points listed above. It will provide specific examples, anecdotes, or vignettes of demonstrated learning and engagement with the class. The paper will be clearly divided into subheadings, either those given or ones the student chooses, which reflect his or her learning. The paper will reveal high engagement with class themes, readings, and activities, even if the student disagrees with what is presented and comes to other understandings and conclusions.

3.0 **A satisfactory paper** will address all the points listed above but may address several points more fully than others. The paper will be clearly divided into subheadings, but will only be relatively clear in understanding each point that needs to be addressed. The paper will provide relevant anecdotes, examples, or vignettes. The paper will reveal a basic engagement with class themes, readings, and activities, and will agree or disagree to a fundamental extent with the ideas presented in the class.

2.0 **An emerging paper** will generally not be adequately subdivided into, or address, the points listed above, or will address the points only in a vague or general way. Examples, anecdotes, or vignettes of learning will be few and only casually related to the topics in the class. References to texts will be weak, nonexistent, or unspecific. The paper will reveal little engagement with the class, either in agreement or disagreement with the ideas presented in the class.

1.0 **An unsatisfactory paper** will not address the themes listed above. It will reveal minimal engagement with the four elements required. It reveals no engagement with the class material, class activities, or the assigned readings.

I have used the Self-Assessment in my final five years of high school teaching and in my 18 years of college teaching and no student has ever asked to do an exam instead. I did get some initial resistance in high school from the self-identified "good" students when I introduced Authentic Assessment after transferring to a new school. Authentic Assessment challenged the system by which they got the easy A and it became apparent that the work of supposedly good students, as presented in their portfolio, wasn't very good. After a time, however, they caught on and did not want to go back to examinations. I need also note that Authentic Assessment requires that students are working in good faith in the class. I always have a provision in my course guidelines or syllabi that if a certain percentage (say 65 or 75 percent) of students are not working in good faith, that I reserve the right to return to more traditional schoolish modalities and give quizzes and examinations. In about 21 years of using Authentic Assessment this happened once during a particular difficult summer class for New York City Teaching Fellows. I gave them an examination. They didn't like it.

Thinking About Learning and Doing Teaching: Using Art and the Visual in Aesthetic Reading

A group of 18 students, who were student teachers in an English Education methods course, were sitting on the floor of the college's library in the entranceway to one of the reading rooms in front of a mural about the borough of Queens called "Procession" (see Figure 5.1). The mural, measuring 8 by 16 feet is based on the personal narratives collected by an art education class led by

FIGURE 5.1

professor Rikki Asher, whose class then composed a mural about where they lived and worked (Asher, 2003).

The following are the Instructional Objectives (IOs) that would be found in a traditional lesson plan, if you want to go that way. Students will be able to (Swbat):

1. Engage in open-ended exploratory talk as an aesthetic reading transactional modality in the tradition of Aesthetic Education (AE);
2. Explain how aesthetic approaches to the text of a visual work of art can be essentially the same as those used with a written text on a page ordinarily associated with the ELA curriculum; and,
3. Enumerate the ways in which elements of aesthetic and transactional reading can be a narrative part of the ELA classroom.

The Line of Inquiry used in Aesthetic Education for the class would be: "How does the Procession mural introduce us to, and engage us with, transactional and aesthetic reading practices?" (Terms and concepts: *Reader response theory and practice; transactional reading; aesthetic reading; Aesthetic Education (AE); exploratory talk, work of art (WOA), Line of Inquiry (LOI)*).

In the previous class, one week earlier, the class had been asked to freewrite about the borough in which they lived and/or went to school. The prompt or "starter" was: "Take a few moments and write about the Borough of Queens where you live and/or work and/or go to school. What do you know about it? What kind of relationship do you have with this geographical place? How do you feel about it? What questions do you have about it? What more do you want to know about it?"

The students shared their understanding of the importance of this vibrant, multicultural geographical place in their lives. Most students lived in Queens and felt that it was a special place because of its many diverse neighborhoods and people. It should be noted that Queens is the second largest of the five boroughs of New York City, is the second most populous county in the United States, and, if it were a city in itself, would be the nation's fourth most populous, after Los Angeles, Chicago, and Brooklyn (if Brooklyn were also a city and not a borough). It had 2,333,054 residents in the 2016 census and approximately 48 percent of them were foreign-born. It is the most ethnically diverse urban area in the world with roughly 160 different languages spoken (https://en.wikipedia.org/wiki/Queens). (Queens is also the home of Peter Parker, aka Spiderman, who resides with his Aunt May at an actual address, 20 Ingram Street, Forest Hills Gardens, Queens.)

After volunteer students shared their responses about the borough, the instructor told them that next week they would meet in the atrium of the school library for a brief introduction, and then would go down one floor to have an aesthetic reading, or aesthetic transaction, with a mural an Art Education class had created a few years before. They were also instructed to bring something to write on, a pen, that they'd need their college ID to enter, and that food and drink were forbidden.

The next week, in the atrium, the students were given a large index card and asked to write briefly on the following questions:

1. What do you know about Queens? Or, what do you think is important about the borough of Queens?
2. What are your feelings toward the borough of Queens?
3. What would you like to know, or what do you need to know, about the borough of Queens?

The group then went down to the lower level reading room and sat in a semicircle around the mural. The instructor asked the class to, "Actively observe the mural for about three to five minutes. Just look around the mural and make a mental note of what you see. Try to formulate questions about the mural."

There were many noticings and questions. Among these, some students wondered if that was Louis Armstrong and what was his relationship to Queens? Others wondered who was Chester Carlson and what did he have to do with Xerox Machine? Why were those planes flying into the burning building? Was that singer Billie Holiday? Much attention was given to the different and colorful costumes on the people in the lower center of the picture. (Here the reader of this book can take a look at Figure 5.1 and come up with his or her own "noticings" or questions.)

When each student made an observation or stated a question, the instructor was careful to ask several open ended, exploratory questions, such as, "Why do you think that is Billie Holiday?" "What do you notice about the types of people who are processing over the bridge?" "What makes you say that the pedicurist on the left is probably a recent Asian immigrant?" The instructor did not make any declarative statements, rather he attempted to draw out understandings of the mural through questionings and exploratory talk.

After about ten minutes, the instructor handed out sixteen cards to pairs of students. The cards were each a cut up section of a postcard of the mural. The students were asked to stand up and approach the mural (but not touch it) and examine that specific section to see what they also noted. They could take notes on the back of the index cards on which they wrote at the beginning of the class.

When they sat down again after about five minutes of further close exploration, the student was surprised by what additional things they noticed. One student stated, "I didn't see at first that there are eyes all around the mural, and all the eyes are different." Another stated that he had not noticed that there were men playing Bocce. Another noticed that there were state and city seals or insignia in the borders of the mural.

The instructor then asked the students to freewrite for a few moments about their experience with the mural so that they could remember things for a final in-classroom discussion. When they returned to their regular classroom, the instructor led the discussion by first discussing the process of the lesson (rather than the *content* of the mural), which included exploratory talk, noticings, questionings, and avoidance of the instructor giving answers. Then the instructor asked how reading this visual text was similar or dissimilar to how they had observed teachers (or themselves) teaching the written text of a novel, play, story, or poem. The students related that when they taught or saw other teachers teaching literature (works of art), the teacher usually had the message or the theme already in her head and led the student through guided so-called *Socratic questions* to get the predetermined message of the text. Here, however, the power of open-ended questioning led the student to have a more powerful aesthetic apprehension of the text of the mural. The professor then asked the students to discuss the ways in which the aesthetic reading of the visual text could be also applied to a written text of a work of art (literature) in the ELA classroom. The students seemed to agree that allowing students to notice, ponder, and wonder would lead them to more powerful transactions with the text, rather than just "getting" the message or point that the teacher had predetermined was in the text.

Once this discussion had run its course, the instructor felt it was the time to answer information- or fact-based contextual questions. Yes, Louis Armstrong had his archives at the college they attended, and the college as well maintained his house in Queen as a historic site. No, the instructor did not know why the Statue of Liberty was included if it is not technically in Queens (then, why did they think the artists included it?). Yes, Chester Carlson invented the Xerox Machine in Queens, and yes that was Billie Holiday. Yes, that "disk building" was the New York Pavilion for the 1968 World's Fair by the famous architect Philip Johnson and it was the place that Edgar the alien bug stashed in a flying saucer in the movie, *Men in Black*.

The class ended with the students creating a six to twelve-line poem (they were asked not to rhyme) about their experience with Queens. They could create the poem individually or in pairs (for support). They could use their notes on the index cards, their writing from last week's class, and anything they remembered from the mural, or anything from their own apperceptive mass of thoughts and feelings about the borough.

> I ride the 7-train local stop after stop from Flushing to Astoria,
> And engage the hundred voices and miraculous faces that go by:
> Mexico, Italy, Korea, Ireland, and Sichuan Province. And in a hundred Greek diners
> I am offered jellyfish salad, dolma, calzone, curried goat, and Guinness on draught,
> And prayer rugs and cymbals, and a Star of David, and David Wright's glove.
> I am the hundreds getting off the plane at LaGuardia and Kennedy
> And searching for a cab.
> To take me through the Boulevard of Death and over the Queensborough Bridge
> So that I'll always have the hope
> For next year's Mets
> and the sunrise over Jamaica Bay.

(Vocabulary words: Boulevard of Death = Queens Boulevard, a 12-lane thoroughfare that bisects the borough and is known for pedestrian accidents; David Wright = Third baseman and captain of the Mets; LaGuardia and Kennedy = Two international airports in the borough.)

References

Applebee, A. (1996). Deadly Traditions. In A. Applebee, *Curriculum as conversation: Transforming traditions of teaching and learning* (pp. 21–34). Chicago, IL: University of Chicago Press.

Asher, R. (2003). Murals as interdisciplinary teaching. In D. Kaufmann, D. M. Moss, & T. A. Osborne (Eds.), *Beyond the boundaries: A transdisciplinary approach to teaching and learning* (pp. 131–144). Westport, CT: Praeger Publishers, Greenwood Publishing Group, Inc.

Beach, R., Thein, A.H. & Webb, A. (2016). *Teaching to exceed the English Language Arts Common Core State Standards: A critical inquiry approach for 6–12 classrooms* (2nd ed.). New York: Taylor & Francis.

Berliner D. C. & Biddle, B. J. (1995). *The manufactured crisis: Myths, fraud, and the attack on America's public schools.* New York: Basis Books/Perseus.

Berliner, D. C. & Glass, G. V. (2014) *50 myths and lies that threaten America's public schools: The real crisis in education.* New York: Teachers College Press.

Braithwaite, E. R. (1959). *To sir, with love.* London: Open Road Integrated Media.

Common Core State Standards Initiative [CCSSI]. (2014). English Language Arts standards, anchor standards, college and career readiness anchor standards for writing.

USA: Common Core State Standards Initiative. Accessed 01/12/16 at: www.corestandards.org/ELA-Literacy/CCRA/W/.

Costigan, A. T. (2014). Demythologizing educational reforms: Thirty years since *A Nation at Risk*. In A. T. Costigan and L. Grey (Eds.), *Demythologizing educational reforms: Responses to the political and corporate takeover of education* (pp. 1–19). New York: Routledge.

Costigan, A. T. (2017). "I'm not teaching English, I'm teaching something else!": How new teachers create curriculum under mandates of educational reform. *Educational Studies*. Available at: www.tandfonline.com/eprint/YW6Y5F2UhED4vHVF5B3p/full.

Costigan, A. T. & Grey, L. (Eds.). (2014). *Demythologizing educational reforms: Responses to the political and corporate takeover of education*. New York: Routledge.

Cronin, A. P. (2014). More on Common Core: Truth is truer than fiction. In J. Pelto, *WaitWhat* (blog). Available at: http://jonathanpelto.com/2014/10/21/common-core-truth-truer-fiction-guest-post-ann-policelli-cronin/.

Cuban, L. (1984). *How teachers taught: Constancy and change in American classrooms, 1890–1980*. New York: Longman.

Eagleton, T. (2008). *Literary theory: An introduction*. Minneapolis, MN: University of Minnesota Press.

Fleischer, C. & Fox, D. (2004). English education in the time of *No Child Left Behind*. *English Education, 36*(2), 99–100.

Freire, P. (1970/2000). Chapter Two. In P. Freire, *Pedagogy of the oppressed* (30th anniversary edition, p. 71). New York: Bloomsbury Academic.

Gabbard, D. A. (2008). *Knowledge and power in the global economy: The effects of school reform in a neoliberal/neoconservative age* (2nd ed.). New York: Erlbaum.

Gallagher, K. (2015). *In the best interest of students: Staying true to what works in the ELA classroom*. Portland, ME: Stenhouse.

Gentry, C. (2011). Imagination, possibility, and wide-awakeness: Maxine Greene's salon at the creativity, imagination, and innovation symposium. In *Arts & Humanities The Department of Arts & Humanities at Teachers College, Columbia University* (website). Available at: http://artsandhumanities.pressible.org/christine_gentry/wide-awakeness-maxine-greene.

Greene, M. (2001). *Variations on a blue guitar: The Lincoln Center Institute Lectures on aesthetic education*. New York: Teachers College Press.

Guerin, W. L., Labor, E. L., Morgan, L., Reesman, J. C., & Willingham, J. R. (2005). *A handbook of critical approaches to literature* (5th ed.). New York: Oxford University Press.

Hunter, E. (1953). *The blackboard jungle*. New York: Open Road Integrated Media, Inc.

Hursh, D. W. (2007). Assessing No Child Left Behind and the rise of neoliberal educational policies. *American Educational Research Journal, 44*, 493–518.

Hursh, D. W. (2008). *High-stakes testing and the decline of teaching and learning: The real crisis in education*. New York: Rowman-Littlefield.

Katz, M. B. (1968). *The irony of early school reform: Educational innovation in mid-nineteenth century Massachusetts*. Boston, MA: Beacon Press.

Kaufman, B. (1964). *Up the down staircase*. New York: Prentice Hall.

Kaufman, D., Moore Johnson, S., Kardos, S. M., Liu, E., & Peske, H. G. (2002, March 2). "Lost at sea": New teachers' experiences with curriculum and assessment. *Teachers College Record, 104*, 273–300.

Kincaid, J. *Girl*. (1978) *The New Yorker*. Available at: www.newyorker.com/magazine/978/06/26/girl.

Kohn, A. (1999). *Punished by rewards: The trouble with gold stars, incentive plans, A's, praise, and other bribes*. New York: Houghton Mifflin and Company.

Lahr, J. (2014). *Tennessee Williams: Mad pilgrimage of the flesh.* New York: W. W. Norton and Company, Inc.

Layton, L. (2014). How Bill Gates financed the Common Core from A to Z. *The Washington Post.* Available at: www.washingtonpost.com/politics/how-bill-gates-pulled-off-the-swift-common-core-revolution/2014/06/07/a830e32e-ec34-11e3-9f5c-9075d5508f0a_story.html?utm_term=.67a715ec6e7c.

McCourt, F. (2005). *Teacher man: A memoir.* New York: Scribner

McNeil, L. (1988). *Contradictions of control: School structure and school knowledge.* New York: Routledge.

McNeil, L. (2000). *Contradictions of school reform: Educational costs of standardized testing.* New York: Routledge.

Mowrer, D. E. (1996). Giving up the grade chase for a competency-based education. *National Student Speech Language Association Journal, 43,* 69–76.

[MLA] Modern Languages Association. (2008). *Report to the Teagle Foundation on the undergraduate major in language and literature.* New York: Modern Languages Association.

[NCEE]. National Commission on Excellence in Education. (1983). *A nation at risk: The imperative for educational reform.* Washington, DC: National Commission on Excellence in Education. Available at: www.ed.gov/pubs/NatAtRisk/index.html

Ravitch, D. (2000). *Left back: A century of failed school reforms.* New York: Simon and Schuster.

Ravitch, D. (2013). *Reign of error: The hoax of the privatization movement and the danger to America's public schools.* New York: Random House/Alfred A Knopf.

Ravitch D. & Maris A. V. (Eds.). (1995). *Learning from the past: What history teaches us about school reform.* Baltimore, MD: The Johns Hopkins University Press.

Raebeck, B. (2002). *The teacher's gradebook: Strategies for student success.* Lanham, MD: Rowman & Littlefield Publishing Group/Scarecrow Press.

Richards, I. A. (1929). *Practical criticism: A study of literary judgment.* New York: Harvest/Harcourt Brace.

Rosenblatt, L. M. (1978). *The reader, the text, the poem: The transactional theory of the literary work.* Carbondale, IL: Southern Illinois University Press.

Rosenblatt, L. M. (1983). *Reading as exploration* (3rd ed.). New York: Modern Language Association.

Schmoker, M. (2014, September 23). The standards are not ready. *Education Week, 34*(5), 22–23.

Scott, W. S. (1963). *Five approaches to literary criticism: An arrangement of contemporary critical essays.* New York: The Macmillan Company.

Smagorinsky, P., Lakly, A., & Johnson, T. S. (2002). Acquiescence, accommodation, and resistance in learning to teach within a prescribed curriculum. *English Education, 34,* 187–213.

Smagorinsky, P., Gibson, N., Bickmore, S. T., Moore, C. P., & Cook, S. (2004). Praxis shock: Making the transition from a student-centered university program to the corporate climate of schools. *English Education, 36,* 214–245.

Smith, F. (1987). *Joining the literacy club: Further essays into education.* Portsmouth, NH: Heinemann.

Smith, M. W., Appleman, D., & Wilhelm, J. D. (2014). *Where the authors of the standards go wrong about instruction—and how you can get it right.* Thousand Oak, CA: Corwin.

US Congress. (2001). *Elementary and secondary education act: No child left behind act of 2001.* Washington, DC: US Congress.

US Department of Education (2009). *American recovery and reinvestment act of 2009, race to the top* (RTTT). Washington, DC: US Department of Education.

US Department of Education. (2015). *Every student succeeds act* (ESSA). Washington, DC: US Department of Education.

Wells, P. (2012, November 13). As not seen on TV. Restaurant review: Guy's American Kitchen & Bar in Times Square. *New York Times.* Available at: www.nytimes.com/2012/11/14/dining/reviews/restaurant-review-guys-american-kitchen-bar-in-times-square.html

6

MULTIPLE LITERACIES AS CULTURALLY SUSTAINING PEDAGOGY IN ENGLISH LANGUAGE ARTS

Limarys Caraballo

> I want to definitely improve my ELA grade. For starters, I want to read the book completely because I tend not to like the books and not read them. But this semester, I am going to suck it up and read all the books that I am assigned to read.

In this excerpt from a journal entry in which students were asked to write about their individual goals for their eighth grade English Language Arts class (ELA), Jason expresses the desire to improve his ELA grade despite his tendency "not to like the books and not read them."[1] His determination to "suck it up" and read what he is "assigned to read" casts the ELA curriculum as a series of required readings and assessments to be endured rather than enjoyed. He does not expect to relate to the reading, but he knows he needs to get through it in order to "improve [his] ELA grade." As part of a research study that I was conducting in a middle school English class at Northeastern Urban Academy (NUA) on students' experiences of the ELA curriculum, I had the opportunity to read Jason and his classmates' statements and journals, as well as interview many of his peers. Unfortunately, Jason's sentiments above were quite common.

What was perhaps most striking to me, however, was the contrast between students' responses to the curriculum and the purposes and desires of their teachers. For example, in an interview, Ms. Brian, the energetic first-year teacher who would teach Jason and his peers, described her goals for her class as follows:

> I really want to create lifelong readers. . . . I feel like there's a certain . . . point in school where you start thinking about reading as a chore. You know, it's like, "I have to do this, and then I have to write a report" . . . I want to keep it fun and, and I want to keep them—I want them to want to read for the rest of their lives.

For Ms. Brian, ELA curriculum involved cultivating a certain kind of person and particular desires about reading. Nonetheless, she recognized that she was required to negotiate administrative expectations regarding standardized test scores that also seemed to make sense to her: "I worry about test scores. . . . I know that that's like a big deal for [the administration]. . . . And, I mean, it makes sense, right?" Like many committed and conscientious educators, Ms. Brian wanted to help her school meet its academic goals, and she wanted her students to succeed in school as well as be "college and career ready." Furthermore, while standardized assessments were not always a major emphasis at this school, the school had received lower marks for their assessment scores in recent accountability reports because students remained at the "Proficient" level rather than progressing to "Advanced." Due to the value-added evaluation and progress reporting system in place in the city, therefore, the administration became increasingly concerned about testing in order to raise the school's "progress grade" in public accountability reports (Darling-Hammond, 2004). Thus, the contradictory perspectives of students, teachers, and administrators conveyed in these excerpts highlight some of the varied circumstances and understandings about ELA instruction that ultimately impacted how Jason and Ms. Brian experienced the ELA curriculum.

An Introduction to Multiple Literacies and Culturally Sustaining Pedagogies

As discussed in previous chapters, the discipline of English consists of much more than the texts to be read or the literacy skills to be mastered. Although it may be disconcerting to learn that a well-meaning teacher and her student may have had such divergent responses to the same ELA curriculum, my argument in this chapter is that literacies are multiple and socially-constructed ways of reading and composing texts, rather than a set of skills to be mastered. Our conception of literacy underlies all decisions about how we approach curriculum design and implementation in ELA. Once we recognize that literac(ies) and language(s) are socially constructed, with particular values and interests that are also embedded in their given social contexts, it becomes easier to understand how a curriculum that seems relevant and culturally responsive to a teacher may not seem so to a student. Approaching the discipline of ELA via a multiple literacies lens thus challenges teachers to interact dynamically with literature as well as the wide range of texts that students (and teachers) "read" and "write," in the broadest sense.

A multiple literacies approach is important because it broadens what counts as literacy and whose language(s), and ways of engaging with texts, matter. For example, students construct perceptions of themselves and others in relation to the hierarchies of knowledge and power that are implicit (and explicit) in curriculum (Kumashiro, 2000), and their curricular experiences are embedded in multiple raced, classed, and gendered identities. In my long-term inquiry into how students of color experienced the academic curriculum and negotiated such hierarchies in the context of NUA, a racially, ethnically, and socioeconomically diverse urban public middle school, I found that narrow conceptions of what it means to be "literate" lead to restrictive learning environments for minoritized students, namely those whose literacy practices are not typically reflected in or valued by the academic curriculum. In addition, the increase in surveillance and accountability measures discussed in Chapter 5 leads to an overregulation of curriculum and over-testing in schools that are marked as "at-risk"; the students in these schools, many of whom come from lower socioeconomic backgrounds, are then deprived of the more creative, engaging, and "real world" experiences of ELA that are available to students in more affluent or well-resourced schools. In this way, these reforms actually perpetuate the gaps in opportunity between White middle-class students and communities that have been historically marginalized by traditional schooling and society.

Furthermore, if we pay attention to students' multiple literacy practices (and identities), we see that many resist and subvert a single definition of literacy. In my research, I found that youth critiqued the curriculum in sometimes subtle and other times not-so-subtle ways. For example, in and out of academic spaces, multiple sites of resistance are visible when students critique their own assignments (Caraballo, 2016), or use hip hop to challenge the status quo (Caraballo & Lyiscott, 2018). In these instances, students may be drawing upon literacies that are not typically honored in school. Recognizing the multiple ways in which students and teachers can create as well as respond to texts serves the multiple purposes of amplifying youth voice in education, and preparing them for future study, career, and civic participation, but also sustaining the cultural resources that students bring from their homes and communities into our academic spaces (Paris & Alim, 2014). Whether it be by translating texts for their families, challenging each other in rap battles, documenting with photography, or producing short films, recognizing multiple literacies challenges us to think about what ELA curriculum is meant to be. By promoting challenging, relevant learning experiences and pedagogical practices that are situated in students' social realities, this chapter invites you, as teachers, to be agents of change, and to lead the reconceptualization of traditional notions of ELA curriculum.

In the first section, I discuss the terms *multiple literacies* and *multiliteracies* as ways to frame individuals' interactions with texts that extend beyond the traditional skills we typically associate with reading and writing. In the second section, I introduce the idea of culturally sustaining pedagogies in order to make the argument that it is not enough to simply acknowledge that students come from multiple backgrounds and might have access to literacy practices that are not currently part of the "standard" ELA curriculum, however that may be defined. A culturally sustaining pedagogy also engages students in the critical analysis of how hierarchies of language and power operate in society in order to codify what is considered "mainstream" literacy and "proper" grammar. Third, using the idea of assemblage as a heuristic, I apply both of these constructs, multiple literacies and culturally sustaining pedagogies, as lenses through which teachers can examine and critique their own ideas about the discipline of ELA and how those can impact teaching and curriculum. I draw from my research at NUA, in a middle school English classroom, to create an example of such an assemblage of ELA. Finally, in the last section, I discuss several entry points into teaching multiple literacies and suggest some activities and examples that serve the dual purpose of illustrating this approach and helping teachers to think more broadly about ELA curriculum and pedagogy.

Conceptualizing Literacies as Multiple and Dynamic: A Culturally Sustaining Approach to ELA

A major debate in the discipline of ELA is concerned with what theories, research studies, and "best practices" should guide the teaching of ELA and the preparation of English teachers. While you may be less likely to think about your teaching in terms of these broader debates, you are probably feeling the push-and-pull from these ideas without necessarily being aware of them. Recognizing how their own questions and conundrums about teaching fit into a broader discourse in the field of English can help teachers make decisions and choices that both feel "right" to them and also take into account how teaching and curriculum can serve (or not serve) students—particularly those that come from communities that are different from the teacher's own background.

In *Being and Becoming a Teacher of English Language Arts*, Christenbury challenges teachers to think beyond "that novel or play [they] loved so much, that poem that changed [their] lives, that writing experience that was powerful, that insight about language that seems to stay in [their] mind" (2006, p. 6). She raises a crucial point about how ELA is taught in a broader, more relational context (beyond a teacher's experiences in English classes, for example), which itself has a major role in shaping students' understanding of their surroundings:

> teachers are only one part of a triad that also features a bewildering array of students, all of whom have fierce needs and aspirations and brilliance and weaknesses and problems and cultural expectations, and a setting, and institutional context, which we soon find can more often than not keep us from teaching and keep our students from learning.
>
> *(p. 7)*

Increasingly, Christenbury and other leaders in the field conceptualize ELA as a discipline that develops students' literacies as they interact with their immediate contexts and society at large. This view stands in contrast to more traditional conceptions of the subject, organized around the rhetoric that all students should be exposed to the best works of literature and critical thinking skills, assuming that reading is a process that requires the same set of skills for all students (Hirsch, 1987).

While references to multiple literacies and multimodality have become increasingly common, literacy has historically been conceptualized in fairly functional terms. According to Burroughs & Smagorinsky (2009), "attention to literacies has largely been confined to knowledge and practices involved in the reading of literature" (p. 171). Au & Raphael have noted a common assumption that "the essayist form of literacy—dominant in western academic circles—is the only desirable form" (2000, p. 170). Such assumptions privilege an *autonomous* literacy model that presumes literacy is that which can be measured, in alignment with the way students' skills are assessed in state tests and exams, as discussed below (Street, 1984, 1995). Much of the literacy instruction offered in schools has been historically grounded in an autonomous model. Similarly, the categorization of individuals as functionally literate (or illiterate) has been based on their ability to decode texts as well as master and apply the conventions of what has been deemed "standard" and/or "academic" English. The assumption is that mastery of the skills associated with reading, writing, and critical thinking will not only lead students to success in ELA and college, but also to the levels of logical and critical reasoning needed to become mature adults (e.g., as portrayed in the Common Core State Standards (CCSS)). On the Common Core website, the standards are described as follows:

> Building on the best of existing state standards, the Common Core State Standards provide clear and consistent learning goals to help prepare students for college, career, and life. The standards clearly demonstrate what students are expected to learn at each grade level, so that every parent and teacher can understand and support their learning. (Retrieved February 20, 2018, from www.corestandards.org/the-standards.)

Based on this rhetoric, ELA curricula have traditionally been designed to cultivate a particular kind of literate and successful individual by focusing on reading and writing skills and universalist themes in literature that everyone should know.

On the other hand, an ideological literacy model (Street, 1984), in which the social contexts, choices, and factors that influence who students are and become are viewed through the lens of the multiple social practices that students bring with them to the classroom, exposes the interests embedded in any given interaction with texts. For example, standardizing assessment of students' reading and writing has been promoted as a way to maintain "rigorous" and "objective" standards for all students—but we also know that our society depends on schools to produce an appropriate workforce for our economy to flourish, and an educated citizenry to lead and shape our democracy.

Therefore, while the current academic paradigms, as exemplified by the CCSS, for instance, has been touted to offer students in the most underresourced schools and districts access to the same rigorous curricula as their more affluent peers (and ultimately, access to the same opportunities in higher education and in future careers), in fact, a belief in the "neutrality" of the CCSS, and its narrow definition of literacy, inadvertently discredit what is outside the Common Core norms as inferior, substandard, or not "rigorous" enough (Ladson-Billings, 2000). The assumption continues to be, in line with the rhetoric that all students should be exposed to the best works of literature and critical thinking skills, that reading and writing are neutral and objective processes—that students who know how to read and write well, and are good "critical thinkers"—can do so because they have mastered a specific set of skills that can be measured by standardized tests. However, most of us know that our society's leaders in almost every discipline are those who can think creatively, *outside* the box. As such, narrow conceptions of literacy, and the accountability measures that enforce them, perpetuate the disparity between the educational opportunities and the type of learning available to students from more affluent backgrounds in schools that are less tied to standardized tests.

In contrast, McLaren argues that *critical literacies*, which interrogate whose interests are served by particular texts, have the potential to "create a citizenry critical enough to both analyze and challenge the oppressive characteristics of the larger society so that a more just, equitable, and democratic society can be created" (cited in Carlson, 1993, p. 238). This premise is grounded in the assumption that identities are multiple and contextual, always being negotiated in particular cultural words, which Dorothy Holland and her colleagues have theorized as *figured worlds* (Caraballo, 2011; Holland et al., 1998). Similarly, literacies are also socially forged in the figured worlds in which people interact with texts and with each other, and the process is related to the construction of identities.

In an essay about why identity matters in literacy research, McCarthey and Moje (2002) conclude that "identity changes and challenges are, in fact, what literacy learning is all about" (p. 237). They consider both the possibility that identities shape people's textual and literate practices, as well as its converse—"that literate practices play a role in identifications and positionings" (p. 229). As an example, they note that mainstream readers discount graffiti as a textual form, even though it involves letters and related symbol systems, because of its association with deviant behaviors. Similarly, teachers make decisions about what texts (and even how much reading) to assign based on their beliefs about students and their identities as readers. In the "real" world, literacy is always conveyed in some social purpose or form such as "letter writing, charters, catechisms, business styles, academic 'texts', etc., and it is always learnt in relation to these uses and in specific social conditions" (p. 43), not in the form of a five-paragraph essay. As Freire and Macedo (1987) succinctly stated, literacy is that which pertains to students' readings of the *word* and the *world*—their responses to texts and the texts that they create offer insights into students' identities and how they position themselves in their own lives and figured worlds. As Luke (1996) argues, "every text is a kind of institutional speech act, a social action with language with a particular shape and features, force, audience, and consequences" (p.15). According to Brian Street (1984) and many literacy scholars in contemporary times, literacy is a social practice that cannot be separated from the context in which individuals make meaning of texts and interact with their surroundings, the institutions that they interact with, and other people, to name a few examples.

Building upon this idea of literacy-as-social-practice, in the mid-1990s an international group of scholars met in New London, New Hampshire, to address a growing anxiety in the field of literacy due to deepening socioeconomic disparities in the midst of an increasingly globalized and technological society. This group of scholars, who called themselves the New London Group, published a seminal article in 1996 in which they coined the term *multiliteracies* to describe two important arguments that they might engage "with the emerging cultural, institutional, and global order: the multiplicity of communication channels and media, and the increasing saliency of cultural and linguistic diversity" (New London Group, p. 63). While "mere literacy" might focus on literacy in terms of language alone, a pedagogy of multiliteracies would focus on much broader modes of representation, and therefore make classroom boundaries just that much more permeable. In coining this term, the New London Group offered scholars a framework to support a much-needed exploration of how "technologies of meaning" are changing each day; it also honors the myriad ways in which students already make meaning of and produce texts in their homes and communities for authentic purposes.

What This Means for English Teachers

One major benefit of understanding how identities and literacies are forged in the context of particular figured worlds, or cultural contexts, is that teachers can strive to create a classroom environment that is: a) deliberately welcoming to students whose languages and literacies are not typically valued or honored in academic spaces; and b) incorporates multiple design elements in the meaning-making process, beyond the linguistic, including forms such as spatial and multimodal. In addition, engaging in this kind of critical practice deepens the understanding of literacies for students from mainstream backgrounds, who may otherwise never question the raced, classed, and gendered context that has led to "proper" English being known as such. Teachers who are equipped to do this can contribute to what Morrell (2005) has described as *powerful English.*

Morrell's (2005) notion of powerful English takes on an even greater significance today because popular culture, social media, and digital modes continue to have such large impact in shaping and disseminating the perspectives, voices, and literacies of teachers and students alike. Describing what he describes as critical English education, Morrell argues that ELA must be "explicit about the role of language and literacy in conveying meaning and in promoting or disrupting existing power relations" and "encourages practitioners to draw upon the everyday language and literacy practices of adolescents to make connections with academic literacies and to work toward empowered identity development and social transformation" (Morrell, 2005, p. 313). A critical English education engages students' home and youth culture and literacies in conversation with traditional academic language and literacies in order for students (and teachers) to be ready to make meaning in what the New London Group identifies as three dynamic realms of existence—our working, public, and private lives. To be very clear, the argument here is *not* that teachers should refrain from teaching traditional academic language and literacies. On the contrary, I am making a case for teaching these academic conventions *critically*, by positioning them among a broader and more inclusive array of literacies. In becoming aware of how those literacies became the dominant mainstream in our society in the first place, students are better poised to be able to leverage multiple literacies to serve their own various purposes and interests. Furthermore, as Paris and Alim (2014) contend, while students and teachers have traditionally been taught that White middle class language and literacy practices alone are the key to power and access in mainstream society, as society becomes increasingly diverse, an inability to leverage multiple literacies in the diverse social and political realms that we navigate in society might actually reduce that access.

Fostering Critical Understandings in ELA *with* Students

The identities students construct and/or take up in academic spaces help us understand some of the broader issues at stake regarding the education of students of color. In the long-term study that I described at the beginning of this chapter, I examined how high-achieving students of color experienced the literacy curriculum as mediated by the multiple identities that they constructed and negotiated within their school—and I found that some identities and literacies were implicitly or explicitly favored while others were censured or overlooked. Conceptualizing identities and literacies in this way, as dynamically constructed in the context of classrooms (as figured worlds) has very real implications for how you might conduct your own classroom. For example, a multiple literacies lens leads us to recognize that the academic curriculum tends to include/exclude literacies based on which ones are perceived to be of most worth, who determines their worth, and how the hierarchy that ensues from that valorization marginalizes historically underserved student populations.

Rethinking Literacies in Secondary ELA

In a course that I developed at Queens College, called *Multiple Literacies in English Language Arts,* teachers conduct their own research on an educational issue relevant to the discipline, and experiment with various "literacies" (cultural, digital, critical, hip hop, etc.). Via course readings, discussions, and assignments, I challenge emerging educators to engage in meaningful inquiry into their assumptions about students and curriculum while simultaneously providing them with strategies and approaches that they may use in their own classrooms.

In the previous chapter, Arthur Costigan explained how public policies and debates about standards and accountability measures inform and impact teachers and teaching. In the same vein, my work in English education is premised on how ELA, as a discipline and academic subject, is informed by specific discourses, or public narratives, that: a) correlate achievement with ability and effort regardless of context; b) promote colorblind perspectives; and c) mute the discussion of racial patterns in students' academic performance. These discourses produce certain versions of ELA, versions that are interrelated and overlapping, and invoke particular identities among students and teachers in classroom contexts.

However, as different waves of reform come and go, it is what happens in classrooms that will make the greatest impact in students' engagement with language and literature. While the national discourse about testing and accountability, as well as college readiness, certainly inform the work of educators across the nation, it is important for you, as teachers, to question, examine, and consider what these discourses make possible or impossible in your own classrooms—and how they impact our students. Therefore, I argue that recognizing literacies as multiple and dynamic not only allows us to consider, for example, how students from nondominant backgrounds make meaning with and of texts, but it also challenges us to rethink how we determine what "counts" as English language arts.

Question(s) for Teachers: What is ELA?

> Is ELA the study and appreciation of literature from various genres?
>
> Is ELA about learning to write using a particular grammar, to communicate with others, or to express ones' thoughts and ideas?
>
> Is the purpose of ELA to prepare students for future careers?

I posit that if we surveyed dozens of English teachers, we would have dozens of different combinations of responses to these questions. Indeed, in a seminal article written on this topic, *The Trouble with English*, Allan Luke (2004; who also happens to be one of the New London Group), examined the various interests and purposes of English education over many decades as well as its relationship to the study of college English. He concludes that, in light of such divergent ideas about the field,

> what is needed is a renewed sense of the purposes and consequences, powers and practices of English, of the intellectual, ideological, and moral force of all forms of representation and, equally, a strong sense of "English" as language, as mode of information, as a multifaceted and ambivalent cultural force within and across the practices and technologies of economic and cultural globalization.
>
> *(p. 94)*

Historically, the ways in which teachers design and implement instruction have been primarily shaped by the assumptions and expectations, literacy models, and discourses that are implicit in the production of "English" as an academic subject, but less so based on the input of the students themselves. Yet, without students' own voices and perspectives, particularly those who have been underserved in schools and historically marginalized by the traditional curriculum, educators will continue to miss the mark when it comes to designing and implementing effective curricula that serve all students well.

In the next section, I explore how we might consider students' experiences of and perspectives on the ELA curriculum, as well as attempt to stitch together the "big ideas" that I have discussed thus far. To summarize the big ideas: identities and literacies are interrelated and embedded in social practice; literacies are multiple and contextual; and a multiple literacies approach can lead to pedagogies that are culturally sustaining for students from diverse backgrounds. In order to do this, I provide another example from the long-term study of the middle school English class at NUA. Drawing from the journal entries of students like Jason, and employing a multiple literacies approach, I create a visualization using excerpts from students' writing that documents how students experienced the ELA curriculum. This visualization serves two purposes, as it is both an example of how alternative literacy approaches can contribute to meaning-making, as well as a method for examining how students' experiences and perspectives can and should inform our understanding of ELA curriculum and pedagogy.

Conceptualizing ELA *as Assemblage* at NUA

Before addressing what an assemblage is and how it can help us make sense of multiple literacies in ELA, it is important to center the discussion in our definition of curriculum. A curriculum, in any discipline, is an important socializing device that informs students' thinking in multiple ways, and from different perspectives, and thus shapes identities in school and beyond. In any subject area, at the surface level is the explicit curriculum, otherwise known as the "official" course of study, scope, and sequence, etc. (Britzman, 1989; Eisner, 1985). However, the curriculum that students and teachers experience may differ greatly from what is outlined as the explicit curriculum. In the context of classroom practice, the curriculum is transformed as it is operationalized: specifically, the *planned* curriculum may differ significantly from the enacted curriculum, which is what students and teachers actually experience as the planned or official curriculum takes on new life in the context of classroom instruction (Snyder, Bolin, & Zumwalt, 1992). The enacted ELA curriculum encompasses the teacher and students' experiences of this assemblage in their context of practice, the classroom. In the current figured world of many classrooms, and certainly so at NUA, the current high stakes accountability context in US schools has been highly preoccupied with the measurable achievement results of students as well as teachers.

Now, what is an assemblage and how does it help us understand ELA curriculum? In art, an assemblage is an assembly or grouping of unrelated objects, parts, and materials as some form of composite. In theory, the notion of assemblage takes on more abstract qualities, but is similarly a collective of elements that are not necessarily similar to each other, yet when assembled, assume a different identity as a collection. I draw upon Deleuze and Guattari's (1987) notion of *assemblage* to present students' narratives of identities and experiences in ELA as nonlinear and produced within continuously shifting relations. Like the individual images in a collage, each of which conveys a particular idea on its own, yet may take on other meanings as part of the larger whole, an assemblage of curriculum is an organic, self-organizing composite of the various discourses, purposes, desires, and struggles in the figured world of the classroom. However, unlike a collage, an assemblage is not static—"[a]n assemblage is precisely this increase in the dimensions of a multiplicity that necessarily changes in nature as it expands its connections" (Deleuze & Guattari, 1987, p. 8). Rather than a "fixed or static" set of representations and relations, assemblages depict a "constantly shifting set of relations" (Walkerdine, 2007, p. 33). I propose that understanding curriculum-*as-assemblage* de-centers mainstream knowledge and creates dialogic spaces for other knowledges, literacies, and identities. When teachers think of curriculum strictly as a collection of "best practices" (even if the practices are good ones), whether those practices are driven by high stakes testing or cultural relevance, they still have the potential to essentialize and minimize. As Ladson-Billings (2014) argues, "teachers undertaking culturally informed pedagogies take on the dual responsibility of external performance assessments as well as community- and student-driven learning" (p. 83).

Curriculum-as-assemblage thus becomes a heuristic that allows us to understand curriculum as a nonlinear and multidimensional composite of multiple interests, as well as ways of knowing and reading and writing the world. Walkerdine's use of assemblage disrupts the tendency to accept narratives as linear and orderly accounts of experience, yet honors the narrative as a construction of self, experience, or meaning-making at a given point in time. Similarly, I draw upon students' narratives to document their versions (and my interpretations of their versions) of literacies in ELA. Presenting their narratives as an assemblage engages us more fully into an alternative literacy process and challenges us to make meaning out of these narratives in new ways.

Similarly, conceptualizing ELA as assemblage renders visible a multiplicity of perspectives that are simultaneously available in the classroom as teachers and students enact the curriculum. For example, conceptions of success and failure are embedded in the enacted curriculum, and "teachers' and students' spoken and written texts shape and construct policies and rules, knowledge, and, indeed, 'versions' of successful and failing students" (Luke, 1996, p. 11) in the middle school classroom.

Some Background—The Curriculum and the Teacher at NUA

Given the size of the school, many teachers at NUA taught a single academic subject to all of the students in a grade. This was the case in eighth grade ELA—Ms. Brian, a White woman in her mid twenties, was a recent graduate from a teacher preparation program and was also new to the school. Initially a film major, Ms. Brian "took the first job that came along" after college. After a couple of years, she felt that her work in media and communications lacked purpose and considered becoming a therapist or a teacher. She eventually became certified in secondary English education (she thought it would allow her to pursue her interest in writing) and enrolled in a graduate teacher education program. Prior to teaching at NUA, she student-taught in a sophomore English class at a large comprehensive high school in the same city. At NUA, she was hired to teach ELA to the eighth grade cohort (three classes, 94 eighth grade students in total, as well as two electives). Ms. Brian was enthusiastic about teaching and "connecting" with students.

Ms. Brian's ELA classes followed the scope and sequence faithfully, although she expressed anxiety about being able to "cover" the number of texts included in the curriculum. She usually made decisions about when a unit would begin or end depending on how long it took to "get through" a particular text or assignment. She shared that she felt overwhelmed, at times, by the overall demands of her job and wished she could manage some aspects of it better, such as communicating with parents about their students' grades. Although as a first-year teacher Ms. Brian might have be more likely to struggle with these multiple demands of meeting administrative expectations, planning lessons, improving her class management, and managing conflicting ideologies, research on beginning teachers indicates that even beyond the first year, teachers are likely to adjust the concepts they apply in graduate courses and in their student teaching placements depending on their current working context (Smagorinsky et al., 2007). Research has also shown that beginning teachers are more likely to depend on textbooks and existing curricular plans, expectations, and resources (Anagnostopoulos, 2003; Feiman-Nemser & Parker, 1990; Lipman, 2004). In that sense, Ms. Brian, as a first-year teacher, was an ideal participant for my study—she was negotiating the various demands related to the implementation of the school's scope and sequence in ELA, and the objectives for each course, along with her own expectations for the ELA curriculum.

Classroom Environment

The classroom environment in the ELA class at NUA was arranged for comfort and collaboration. The majority of the space was occupied by four square tables that each accommodated eight students. Ms. Brian kept several books on a shelf for students to choose from for independent reading when they were finished early with a test or assignment. A favorite spot in the classroom was the reading area, a large space where Ms. Brian had a lived-in sofa and large area rug brought in, at her own expense, at the beginning of the semester. Students often vied for a spot on the sofa when Ms. Brian instructed everyone to move to the "cozy area" for a discussion or group work. On the white board at the "front" of the room, a section on the right or left was reserved for the assignments for the week under each category, and students were expected to copy their assignments into the appropriate sections of their ELA notebooks or "binders."

These students' ideas about the purposes of ELA are therefore quite different, but both stem from what they think (or have been told) is required in order to be successful in the class. In Figure 6.1, excerpts from students' ELA goal statements are distinguished from each other by font and style, yet juxtaposed to illustrate how an assemblage of simultaneous multiple versions of ELA shapes enacted curriculum. The interweaving of excerpts from students' ELA goals and journal reflections documents a collection of students' responses to a single prompt, yet the juxtaposition of their very divergent goals disrupts the idea of a single understanding or purpose of an ELA curriculum. This narrative visualization incites us to imagine how versions of ELA exist simultaneously in the classroom context and mediate students' experiences of the curriculum. It also marks, by omission, the literacies and identities that are excluded from the curriculum—what Eisner (1985) describes as the null curriculum, or "all that is not selected as well as all that occurs but remains unnamed and unacknowledged" (Britzman, 1989, p. 149).

Students' conceptualizations of ELA and of achieving in ELA illustrates some of the ways in which the discourses that regulate the world of achievement and literacy at NUA function to further stratify students from diverse backgrounds (Au & Raphael, 2000). This visualization highlights the intersections between/among students' multiple conceptualizations of ELA to demonstrate how various discourses of achievement in ELA frame literacy skills as neutral, excluding any references to whose "English" is privileged in class, and implying that success is within reach for those who put in the effort. What remains unstated, furthermore, is that for those who claim standard English is their home language, the path to such "success" is much shorter than those who do not speak standard English at home. Furthermore, in contrast to a culturally sustaining pedagogy, this assemblage makes no reference to the cultural and youth literacies that many students already master.

At NUA, as in secondary (middle and high school) English curriculum in general, reading and writing were generally grounded in a liberal humanist academic tradition of literary appreciation and analysis of what are considered great and classic texts, as implied by the quote from Jason's journal that I cited at the beginning of this chapter. With respect to writing, we can gather from the students' statements that they find the kinds of writing they are expected to produce to be formulaic and artificial. Although the ELA curriculum at NUA encouraged students' creativity and explored various means of self-expression in the lower grades by incorporating projects such as an interview project and a "rap" writing

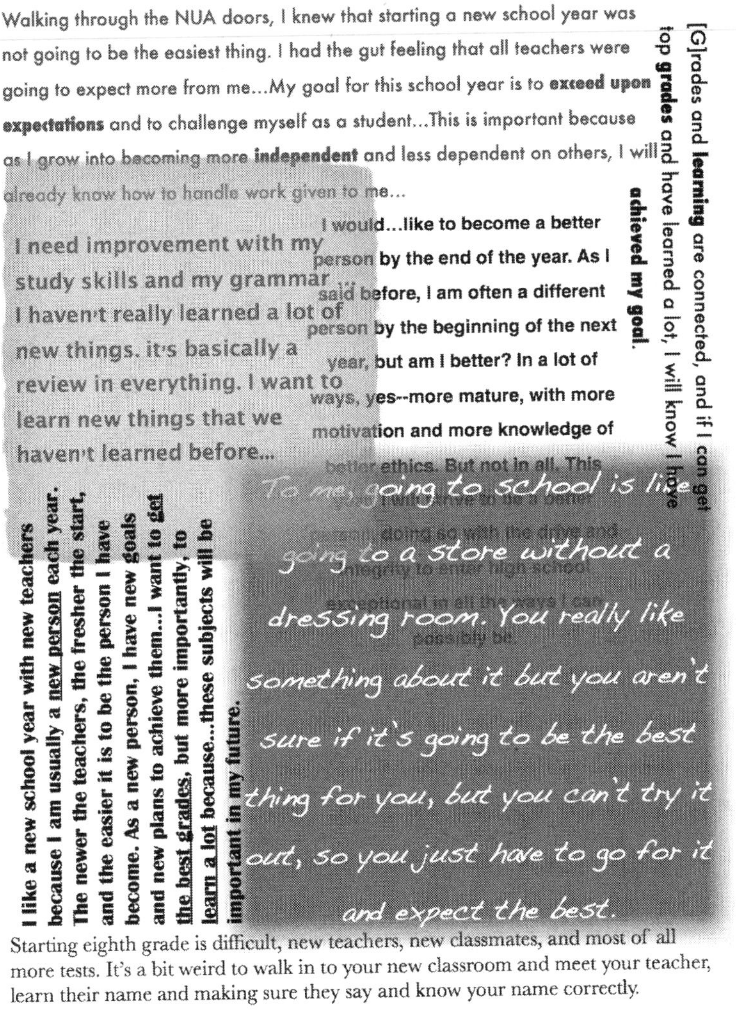

FIGURE 6.1 Visualization of ELA as assemblage.

assignment as part of their sixth grade year-long thematic study of "Identity" (see Figure 6.2), the focus in the upper grades became increasingly circumscribed by the pressures of accountability and the need for the school to stand out as a college- and career-preparatory school.

Entry points for Multiple Literacies for ELA Classrooms

In this section, I describe various methods through which you can engage multiple literacies in your ELA classroom. Some may be new to you, and others

FIGURE 6.2 Bulletin board display of sixth grade ELA and hip hop assignment at NUA.

you may recognize or perhaps have tried in your own classrooms. Whether or not you have tried these activities or considered these prompts before, their significance lies in the framing. I encourage all of us to think of these exercises not simply as activities or strategies to try, although there is certainly merit in trying out new methods. The challenge is in reflecting, in light of each activity:

- What products are generated in connection to each approach, activity, or method?
- How do these various products "count" as texts and what literacies are engaged?
- In what ways do these new literacy engagements deepen or add to our understanding or experience?

The Self in Context: Autoethnography

Recent events worldwide regarding conflicts connected to race and religion, in particular, contribute to a generalized climate of tension and anxiety in society, and education is no exception. Despite the general acceptance of multiculturalism in education and widespread adoption of culturally relevant and culturally responsive pedagogies (Ladson-Billings, 1994; Gay, 2000), how multiculturalism is defined and enacted varies greatly. In some cases, the rhetoric of multiculturalism and superficial enactments of cultural relevance actually mask the complexity of diversity in institutions and in society. In some cases, generalizations about cultural or racial groups perpetuate deficit or marginalizing perspectives about communities of color (Paris, 2012; Ladson-Billings, 2014).

In addition, the focus is often almost exclusively on students, as if teachers did not themselves have cultural identities. For example, despite known incidents of religious discrimination among teachers, such as Muslim teachers in public school who have been prevented from wearing religious garb ("Mark Leon . . .", 2012), rhetorics of diversity and multiculturalism in education often focus on students' cultural identities to some extent but generally overlook the role of teachers' cultural, ethnic, and religious identities. Even when teachers' cultural identities are a main focus, their identities are framed primarily in terms of teachers' ability to relate to students (Ndura, 2004).

Recently, one of my students in an ELA methods course, Elma Rahman, experienced some very troubling interactions with schools and testing centers as she was completing her clinical practicum as well as her exams for an initial teaching certification. Prompted by these experiences, she decided to focus her inquiry project in my class to explore issues of teacher identity. After she completed her project, she wanted to deepen her inquiry into her experiences as a Muslim woman and English teacher candidate in the context of the broader narrative of multiculturalism and teacher education.

Because Elma was reflecting on her own experiences as embedded in a broader cultural and sociopolitical context, she gravitated toward autoethnographic methods. In an article that she and I recently coauthored for *English Journal* (Caraballo & Rahman, 2016), we chose an excerpt from this vignette, which Elma developed from one of her journal entries about her experiences:

> My experience in the education system has shown me that sometimes there are people within the school society who expect teachers to fit into a certain mold. But what if one does not fit into the mold? Because of my religious and cultural background, I have not been able to fit this mold, nor do I want to. Thus, I have had many doors close in my face in the public school system, primarily because I am a Muslim woman who wears the *niqab*, face veil. During my first student teaching semester, I was assigned to a middle school in the borough of Queens in New York City. The day I arrived at the school to speak with the assistant principal, I remember waiting in the office for two hours until I found myself in her office. As I waited in the main office with two other college students looking to student teach at the school, I remember them both being called in at the same time by an administrator. Before I could

> ask if I should go along as well, a secretary instructed me to wait to be called in. After I asked a second time, I was directed to the administrator's office, who said: "Oh, I saw you sitting in the office, but I did not know that you were here for student teaching." She then asked me what I would like to teach. When I explained my program's requirement to first observe and then teach, she told me that she would let me observe, however, I may not be able to teach. A month later, I was reassigned to another school, where I had the opportunity to only teach for a week when I was actually supposed to have taught for one or two periods a day for three months.

Borrowing from autoethnography, a genre in which the writer/researcher engages in the layered process of connecting the personal and the cultural (Duarte, 2007), Elma examined the interrelatedness of her identities and experiences in and outside of schools—identities and experiences that challenge (in)visibility—and extended her inquiry into her multiple identities as a Muslim, a woman, and a teacher to build curriculum that fosters critical literacies and promotes social justice. This inquiry also incited the development of curriculum that brought some of these tensions forth in literature, namely *The Minister's Black Veil*, by Nathaniel Hawthorne, as a way to scaffold the conversation about identities in particular cultural contexts. As Camangian (2010) suggests, these methods led Elma to "start with the self" and as she worked to incorporate concepts from autoethnography, as well as critical literacies, into her teaching.

A similar process of self-reflection and sociocultural analysis might work for your students as well. If we see writing as a socially constructed and meaning-making activity (Sperling, 2003), responses to autoethnographic journal prompts can be particularly useful and draw from literacies in relation to the personal, cultural, and autobiographical in critical and culturally sustaining ways. Below are some of the journal prompts that I use in my courses to introduce teachers to autoethnographic methods:

- Each of us experiences particular moments in our educational trajectories, whether as learners or educators, that change how we think about English. Please reflect on such a moment, and write a narrative description of that moment. Keep writing without stopping for 30 minutes, adding as much detail as possible.
- Please respond to one or more of the arguments about literacies discussed in this chapter. Where do you stand? Ground your response in examples from your own education, classroom experience, and/or research, whatever is applicable. Add to this journal entry after you have discussed your classmates' responses as well.

- What are some of your assumptions about literacies? Where do you think these assumptions come from? Draw from your language experiences in past and present home as well academic contexts.
- What experiences, concepts, or issues would your own autoethnography focus on?

Critical Multilingualism

Recently, I had a discussion with the graduate students in my research seminar in response to Martinez's (2017) article on critical language solidarity. Martinez argues that teachers, however well-meaning, perpetuate violence against the home and youth language practices of many of their Latinx students, either by correcting their language according to standard American English, revoicing their contributions in class to "model" academic English, or disallowing personal connections to the readings unless they were directly connected to textual evidence. I listened in as these committed teachers grappled with these provocative ideas about practices that are so commonplace in ELA instruction, particularly among students who are labeled as English language learners. Some of them agreed readily with Martinez's arguments, and others agreed in theory, but countered that if students were not taught "professional" and "academic" grammar and conventions, then students would be at a disadvantage in the "real" figured worlds of higher education and future careers. They seemed to come to an impasse at that point, enacting in real time the complex tensions of our discipline. While many teachers recognize that incorporating students' home and cultural languages could be more engaging to reluctant readers and writers, they fear that they must dedicate all of their attention to mastery of the dominant language in order to make sure that students meet benchmarks as well as gain all of the necessary skills to be successful in future study and employment. There is nothing wrong with that, right? Well, what if it is not quite that simple?

If we understand literacies and languages as socially constructed, we must also recognize that the norms and conventions that we might consider "standard" are grounded in hierarchies of power in society. When students learn that the language of power, which is primarily grounded in White and middle class norms, is worthy of study, while their own oral traditions and ways of interacting with texts are relegated to the margins of the curriculum, if they are present at all, they are not just learning about what is "professional"; they are also internalizing messages about whose literacy practices are of most worth. For example, English language learners and first generation students are often defined according to the language skills that they lack, when in fact many are engaged in complex literacy events in the context of their family lives. The authentic literacy practices in students' home lives offer them opportunities to participate in their family's social literacies, such as taking on the role of translator for one's parents. For example, Jonah, a bilingual NUA student, described his role as a translator in his family with palpable pride:

Jonah: I'm basically always a translator for my parents and my grandparents, and I'm always dealing with their problems, like if I have to call some place. So I'm very independent, like, I'm not very timid of having to do something.

Limarys: And how do you feel about doing that? About having that role in your family?

Jonah: It makes me feel, like, important because that means that I'm kind of necessary. But sometimes they use my little sister, so she can learn, too.

(Caraballo, 2012, p. 49)

Beyond these complex identities with respect to language and bi/multilingualism, students also demonstrated engagement in meaning-making and an emergent sense of "voices" (Cook-Sather, 2006) in literacy practices beyond those measurable by grades and standardized tests. At NUA, for example, students constructed identities-in-practice within and beyond the classroom that reflected the multiple literacies they leveraged and the contexts that they negotiated on a regular basis. And while the work of translation has long been highly regarded in the context of adapting literary works for a global audience, first generation youth who must translate documents for their parents do not typically receive "credit" for the complex work with language and literacies that they do at home, and this has more to do with sociopolitical status of particular immigrant groups than about discourses of multilingualism.

Most importantly, students often miss opportunities to learn about the structure and norms of their own home languages—to deepen their understanding of a wide range of sociolinguistic patterns. Furthermore, conventions about the teaching of language and writing that many of us internalized in grammar school tend to ignore the changing demands of an increasingly globalized world, where linguistic and cultural dexterity are gaining political and intellectual relevance and status in mainstream society. As Alim and Smitherman (2012) discuss in *Articulate while Black: Barack Obama, language and race in the US*, a major factor in President Obama's success as an orator was due to his ability to communicate with very different audiences, whether they be in multigenerational congregations in southern Black churches or international diplomats. While some teachers may think they are taking time "away" from the primary curriculum when they explore students' co-curricular, cultural, or social engagement in literacies (such as writing or discussing song lyrics with friends), this work actually supports students' ability to examine the power and purpose of language and literacies in the various milieus they will ultimately need to navigate. If broadening and cultivating students' consumption and production of different kinds of written, oral, and digital texts is part of your understanding of what an ELA curriculum should include, then students need to also be engaged in analyzing and critiquing the complex power relations that shape those language conventions in the context of their own lives. Some questions to consider are:

- Reflecting on your sociocultural, national, religious, racial, gendered, classed, (etc.) background, write about how your experiences as well as values and assumptions about language might inform your work as an educator.
- How might teachers incorporate multiple language/cultural practices in ELA?

Participatory and Youth Literacies

The third and most multi-faceted entry point in this chapter may fit best under the broad category of participatory and youth literacies, often expressed in modalities related to research, digital media, and performance. As we argued in our co-authored article in *English Leadership Quarterly*, engaging multiple literacies helps us to see youth culture as another valid factor in literacy development, rather than as subordinated to academic or dominant culture (Caraballo & Hill, 2014). As such, embedding standards-based learning in the context of students' own experiences builds active learning toward literacies that transcend classroom walls. We argue that

> creative liberty with the Standards is a *requirement*, not just an option, of literacy instruction for social justice. If we want to engage students in rules of language that cultivate creativity, community, and authenticity, we must breathe these values into our content and approach to literacies.
>
> *(p. 6)*

These values are manifest in many ways, especially in interdisciplinary projects such as Hill's garden-based curriculum, which culminated in a digital magazine in which students based their reporting, editorials, recipes, and visual representations on their work in the school garden: https://issuu.com/prof.hill/docs/fresh.2012.

In a different context, yet similarly place-based example, Kinloch's (2010) critical ethnography documents youth in Harlem as they use their rapidly gentrifying neighborhood as a unit of analysis to develop critical literacy skills such as writing across genres and public speaking. Kinloch explores how YPAR enabled the youth with whom she co-researched to enhance these academic literacies:

> As Khaleeq expanded his literacy narrative during the course of our work together, writing became not only an activity that he performed at school; it became an activity that allowed him to express difficult ideas and emotions in and about the community.
>
> *(p. 47)*

Below, I highlight one more example that demonstrates the depth of analysis that youth from multiple levels of "academic" literacy and language background are willing and able to engage in when provided the autonomy and safe space to do so. In an afterschool program that I co-direct, Cyphers for Justice, students draw from their experiences with multiple literacies in order to demonstrate the interrelatedness of research, art, self-expression and social action in their Youth Participatory Action Research (YPAR) projects. According to Morrell (2006), YPAR builds on decades of participatory action research and consists of the collective investigation of a problem; relies on the knowledge of those most directly affected or involved; is driven by a desire to take action; and engages youth in addressing issues of social inequality.

In our collaborative, youth and pre-service teacher participant-researchers engage in every phase of inquiry, from design to implementation to critical reflection, analysis, and performance, using a range of rhetorical modes, from digital literacies to hip hop and spoken word. In addition to having the opportunity to relate to their teachers and peers on a more personal level, students have responded to questions that prompted them to take a stand. We may start a session with the question: "What is it that you refuse to be silenced about?" The responses have ranged from "racism, and how people are in denial" about its existence in our society, to a student sharing that "some people feel intimidated by me, because of the way I look" as a young Black man. Once students have voiced these weighty and relevant concerns that matter to them, a next step is to allow them the space and time to explore those ideas through rap or freestyle, spoken word, dramatic sketches, or short films.

Inviting students to experiment with different rhetorical modes (beyond conventional formats used in schools) that students can use to communicate their research and ideas has the dual purpose of including those who are less likely to see themselves as researchers and writers, as well as deepening the skills mandated by traditional academic standards. For example, in Caraballo & Lyiscott (2018), we discuss how we tap into student schemas and generate ideas for suggested YPAR topics by using the hip-hop culture tradition of the cypher, a hip-hop cultural practice that is rooted in West African traditions. The art form consists of rhythmic dialogue and improvised clever banter all while the participants are part of a sacred circle that taps "into student schema, inclusivity, and attend[s] to group dynamics" (Kirkland, 2013). We invited our students to draw on the elements of hip hop that they witness and encounter daily in their favorite artists to inspire the creativity and boldness that they would need to engage in social action.

Similarly, when creating spoken word poems, students are asked to focus not only on the content of their verses and the structure of their stanzas, but also how the embodiment of that poem, its spoken performance, contributes to its meaning and impact. Furthermore, there are many more ways to access such creativity and boldness involving other performative literacies as well, such as tableaus. Increasingly a popular activity, I think tableaus are particularly interesting when

FIGURE 6.3 Tableau entitled "Literacies over Time".

they challenge students to depict fairly abstract concepts. When presenting a tableau, participants are not allowed to move or talk, but can use their bodies and facial expressions to communicate. In my ELA curriculum courses, I challenge educators to create a tableau to explain the how literacies are embodied or physically experienced. In a tableau that they entitled "Literacies over Time" (see Figure 6.3), teachers collaborated on a "live portrait" depicting the various ways in which students are currently able to interact with texts. The question mark image included in the tableau reflects the uncertainty (and possibility) of forms yet unknown.

So, what can be gained from these community-based practices, in the context of more traditional classrooms? The following questions may help you think through the affordances and challenges of taking up these approaches in your own classrooms:

- Whose voices are typically privileged in your or your colleagues' classrooms?
- How might you and/or your students effect change in your communities?
- What would be the key elements of a lesson plan that you might use in your classroom to incite social change?
- In what ways are literacies embodied in our schools and communities?
- How can research and performance lead to the development of critical literacies?

Thinking About Learning and Doing Teaching

As seen in my sample assemblage earlier in this chapter, students were candid about their goals and their challenges in ELA. The process of creating an assemblage of the various purposes of ELA that were manifest in students' writing prompted me to examine what literacies seem to "count" and which seem to be excluded or marginalized in a particular ELA curriculum. If you are currently teaching, student teaching, or observing in a classroom, consider choosing one assignment in which students are reflecting on their reading, writing, or discussions. Then,

- Make a copy of a full class set, or as many student writing samples as you have access to;
- Read all of the students' work, making notes separately of their ideas about texts, their responses to texts, or completing assignments about texts;
- Choose several quotations or excerpts that represent the full range of ideas in the sample set;
- Cut out these quotes or excerpts and create a visualization or assemblage (however crude or messy), such as a collage, chart, or diagram;
- Read all of the quotes or excerpts again, but strictly as part of the visualization;
- Consider how the sum of these parts characterizes the ELA class in which these students belong—how would you describe the curriculum in that ELA class, after completing this exercise?

Once your assemblage is completed and you have a sense of what literacies might be emphasized or sustained in your classroom community, you may want to explore various online resources to plan next steps:

- The National Council of Teachers of English has several statements on the teaching of multiple literacies: www.ncte.org/policy-research/wwk/multipleliteracies
- The *Canadian Journal for Teacher Research* provides suggestions for teaching multiliteracies, and it is hosted by a site that features teacher research: www.teacherresearch.ca/blog/article/2014/07/03/245-how-to-teach-multiliteracies
- Among many other resources available on the readwritethink.org site, this lesson plan engages multiple modalities in the teaching of autobiography: www.readwritethink.org/professional-development/strategy-guides/teaching-with-multiple-modalities-30101.html

Putting It All Together

As students today are positioned and position themselves as negotiators of multiple figured worlds, it is imperative for educators to help them develop the tools they will need for those negotiations by thinking about the multiple literacies that students must be able to leverage in each of those cultural contexts. Theorizing ELA as assemblage may be one such tool—it renders visible how students' identities and experiences are interrelated in figured worlds in and out of school, and how the curriculum either recognizes or excludes the multiple literacies associated with those identities and contexts.

Conceptualizing the curriculum as an assemblage informed by multiple literacies and discourses, thus, serves multiple purposes and generates many possibilities. For example, it demonstrates how discourses of achievement regulate which literacies are considered "professional" and "academic." It also highlights other literacies, such as those related to students' home and community social practices like translating documents for their parents, reflecting on a sermon at their house of worship, or rapping and emceeing with their friends. These are emergent sites of struggle and resistance where youth carve spaces in which to reframe the curriculum and how it positions them as readers, writers, and achievers. The latter is evidence of the budding "critical" literacies in the midst of educational institutions steeped in the most immutable structures of schooling. But it also suggests the possibility of movement and change when educators as well as students begin to interrogate and interact with the discourses that shape their figured worlds. What kind of educator would you want to be?

Several scholars have discussed how the current accountability-driven context of standards and achievement is narrowing the scope of conversations about what students should be learning in schools and how learning might be assessed or measured. Although the expectation that all students should be given equal opportunities to succeed is certainly appropriate, and there are plenty of teachers who are able to incorporate preparation for assessments into their existing curricula (Zumwalt, 2004), the pressure of the testing movement has generally led to the prioritization of math and particular forms of literacy in ways that accentuate the divide between privileged and underprivileged children (Lipman, 2004). The "divide" between privileged and underprivileged children is complex because it extends beyond resources and other socioeconomic factors, such as assumptions about which curriculum is appropriate for which students. Research has indicated that students in more affluent and/or selective schools are exposed to rich experiences and curricula in the arts, social studies, and sciences (Lipman, 2004), and that the emphasis on higher-order thinking and innovation prepares middle- and upper-class students for future positions of authority and leadership (Anyon, 1980).

One way in which teachers can begin to ameliorate the impact of hidden curricula involves assuming an ethnographic approach toward teaching and learning in schools and classrooms. For example, in their reviews of ethnographic studies, Wills, Lintz, and Mehan, (2004) and Suarez-Orozco, Suarez-Orozco, and Doucet (2004) discuss ways in which theory and practice converge in classrooms, and then make space for the home and community literacies that students bring to the classroom. Noting that the principles of multiculturalism are constantly converging with the reality of schooling, Wills et al. maintain that instructional practice involves more than cultural knowledge about students' backgrounds; teachers should "learn about the details of their students' lives in particular" and "adapt general principles to local circumstances" (p. 179).

By assuming an inquiry stance (Cochran-Smith & Lytle, 1999)—such as making it a habit of asking yourself tough questions about your curriculum and your teaching—teachers can facilitate connections between school knowledge and students' cultural knowledges in ways that eliminate false boundaries between what is considered academic and non-academic. One last example from my study: in a journal entry in which Ms. Brian asked her students to comment on their use of slang (as part of their study of *The Outsiders*), two students wrote that they use slang only when it is "appropriate" to do so—namely, outside of "formal" spaces such as the classroom and other evaluative contexts. While it was great that the journal prompt engaged multiple literacy practices by asking them to reflect their own language use, there was no place in the curriculum to discuss the structures of power that contribute to the demarcation between what is "standard" language or "slang." Facilitating these connections might mean creating spaces in which students are encouraged to critically consider how school knowledges came to be considered as such, and what such knowledges exclude or render invisible or unknowable (Pinar & Bowers, 1992). Raising a critical consciousness about existing power structures is often equated with opportunities for dialogue and privileged as a way to elicit the "voices" of youth (Cook-Sather, 2006). However, it is important to note that no conversation is devoid of power relations (Ellsworth, 1989), particularly in evaluative contexts such as classrooms. Furthermore, conventions about dialogue and participation are themselves culturally and socially situated, and seldom consider silence as a form of participation (or resistance). Greater awareness of how these (in)visible factors contribute to raced, classed, and gendered patterns of achievement in ELA would invite the examination of the literacies that reify existing patterns of achievement. Combined with an inquiry stance in which teachers see themselves as co-constructors of knowledge alongside students, such approaches to ELA curriculum and teaching can lead to opportunities for students to construct, but also interrogate and reframe, their multiple literacies.

Note

1 All student and school names are pseudonyms. Goal statements such as Jason's were assigned as journal prompts throughout the academic year.

References

Alim, H. S. & Smitherman, G. (2012). *Articulate while black: Barack Obama, language and race in the US*. New York: Oxford University Press.

Anagnostopoulos, D. (2003). Testing and student engagement with literature in urban classrooms: A multi-layered perspective. *Research in the Teaching of English*, *38*(2), 177–212.

Anyon, J. (1980). Social class and the hidden curriculum of work. *Journal of Education, 62*(1), 67–92.

Au, K. H. & Raphael, T. E. (2000). Equity and literacy in the next millenium. *Reading Research Quarterly, 35*(1), 170–188.

Britzman, D. P. (1989). Who has the floor? Curriculum, teaching, and the English student teacher's struggle for voice. *Curriculum Inquiry, 19*(2), 143–162.

Burroughs, R. & Smagorinsky, P. (2009). The secondary English curriculum and adolescent literacy. In L. Christenbury, R. Bomer, & P. Smagorinsky (Eds.), *Handbook of Adolescent Literacy Research* (pp. 170–182). New York: Guilford Press.

Camangian, P. (2010). Starting with self: Teaching autoethnography to foster critically caring literacies. *Research in the Teaching of English, 45*(2), 179–204.

Caraballo, L. (2011). Theorizing identities in a "just(ly)" contested terrain: Practice theories of identity amid critical-poststructural debates on curriculum and achievement. *Journal of Curriculum and Pedagogy, 8*(2), 155–177. doi:10.1080/15505170.2011.624939

Caraballo, L. (2012). Identities-in-practice in a figured world of achievement: Toward curriculum and pedagogies of hope. *Journal of Curriculum Theorizing, 28*(2), 43–59.

Caraballo, L. (2016). Students' critical meta-awareness in a figured world of achievement: Toward a culturally sustaining stance in curriculum, pedagogy, and research. *Urban Education, 52*(5), 585–609. doi:10.1177/0042085915623344

Caraballo, L. & Rahman, E. (2016). Visible teaching, (in)visible teacher: An educator's journey as a Muslim woman. *English Journal, 106*(2), 47–53.

Caraballo, L. & Hill, M. (2014). Curriculum-in-action: Cultivating literacy, community, and creativity in urban contexts. *English Leadership Quarterly, 37*(1), 5–11.

Caraballo, L. & Lyiscott, J. (2018). Collaborative inquiry: Youth, social action, and critical qualitative research. *Action Research*, 1–18. Online First. doi:10.1177/1476750317752819

Carlson, D. (1993). Literacy and urban school reform: Beyond vulgar pragmatism. In C. Lankshear & P. McLaren (Eds.), *Critical literacy: Politics, praxis, and the postmodern* (pp. 217–246). New York: State University of New York Press.

Christenbury, L. (2006). *Making the journey: Being and becoming a teacher of English language arts* (3rd ed.). Portsmouth, NH: Heinemann.

Cochran-Smith, M. & Lytle, S. (1999). Relationships of knowledge and practice: Teacher learning in communities. *Review of Research in Education, 24*, 249–305.

Cook-Sather, A. (2006). Sound, presence and power: Student voice in educational research reform. *Curriculum Inquiry, 36*(4), 1–16.

Darling-Hammond, L. (2004). Standards, accountability, and school reform. *Teachers College Record, 106*(6), 1047–1085.

Deleuze, G. & Guattari, F. (1987). Introduction: Rhizome. *Thousand plateaus: Capitalism and schizophrenia* (pp. 3–23). Minneapolis, MN: University of Minnesota Press.

Duarte, F. P. (2007). "Using autoethnography in the scholarship of teaching and learning: Reflective practice from 'the Other Side of the Mirror.'" *International Journal for the Scholarship of Teaching and Learning, 1*(2), 1–11.

Eisner, E. (1985). *The educational imagination.* New York: Macmillan Publishing.

Ellsworth, E. (1989). Why doesn't this feel empowering? Working through the repressive myths of critical pedagogy. *Harvard Educational Review, 59*(3), 297–324.

Feiman-Nemser, S. & Parker, M. B. (1990). Making subject matter part of the conversation in learning to teach. *Journal of Teacher Education, 41*(3), 32–43. doi:10.1177/002248719004100305

Freire, P. & Macedo, D. (1987). *Literacy: Reading the word and the world.* Westport, CT: Bergin & Garvey.

Gay, G. (2000). *Culturally responsive teaching: Theory, research, and practice.* New York: Teachers College Press.
Holland, D., Lachicotte, W., Skinner, D., & Cain, C. (1998). *Identity and agency in cultural worlds.* Cambridge, MA: Harvard University Press.
Hirsch, E. D. (1987). *Cultural literacy: What every American needs to know.* Boston, MA: Houghton Mifflin.
Kinloch, V. F. (2010). *Harlem on our minds: Place, race, and the literacies of urban youth.* New York: Teachers College Press.
Kirkland, D. (2013). *A search past silence: The literacy of young Black men.* New York: Teachers College Press.
Kumashiro, K. (2000). Toward a theory of anti-oppressive education. *Review of Educational Research, 70*(1), 25–53.
Ladson-Billings, G. (1994). *The dreamkeepers: Successful teachers of African American children.* San Francisco, CA: Jossey-Bass.
Ladson-Billings, G. (2000). Racialized discourses and ethnic epistemologies. In N. K. Denzin & Y. S. Lincoln (Eds.), *Handbook of Qualitative Research* (2nd ed., pp. 257–278). London: Sage.
Ladson-Billings, G. (2004). New directions in multicultural education: Complexities, boundaries, and Critical Race Theory. In J. A. Banks & C. A. M. Banks (Eds.), *Handbook of research on multicultural education* (2nd ed., pp. 50–68). San Francisco, CA: Jossey-Bass.
Ladson-Billings, G. (2014). Culturally relevant pedagogy 2.0: A.k.a. the remix. *Harvard Educational Review, 84*(1), 74–84.
Lipman, P. (2004). *High stakes education.* New York: Routledge Falmer.
Luke, A. (1996). Text and discourse in education: An introduction to critical discourse analysis. *Review of Research in Education, 21,* 3–48.
Luke, A. (2004). The trouble with English. *Research in the Teaching of English, 39*(1), 85–95.
"Mark Leon Essex Smith, Arkansas Teacher, Loses Case against District Claiming Religious Discrimination." *The Huffington Post,* 19 November 2012. Available at: www.huffingtonpost.com/2012/11/19/mark-leon-essex-smith-ark_n_2160124.html.
Martinez, D. (2017). Imagining a language of solidarity for Black and Latinx youth in English language arts classrooms. *English Education, 49*(2), 179–196.
McCarthey, S. & Moje, E. (2002). Identity matters. *Reading Research Quarterly, 37*(2), 228–238.
Morrell, E. (2005). Critical English education. *English Education, 37*(4), 312–321.
Morrell, E. (2006). Critical participatory action research and the literacy achievement of ethnic minority groups. In J. V. Hoffman, D. L. Schallert, C. M. Fairbanks, J. Worthy, & B. Maloda (Eds.), *55th Yearbook of the National Reading Conference Yearbook* (pp. 1–18). Oak Creek, WI: National Reading Conference.
Ndura, E. (2004). "Teachers' Discoveries of Their Cultural Realms: Untangling the Web of Cultural Identity." *Multicultural Perspectives, 6*(3),10–16.
New London Group: Cazden, C., Cope, B., Fairclough, N., & Gee, J. (1996). A pedagogy of multiliteracies: Designing social futures. *Harvard Educational Review, 66*(1), 60–92.
Paris, D. & Alim, H. S. (2014). What are we seeking to sustain through culturally sustaining pedagogy? A loving critique forward. *Harvard Educational Review, 84*(1), 85–100.
Pinar, W. F. & Bowers, C. A. (1992). Politics of curriculum: Origins, controversies, and significance of critical perspectives. *Review of Research in Education, 18,* 163–190.

Smagorinsky, P., Wright, L., Augustine, S. M., O'Donnell-Allen, C., & Konopak, B. (2007). Student engagement in the teaching and learning of grammar: A case study of an early-career secondary school English teacher. *Journal of Teacher Education, 58*(1), 76–90.

Snyder, J., Bolin, F., & Zumwalt, K. (1992). Curriculum implementation. In P. W. Jackson (Ed.), *Handbook of research on curriculum* (pp. 402–435). New York: MacMillan.

Sperling, M. (2003). Tenth-grade literacy and the mediation of culture, race, and class. In S. Greene & D. Abt-Perkins (Eds.), *Making Race Visible: Literacy Research for Cultural Understanding* (pp. 131–148). New York: Teachers College Press.

Street, B. (1984). *Literacy in theory and practice.* Cambridge: Cambridge University Press.

Street, B. (1995). *Social literacies: Critical approaches to literacy in development, ethnography and education.* Boston, MA: Addison-Wesley Publishing.

Suarez-Orozco, C., Suarez-Orozco, M. M., & Doucet, F. (2004). The academic engagement and achievement of Latino youth. In J. A. Banks & C. A. M. Banks (Eds.), *Handbook of research on multicultural education* (2nd ed., pp. 420–440). San Francisco, CA: Jossey-Bass.

Walkerdine, V. (2007). *Children, gender, video games: Towards a relational approach to multimedia* London: Palgrave Macmillan.

Wills, J. S., Lintz, A., & Mehan, H. (2004). Ethnographic studies of multicultural education in US classrooms and schools. In J. A. Banks & C. A. M. Banks (Eds.), *Handbook of research on multicultural education* (2nd ed., pp. 163–183). San Francisco, CA: Jossey-Bass.

Zumwalt, K. K. (2004). Choosing to make a difference. In A. T. Costigan, M. S. Crocco, & K. K. Zumwalt (Eds.), *Learning to teach in an age of accountability* (pp. 247–262). Mahwah, NJ: Lawrence Erlbaum & Associates.

INDEX

Page numbers in italics and bold refer to information in figures and tables respectively.